THE STRUCTURE AND GOVERNANCE
OF HIGHER EDUCATION

D0338931

THE STRUCTURE & GOVERNANCE OF HIGHER EDUCATION

Michael Shattock
(Editor)

Burton R. Clark   Lord Crowther-Hunt
Robert Berdahl   John Pratt   John Bevan
Guy Neave   David Morrell
Peter Scott

SOCIETY FOR RESEARCH INTO HIGHER EDUCATION

Research into Higher Education Monographs

The Society for Research into Higher Education,
At the University, Guildford, Surrey GU2 5XH

First published 1983

ISBN 0 900868 91 0

Printed in England by Direct Design (Bournemouth) Ltd. Printers
Butts Pond Industrial Estate, Sturminster Newton,
Dorset DT10 1AZ

THE LEVERHULME PROGRAMME
OF
STUDY INTO THE FUTURE OF HIGHER EDUCATION

This is the ninth publication of a programme of study focusing informed opinion and recent research findings on the major strategic options likely to be available to higher education institutions and policy-making bodies in the 1980s and 1990s. The programme as a whole has been made possible by a generous grant from the Leverhulme Trust to the Society for Research into Higher Education and is entirely independent of governmental or other organizational pressure. The present monograph arises out of a specialist seminar on the structure and governance of higher education. We are extremely grateful to Lord Norman Crowther-Hunt for his lively chairmanship of the seminar, for important contributions to the present volume and for his considerable interest in the whole programme.

A fundamental question facing higher education is the extent to which consensual arrangements and assumptions that generally worked well during the long postwar period of its expansion can cope with the much more stringent conditions likely to prevail in the 1980s and 1990s. Is there sufficient common purpose amongst the various institutions and interest groups that constitute 'the higher education system' to permit the development of viable long-run policy objectives, or must higher education policy increasingly become merely the outcome of a struggle for survival and dominance among conflicting interests and ideas?

This is both a substantive and methodological question. Substantively it will be faced squarely in the final report of the programme of study. Methodologically it will be tackled in the way the conclusions of that final report are reached.

In brief, the study is an experiment in formulating long-term strategies openly, taking into account the best specialist knowledge about a complex system, the legitimate interests of a wide range of conflicting pressure groups, and wider public interests as perceived by disinterested individuals with no direct day-to-day involvement in higher education. The final recommendations will be the result of an iterative process in which proposals are made, then discussed, then revised, then reconsidered. Stage one is to commission research reviews by acknowledged experts in various specialist areas. Stage two is a seminar at which others with detailed knowledge and experience of the area discuss these reviews. Stage three is publication of the reviews together with a report of the discussion and of the policy implications highlighted by it. Stage four is wider debate in the press and in specially convened conferences. Stage five is reconsideration of the policy issues in the light of the wider reaction. Stage six is the preparation of a final report. A seventh stage is of course intended, in which public authorities and institutions of higher education will take up the report's recommendations.

Publication of this monograph represents the conclusion of our inquiries into particular issues. Our final report, proposing a strategy for the long-term development of higher education, will appear in June 1983.

Previous volumes in the series have dealt with higher education and the labour market, access to higher education, institutional change, the future of research, the arts and higher education, professionalism and flexibility in learning, accountability or freedom for teachers, and resources and their allocation.

The scope of the SRHE Leverhulme programme is very wide. The need for a major review of higher education has been recognized by informed commentators for some time, and the financial stringency of recent years has made the matter urgent. In its report *The Funding and Organisation of Courses in Higher Education* the Education, Science and Arts Committee of the House of Commons commended the SRHE Leverhulme programme of study, and concluded, 'We believe that higher education is at a watershed in its development and that the time is ripe for a great national debate....' The SRHE Leverhulme programme is intended to contribute to that debate by offering both a structure within which the main issues can be considered and an assessment of the evidence on which future policy should be based.

Gareth Williams
Programme Director

FOREWORD

by Lord Crowther-Hunt

The seminar on the structure and governance of higher education was the last in the SRHE Leverhulme series, but possibly the most important. Its main theme was the future relationship between the government and the various institutions of higher education for which, inevitably, the government will remain the chief paymaster. Unless we get that relationship right the rest of the SRHE Leverhulme programme will be so much pie-in-the-sky.

It was a pity, therefore, at least in presentational terms, that at a late point in our proceedings the seminar decided to give pride of place in our recommendations to the traditional call for institutional autonomy. This has tended to make our recommendations appear very much less radical than in fact they are. So in this Foreword I propose to draw attention to what in my view should have hit the headlines.

Of primary importance is our proposal to deal with the obvious failure of the departments of education under successive governments to work out positive and comprehensive policies for higher education. There was general agreement that the day-to-day, piece-meal, reacting to events (which has masqueraded over the years as departmental long-term higher education policy making) was totally inadequate to meet our national needs. So we recommend the establishment of a Higher Education Policy Studies Centre for a continuous long-term exploration of policies and policy options in higher education. Its focus will always be on the far horizons — but it will need to keep a sharp eye on current policy making to ensure it is in line with the longer-term national needs it is identifying. Its focus, too, will include the plans of our international competitors, of which the Department of Education and Science so often seems so ignorant. This new Higher Education Policy Studies Centre will have no formal powers, but will derive its influence from the quality of its reports and the extent to which its persuasive operations will affect the day-to-day work of the DES, the UGC, NAB, and the House of Commons Select Committee on Education. Indeed, one might expect the Select Committee in particular enthusiastically to welcome such a powerhouse of ideas and policy.

Next in order of importance was our general agreement about the future of the UGC and NAB and their relationship with the government. Thus we recommend that the UGC and NAB should include within their remit the entire higher education provision, including direct grant and voluntary institutions. It was also envisaged that the UGC and NAB should work ever more closely together. Some of us recognized that this logically meant the eventual merger of the two bodies — though, alas, this view did not command majority support; its time will come. But what did command general agreement was that the UGC should become more independent of the government by having its own staff appointed independently of the Department of Education and Science; and that the UGC and NAB should publish their advice to the government and the criteria they use to make judgements (including financial) between different institutions. Given developments along these lines we shall have forged a powerful, policy-advisory, executive, and co-ordinating body standing at the centre as a buffer between the government and individual institutions of higher education, over which the UGC/NAB will be able to exercise a good deal of authority. At the same time it will need to recognize the need to protect and encourage all the institutional self-government and initiative needed in the cause of efficient local management and, even more important, in the cause of educational innovation and creativity. But since so much of its (their) staff and membership will be drawn from the individual higher education institutions themselves, achieving the balance between institutional autonomy and central planning ought not to be beyond the wit of man.

That, then, is the essence of the exciting prospect that this seminar envisaged for the future structure and governance of higher education. It was a pity, therefore, in the presentation of our findings that this got overshadowed by the fact that the majority of our colleagues would not face up to the logic of a long-term merger between the UGC and NAB. Instead they recommended an advisory body which would 'overarch' both the UGC and NAB. The new overarching body should not, in their view, 'interfere with the established powers and functions of the UGC and NAB.' But it should 'offer strategic advice to the Secretary of State on matters relating to higher education including the division of funding.' With luck this idea for an additional bureaucratic monstrosity to interpose itself between the Department and the UGC/NAB will wither on the vine.

It was also a pity that underlying a number of our sessions was a widespread view that somehow or other the future of higher education and the institutions that compose it should be left to market forces and 'natural demand'. There is, of course, no such thing in Britain as 'natural demand' for places in higher education when the government determines the level of student grants and whether or not they should be replaced by, or supplemented by, loans. Government decisions in this area determine, or have a major influence on, student demand. And no one is seriously suggesting there should be no loan or grant assistance for would-be students. So let's forget about concepts of natural demand.

These blemishes apart, I have no doubt that in the end this seminar and the papers it discussed will be judged to have made an important contribution to policy making for the structure and governance of higher education. Certainly I enjoyed the privilege and stimulation of chairing it.

Norman Crowther-Hunt
Chairman

CONTENTS

SEMINAR PARTICIPANTS

THE STRUCTURE AND GOVERNANCE OF HIGHER EDUCATION

*The Lord Crowther-Hunt (Chairman), Exeter College, Oxford
Mr Michael Shattock (Convenor), University of Warwick
Mr John Anwyl, University of Melbourne
Professor John Ashworth, University of Salford
Mr Christopher Ball, National Advisory Body for Local Authority Higher Education
*Professor Robert Berdahl, University of Maryland
*Mr John Bevan, National Advisory Body for Local Authority Higher Education
Dr William Birch, Bristol Polytechnic
Dr Donald Bligh, University of Exeter
Dr Clive Booth, Plymouth Polytechnic
Mr Jack Butterworth, University of Warwick
Mr Geoffrey Caston, Committee of Vice-Chancellors and Principals
*Professor Burton R. Clark, University of California at Los Angeles
Dr Ray Cowell, Sunderland Polytechnic
Mr John Davies, Anglian Regional Management Centre
Mr Rowland Eustace, Society for Research into Higher Education
Professor David Gardner, University of Utah
Miss Harriet Greenaway, Bristol Polytechnic
Professor A.H. Halsey, University of Oxford
Mr Peter Holmes, Department of Education for Northern Ireland
Dr Edwin Kerr, Council for National Academic Awards
Mr G.Kloss, University of Manchester Institute of Science and Technology
Professor Maurice Kogan, Brunel University
Dr Robert Lindley, University of Warwick
Councillor N.P. Lister, OBE, Coventry Education Committee
Dr David MacDowall, Polytechnic of North London
Professor Graham Moodie, University of York
Professor Peter Moore, London Business School
*Mr David Morrell, University of Strathclyde
Mr Alfred Morris, Polytechnic of the South Bank
*Dr Guy Neave, Institut Européen d'Education et de Politique Société, Paris
Mr John O'Leary, *The Times Higher Education Supplement*
Mr Brian O'Reilly, Newcastle-upon-Tyne Education Department
*Dr John Pratt, North East London Polytechnic

Mr Christopher Price, MP
Professor Philip Reynolds, University of Lancaster
*Mr Peter Scott, *The Times Higher Education Supplement*
Professor John Sizer, Loughborough University
Mr Martin Stott, National Union of Students
Mr John Thompson, Department of Education and Science
Dr Noel Thompson, Department of Education and Science
Mr Chris Tipple, Leeds Education Department
Professor Leslie Wagner, National Advisory Body for Local Authority
    Higher Education
Mr W.S. Walton, Sheffield Education Department
Mr David Warren Piper, University of London Institute of Education
Mr Phillip Whitehead, MP
Sir Bruce Williams, The Technical Change Centre
Professor Gareth Williams, University of Lancaster
Mrs Jennifer Wisker, Cheshire Education Department

---

*Author of paper

INTRODUCTION AND ACKNOWLEDGEMENTS

The structure and governance of higher education is at any time a large theme. In the context of the sharp reduction in university resources and the 1981 allocation exercise by the University Grants Committee (UGC), the creation of the National Advisory Body (NAB) and the attempt by the Department of Education and Science (DES) further to restructure the colleges and institutions concerned with teacher training, it has become one of the major topics of concern for higher education. Too often such concern within higher education degenerates into a desire for self-protection and an automatic distrust of external intervention. It is increasingly clear, however, that the political and social environment of higher education is changing very rapidly and that by the early 1990s its structure and governance will look very different from today. This volume in the SRHE Leverhulme series, and the seminar which preceded it, were intended to develop some ideas and recommendations as to what the new structure ought to look like.

The seminar owed a significant debt to the work of the Parliamentary Select Committee on Education, Science and Arts under its chairman, Christopher Price, MP, which, in its report *The Funding and Organisation of Courses in Higher Education* (Fifth Report 1979-80 Vols. I, II and III HC 787 — I, II and III) and in its published evidence, opened up the subject of the structure and governance of higher education for national debate for the first time for nearly a decade. It has been a privilege to have been associated as an adviser with the Select Committee and the choice of themes for this book reflects a wish to re-examine in more detail some of the issues which that committee identified. In one major respect, however, the higher education scene has changed since the Select Committee's report was published: with the creation of NAB (very much along the lines recommended by the Select Committee). The implications for the future structure and governance of higher education of this new locus of authority are not easily calculable.

A further intellectual debt must be acknowledged to the experience many of us have gained over the years of the US higher education scene. For far too long the Robbins halo effect has hung around British higher education to the exclusion of new ideas developing in other countries. We were fortunate, therefore, to have amongst our contributors to the seminar Professors Burton Clark and Robert Berdahl from the United States, both of whom are very familiar with British higher education and have made major studies of higher education systems outside the US (Burton Clark on

Italy, Berdahl on the British UGC). In addition we had Dr Guy Neave, one of the few British researchers on higher education who has an extensive experience of European systems. Their contributions, along with those of John Anwyl, David Gardner, Gunther Kloss and Bruce Williams amongst the participants, ensured that our discussions took account of a broader perspective than would otherwise have been the case. A special word is due here to all the participants at the seminar; they were drawn from an unusually broad spectrum of interests and backgrounds which injected a strong element of realism and practical experience into our debates.

I should here like to acknowledge my gratitude to all the authors of the seminar papers making up this volume, and particularly to Lord Crowther-Hunt who uniquely amongst chairmen of the SRHE Leverhulme seminars was persuaded to write a paper for it as well as take the chair. In addition I should like to thank Rowland Eustace, Alf Morris, John Sizer, John Pratt, Donald Bligh and Gareth Williams for commenting on the first draft of Chapter 10. My thanks must also go to the SRHE Leverhulme 'team' of Gareth Williams as director, Betsy Breuer as programme administrator and Sally Kington as publications officer for all their support and advice. Finally I owe a debt to my secretary Sue Elliott who remained unruffled through it all in spite of much which should have provoked her.

Michael Shattock
Editor

THE STRUCTURE AND GOVERNANCE OF HIGHER EDUCATION

by Michael Shattock

The seminar on structure and governance was rightly the last of the topic-orientated seminars in the SRHE Leverhulme programme. Questions of governance and structure cannot be viewed as ends in themselves but only as related to the context of higher education and the demands of political/social accountability. Considerations arising from the labour market, policies towards access to higher education, institutional forms, the organization and funding of research, and resource allocation are all relevant to defining an appropriate structure; national funding mechanisms, relationships with the state, with government departments and with the community, together with the political environment in which higher education operates represent essential components in defining forms of governance. Previous seminars rejected a narrowly manpower-orientated higher education system, and called for a widening of access to higher education and a blurring of the distinction between 'advanced' and 'non-advanced' further education. They recommended an enhanced role for local communities in institutions in their locality, better institutional co-operation, both locally and across the binary line, the creation of a credit transfer system and the greater use of financial mechanisms to induce change and innovation. They urged the need for government to establish and publish broad strategies and guidelines for higher education and showed little enthusiasm for any substantial intrusion of market strategies into the planning of higher education. They believed that government should make more effort to establish research priorities and that a funding mechanism should be introduced which distinguished between support for undergraduate teaching and scholarship and for postgraduate teaching and research.

The structure of higher education in Britain and its governance systems result less from central planning and much more from a process of evolution. Neither the changes brought about by Robbins nor the establishment of the polytechnics (as Peter Scott makes clear in Chapter 9) marked radical changes of direction but rather a reinforcement of existing trends. The recommendations that have emerged from previous SRHE Leverhulme seminars emphasize the importance of ensuring that any system of structure and governance is sufficiently flexible to be able to respond not only to such recommendations but also to any other pressures for change. A second consideration relates to time-scale. Political decision making is notoriously over-concerned with the short term while higher education is inclined to require long lead times, particularly if broad changes of direction are to be brought about. Any recommendations about structure and governance need to provide signposts for the later 1980s and the 1990s rather than for the immediate short term. Nevertheless, the short term cannot be wholly ignored because governments as well as bodies like the University Grants Committee (UGC) and the National Advisory Body (NAB) need to identify the intermediate steps that have to be taken before major changes are made.

The period since 1978 has seen a rate of change in higher education unprecedented since the early 1960s. In December 1978 the Department of Education and Science (DES) issued its discussion document *Higher Education into the 1990s* (DES/SED 1978), following it up a year later with *Future Trends in Higher Education* (DES/SED 1979). Neither publication was particularly useful for its detailed forecasts of numbers in higher education (in common with the 1972 white paper *Higher Education: A Framework for Expansion*), but they signalled the debate over policies for a future contraction in home student numbers which was already in progress within the Treasury and the Department of Education and Science. They also drew public attention to the falling age participation rate and the presence of a considerable unsatisfied demand for higher education from the post 21-year-old population. The Model E proposals for a greater involvement by higher education in continuing education of various kinds, to take up any slack left by a contraction in the 18-year-old cohort, have been examined in various reports by the Advisory Council for Adult and Continuing Education (ACACE). However, the effects of the demographic downturn and the possibility of 'tunnelling through the hump', both foreshadowed in a little noticed, but influential publication from the Central Policy Review Staff (CPRS) *Population and the Social Services* (HMSO 1977), represent an essential backcloth to any consideration of the governance and structure of higher education in the 1980s and 90s.

As higher education continued to expand through the 1970s, interest grew in questions of co-ordination, particularly in relation to the public sector. The Oakes Working Party recommendations for a new public sector body were not proceeded with by the Conservative government when it came to power in 1979, but the whole question of the organization, co-ordination and control of higher education was the subject of a report by the Select Committee on Education, Science and Arts in 1980 (*Fifth Report* HC 787—1 1980). This report recommended inter alia:

1   A Committee for Colleges and Polytechnics (CCP) should be set up by the secretary of state to give advice and make recommendations about the finance, administration and planning of institutions in the maintained sector engaged in advanced further education.
2   The CCP, together with the UGC, should set up a joint secretariat with DES observers, to co-ordinate planning in higher education.

3   When the CCP is set up the government should bring forward proposals under which it is the duty of the UGC and the CCP to make public more information about their activities and methods of administration, and about the formal advice they submit to government.

4   The lay membership of the UGC should be increased to include further representatives of local education authorities (LEAs) and both sides of industry.

5   The government should, after a period of not less than five years and not more than ten years from the setting up of the CCP, review both its functions and those of the UGC.

6   All colleges, polytechnics and universities should submit to the UGC or the CCP, for approval, detailed statements regarding their purposes and objectives. When approved, these statements should be published and used as a 'touch-stone' against which proposals for new developments should be considered.

7   The regional advisory councils should be abolished. Some of their activities, not involving higher education, may need to be continued by a smaller organization.

8   Institutions of higher education and local education authorities should co-operate on an area or sub-regional basis in voluntary planning, particularly for continuing education, and every institution of higher education should be required to publish an annual report on the extent to which facilities are being shared, and draw particular attention to unnecessary duplication.

Problems of co-ordination were repeatedly emphasized in all the evidence to the Select Committee put forward by the major constituent bodies in higher education, and the need for a machinery to encourage co-operation between the UGC and the public sector was even more sharply emphasized when the implications of the reduction in government expenditure on higher education became apparent. The DES' first reaction appears to have been to transfer the public sector institutions wholesale from local authority to DES control. The furore caused by a leaked memorandum to this effect which appeared in the THES, followed by a clearer appreciation of the costs and administrative burdens involved, led to a reconsideration. Pressured further by a decision of the Council of Local Education Authorities (CLEA) to set up its own co-ordinating body for the public sector, the government issued its consultative document *Higher Education in England outside the Universities: Policy, Funding and Management* (DES 1981). This contained a comprehensive discussion of the issues involved and set out two possible models: A, which followed the arrangements proposed by CLEA; and B, the centralized DES proposal. With the arrival of a new secretary of state and parliamentary under-secretary the DES proceeded to establish a National Advisory Body for

Local Authority Higher Education (NAB) for an initial three-year period pending the consultation process, and to provide for representation of the UGC on the NAB and vice versa.

The role of the DES has also been changing. In Chapter 4 Robert Berdahl describes the background to the transfer of the UGC from the Treasury to the DES and the creation of a universities' branch within the DES. In Chapter 3 Lord Crowther-Hunt refers to and endorses criticism by the Organisation for Economic Co-operation and Development (OECD) of DES planning mechanisms at the time of the 1972 white paper. The Select Committee in its 1980 report cast serious doubts on the DES' ability to match its claim to be able to co-ordinate higher education. Since then, however, some significant changes have taken place. Within the DES reorganization has eliminated a separate universities' branch and sought to provide a much closer integration in the forward planning and resource management of university and public sector higher education. The parliamentary under-secretary with responsibilities for higher education has taken the chairmanship of the NAB Committee (which, as John Bevan points out in Chapter 5, has no parallel in the UGC) while the secretary of state, who has played a much more robust role than his immediate predecessor in defending his department's policies and those of the government towards higher education, has issued written and public guidance to the UGC and the NAB and sought in return formal advice on a number of questions. His decisions about further reductions in teacher training numbers have differed significantly from those recommended to him by the advisory committee (ACSET) established for the task. The consultative document stated that higher education needed 'a national assessment of priorities, national planning and a due degree of central control' and it looks very much as if the DES is now in the process of seeking to undertake this task.

The cuts in higher education expenditure have had the beneficial effect of concentrating a good deal of positive thinking on the wider economic role of higher education. With its responsibilities for the training of specialist manpower — doctors, health workers, veterinary scientists, and so forth — higher education has strong links with government departments like the Department of Health and Social Security or the Department of Agriculture. There are also important service and research relationships between higher education and a wide range of government departments. The Select Committee on the Social Services (HC 191 1982) reported critically on the effect the UGC's cuts had had on university medical schools' ability to carry out National Health Service commitments. The Education, Science and Arts Select Committee called for a direct link between the Department of Industry and the UGC to ensure that the Department of Industry, as 'lead department' for the development of biotechnology, can bring direct influence to bear on the UGC side of the 'dual funding' system (HC 289 1982). What has become clear is that higher education's interests and relationships extend far beyond the DES. It is significant that the Finniston inquiry into engineering education was launched by the Department of Industry, which has its own Education Unit, and that the mushrooming programme of vocational training for 16—19-year-olds is carried out by the Manpower Services Commission under the Department of Employment and not the DES. All this raises the question once again as to whether higher education's broad remit is best served by being located within the DES. Would a ministry of higher education, as exists in some countries, take a more comprehensive view of higher education and find a way of relating to and harnessing other government departments' interests more effectively than the DES? The Department of Industry, in a paper submitted to the SRHE Leverhulme programme, made clear that it took a direct interest in three aspects of higher education: in the culture and values it projects, in the curriculum, and in the structure which it believed inhibited change, but there is no machinery through which such interests can be reflected.

Questions of co-ordination tend to come down to who should co-ordinate and what level of co-ordination is required. One model which some find attractive is the Australian (Commonwealth) Tertiary Education Commission (CETC). This body co-ordinates the universities, the colleges of advanced education (CAE) and the technical and further education colleges (TAFE) through three separate committees. Another approach is the state co-ordinating commission developed in the United States and described by Robert Berdahl in Chapter 4. On current evidence the DES seems to favour a strong department co-ordinating a separate UGC and NAB but by 1990, with a contracted higher education system, a merged UGC and NAB might represent a more appropriate piece of machinery. In judging these models, concepts of public accountability or, as the DES puts it in its consultative document, 'public confidence' in the governance of the system are crucial.

Much depends on the extent of the co-ordination. The Select Committee wished to minimize co-ordination at the DES level, relying on UGC/public sector body collaboration (it proposed they should have a joint secretariat), and placed more emphasis on market forces. It quoted with approval the final report of the Carnegie Policy Studies (*Three Thousand Futures: The next twenty years for higher education* 1980) which suggested:

'... that reliance for contraction be placed mainly on the student market, letting the students decide which colleges and major programs within colleges will lose enrolments. We emphasize again nevertheless, as we have done before, that colleges should maintain some reasonable balance among essential programs and not rely on student choices alone. Students, particularly as they get good advice from counselling agencies (and we believe these agencies should be greatly strengthened) can probably make as good decisions, by and large, as can planners.

And the process is so much easier politically — it is easier for the students to make the hard decisions one by one. For this process to work well, there need to be not only well-informed consumers but also fair competition among institutions based on the quality of their service.'

The report also urged greater institutional autonomy within a framework of US style 'mission statements'.

One effect of the cuts has been to put the UGC much more firmly in the driving seat as far as the universities are concerned, and it is difficult to see how the NAB can avoid moving in the same direction. Any change which related recurrent grant more to national research strategies would also reinforce the power of the centre, whether that power were exercised by a tertiary education commission, by DES through UGC, NAB and the research councils, by a combined UGC and NAB, or by some kind of department of higher education hived off from the DES.

Such considerations, however, ignore two important questions which have both practical and political significance. The first is the extent to which higher education should be seen as concentrated within a limited number of say a hundred (or even fewer) institutions. There remains the view, strongly held both by the local authorities and by many educationalists, that education should be seen as a continuum and that higher education should not be separated from its roots in the schools and institutions responsible for the education and training of 16 to 19-year-olds. The 'seamless robe' argument particularly affects the status of the range of institutions which offer both advanced (AFE) and further education (FE) courses. If all such institutions were to be included in a unified higher education system, practical issues of management would become paramount. The second question relates to the way local or regional concerns can be reflected in the governance of higher education. Once again the 'seamless robe' question is important. The dangers of centralization and the importance of local and regional influence are too obvious to require reiteration, but the practical problems of meshing local or regional mechanisms with central co-ordination are considerable both bureaucratically and politically.

2

GOVERNING THE HIGHER EDUCATION SYSTEM

by Burton R. Clark

The question is simple: what is it that we wish to govern? The answer is complex, since the contents of governance, the activities we wish to shape and control, change qualitatively as we move from one sector of society to another. In spite of this obvious fact, we still encounter much opinion to the contrary. Recent graduates from schools of management often expect to govern and administer higher education in the same way as transportation and national defence, and one still hears echoes in the daily press in various countries of traditional principles of governance and management that treat all sectors as the same. Academics then seem to be merely special pleaders when they claim uniqueness for higher education and thereby seek exception from the conventional wisdom of business-school graduates and the editorial writers: just one more interest group asking donors to leave the money on the stump and otherwise accord full self-government and operational autonomy. But, rightly made, the case is powerful. Persons who know how to govern higher education in order to make it productive know what this realm is about and how it is constituted. The interests of academics can certainly have a better marriage than they do now with the enlightened interests of those bureaucrats and politicians who become responsible for much system-wide allocation and order.

My task is to concentrate on the essential nature of the organization of higher education and then to address the problems of governance. I will lump major national systems together, despite their profound differences, in order to emphasize underlying features of this sector of society. I want to emphasize the internal logic of the system, the deepest roots of order and change. I will therefore largely ignore contemporary issues, at least by way of direct attack, and reserve my warranted biases for a set of closing commandments.

If we wish to explicate unique features of higher education, as well as identify those held in common with other societal sectors, we should not begin with statements of purpose. Such statements can be usefully analysed as official rhetorics that serve in many ways: ideologies that legitimate a sector in the eyes of outsiders; doctrines that help link participants and improve their morale; warm blankets thrown over the cold bed of self-interest. But formal purpose must be avoided like the plague if we are to determine what occurs in higher education that heavily conditions the problems of governance. It matters not whether we are in small or large countries, the East or the West. Swedish statements of purpose in higher education, eg 'democracy, personality development, social change', tell us no more than American statements, eg research, teaching, and service: the latter doctrine leaving limitless scope to what can be researched, what can be taught, and what can be applied as a service, with of course some equality and life enhancement thrown in along the way. Such official declarations in Communist nations as those in Poland, 'instruction of qualified personnel for all jobs in the economy, culture, and all sectors of social life requiring credentials of higher education,' and 'education for self-fulfilment,' hardly improve upon the situation (Kerr 1978).

In short, the purposes of a broad sector are increasingly stated in general terms. As stated purpose is widened, it provides little or no guidance in the making of decisions or in otherwise influencing the actions of groups and the behaviours of individuals. Wide-open philosophies leave the answers to operational mandates and interest-group struggles. The first injunction is clear: if we want to know the score about activities in a large sector of society, we should stay away from stated purposes. Especially in education!

THE FACTORY FLOOR IN HIGHER EDUCATION [1]

The first way to go is to the 'factory floor', to production. There we ask about tasks and related technologies. There we ask about what makes the system productive, in operational terms. And then we are positioned to ask which structures of management and governance help the system to be productive and which ones stand in the way.

The factory floor in higher education is cluttered with bundles of knowledge that are attended by professionals. The professionals push and pull on their respective bundles. If they are doing research, they are trying to increase the size of the bundle and even to reconstitute it. If engaged in scholarship other than research, they are conserving, criticizing, and reworking it. If teaching, they are trying to pass some of it on to the flow-through clientele we call students, encouraging them to think about its nature, how it may be used, and perhaps take up a career devoted to it. If engaged outside the 'plant' as advisors, consultants, or lecturers, academics further disseminate knowledge or try to draw out its implications for practical use. What academics most have in common is that they work with and upon knowledge. What they have least in common is common knowledge, since they are at the cutting edge of specialization in high knowledge. They are rewarded primarily for going off in different directions, now and then calling up a theory or an approach that reintegrates but otherwise busily fragmenting as if prestige and their own version of the good life depended on it, which it does.

Our fragmenting professionals long ago discovered a firm foundation for worker self-management, since each cluster knows something that the others do not know and can do something that the others cannot do. Their separate tasks have separate technologies: the clusters become distinctive 'thought groups' supporting different 'thought styles' (Fleck 1979), as well as different specific methods and tools. Each group becomes authoritative in a 'subject' or field of professional preparation. Each virtually owns an area of work by virtue of required expertise. If tenure did not exist, the nature of knowledge control on the factory floor of higher education would call out functional substitutes.

These ever more specialized professionals have little need to relate to one another within the local shop in order to do their work and be rewarded. They can produce on their own: new knowledge in physics, student graduates with a better grasp of history, engineering advice to a specific business firm. Attempts at general or liberal education push them towards one another, to compose larger bundles, but such efforts have been held largely to the first two years of 'college', as in the United States, or, more generally throughout the world, located entirely in secondary education. Producing separately for the most part, the many groups become an extreme case of loosely-linked production. The university is a gathering place for professionalized crafts, evermore a confederation, a conglomerate, of knowledge-bearing groups that require little operational linkage. Members of these groups steadily cell-split to get away from each other — sociologists from anthropologists, biochemists from biologists and chemists, historians of science from historians and scientists — the better to mine a vein of knowledge.

What is most stunning about the operational level in this sector of society is how much the main personnel are oriented to, and controlled by, an affiliation to others like themselves who are located elsewhere. 'Disciplines' and 'professional fields', we call these extra-factory authorities, and we know much about their potency in the minds of academics, their primacy in guiding actions. Wise investigators, like Tony Becher (1981), are now off studying the separate cultures of the individual disciplines. Anyone who does fieldwork inside universities is soon made aware of the vast differences among the many cultural houses. To become a disciplined worker in higher education is to take up residence in one of those houses; or more precisely, to place one's self in a local branch of a widely distributed estate.

Thus we are confronted with a huge master matrix in which the academic person comes under dual authority, simultaneously belonging to a discipline and an enterprise. The discipline is the functional specialty, the primary home. Training is taken here; identification is strongest here. The specialist, in effect, then goes out to a 'project' or 'problem' grouping that we call the university, where various specialists are brought together, commonly for purposes of teaching. But the specialist goes on specializing, indeed often serving locally as a one-of-a-kind expert in such singular slots as historian of the American West, survey methodologist, expert on Japanese politics.

Authoritativeness within the university not only locates at the department level but is also acquired by very small groups and even individualized.

This duality of identification and commitment is not simply a phenomenon of the last several decades. It is at the heart of modern systems, rooted in the great strengthening of the disciplines that occurred in the nineteenth century in Continental Europe, Britain, and America. Germany led the charge: 'By 1840 the new conception of the professoriate which regarded research and disciplinary prestige as the supreme professional values had permeated all the universities of Prussia' (Turner 1971 p.181). Behind the charge was a new ideology, emphasizing creativity and a dynamic concept of learning; a new competitiveness within and among the universities that fostered achievement and the spread of the new mode throughout the German system; *and* the assistance of state officials, especially through intrusion in professorial appointments, that helped to break the hold of eighteenth-century norms and to stimulate the rise of the new professors (Ben David and Zloczower 1962; Turner 1971). The disciplinary imperative has been a basic fact of organizational life in the leading international centres of learning for well over a century.

The location of authoritativeness at the operating level is the natural ground for the most unusual types of academic influence, the personal and collegial forms discussed below. Academic departments consist in part of autocrats who individually run certain operations, even dictatorially, and then come together as equals and part-equals to decide collectively on larger matters, thereby operating in a way not readily duplicated in other sectors of society. The other sectors are different in that they are not simultaneously discipline-based and discipline-diversified. They are not extensively composed as a matrix of disciplines and enterprises.

Thus, we may note in passing, we should not ask a business firm to operate like a university. This is hardly fair. Unless, of course, the firm bases itself on diverse bundles of knowledge and contains diverse groups who know how to use those bundles. As industry moves in this direction, led by high-tech sectors, professional personnel nudge business firms towards the university model. For the sophisticated business executive, relevant lessons may be just down the street, in the university department or laboratory, saving the expense of a trip to Osaka. Top business managers also share with their counterparts in higher education the problem of occasionally getting away from marketing, finance, and merger in order to understand what is going on down where the work of production is located.

The relative weight of the discipline and the enterprise clearly varies across a higher education system. The bonds of speciality become extremely strong under certain conditions, relatively weak under the constraints and rewards of other contexts. The conditions of the research university, carried to the extreme, produce a fanatical pursuit of research and scholarships that amounts to a withdrawal from the university and is the bane of staff co-operation and attentive teaching. The university then becomes a set of research academies. In contrast, the condition of such short-cycle units as the US community college, carried to the extreme, denies expertise, turns the academic into a school teacher, and pulls him or her virtually out of the discipline and perhaps out of the overall academic profession. The college then becomes a secondary school or, more likely, a community centre.

It is the compromises of matrix structures in which academics come under reasonably potent dual authorities and have reasonably viable dual memberships that prevent either of the extremes from dominating. Of course, the organizational problem all along has been to arrange the structure of each national system so that the key personnel can serve two masters. But the problem has been greatly exacerbated in the decades since World War II. The numerical expansion of more-accessible higher education caused a great expansion in the number of institutions and increased their scale. The dynamics of specialization in modern research and scholarship caused a great expansion in the number of disciplines and sub-specialities and also increased *their* scale. Hence we have vastly increased the density of intersects of disciplines and enterprises, the centres of dual allegiance where academic persons work both for their universal field of study and for their local institution.

Any given university or college is then a hothouse of differences. It is not the case that a department is a department is a department. Across all the many fields of the arts and sciences, and the professional schools, different structures of knowledge will condition the styles of operation. As research on departments has already determined, 'any attempt at universal standards for academia will impose a uniformity of activity and output which is inconsistent with the particular subject matter requirements of specific areas' (Biglan 1973 p.213). And, 'any attempt to change the university must take into account the intimate relations between the structure of knowledge in different fields and the vastly different styles with which university departments operate' (Lodahl and Gordon 972 p. 71). Thus, it is not irrational, self-interested academics who stand in the first instance against the wishes of planners who seek greater uniformity and coherence. It is the very nature of the enterprise, the substances on which the system is expected to work and the enormously varied structures of thought and appropriate procedures that follow. The variation in subject matter that is part and parcel of the system produces a need for extreme non-uniformity: in structure and procedure, in policy and governance.

THE PRESS OF EXTERNAL AND INTERNAL BELIEFS[2]
The second way to go in grasping the understructure of higher education is to the symbolic side of organization: the beliefs that participants use to determine the tracks along which action will be led and the values that are pressed upon the system. Here confusion reigns, since there are so many

vague beliefs and values afloat in and around the system. And that is the point: there are many of them, each legitimate and insistent; they are nearly always ambiguous; they contradict one another; they undergo periodic redefinition; and we sense greater uncertainty for the future in what we want done and the norms we should live by in choosing how to do it. All of which conditions how governance does and ought to occur.

Within the system faculty members are heavily influenced by the beliefs of their individual disciplines. They also absorb to some degree the traditions of the institution to which they belong. They receive additional guidance from the norms of the overall academic profession that, for example, define plagiarism as a high crime. They may even come under indistinct styles of a national system in its entirety, eg greater emphasis on the quality of undergraduate instruction in the British system than in the American, more emphasis on humanistic thinking in the Italian system than in the German. These internal sources of academic culture often push the academic in contradictory ways, as in the frequent tension between disciplinary and institutional imperatives.

Then, written larger, there are also broad sets of values that are impressed upon the system by many external groups as well as picked up as virtues by those on the inside. Four such sets are now prominent: cursory review will serve to identify them and indicate their complexities and contradictions.

Virtually all of us want social justice effected in higher education and some among us take this value as the primary concern. Fair treatment for all is pressed upon modern academic systems as a set of issues of equality and equity, first for students and second by and for faculty, other staffs, enterprises, and whole sectors. The definitions vary enormously from one nation to another: for example, equality of access may be taken to mean everyone qualifies or that only those who meet certain standards may enter. The weight of the equality pressure may shift from equal access to equal treatment to equal outcome; or run the reverse route in those countries that began with the promise of a national degree, then moved to make programmes as uniform as possible, and then finally, post-1960, got around to worrying about who entered. Whatever their specific definitions, the equity values are inescapable. Actors must cope, structures must be adjusted, to the claims of have-nots for access, and the protections that are contained in the norms of fairness.

As a second value, nearly all of us want competence in the system. The preference for competence comes in many sizes and shapes: in the work of individual professors and their departments; in the quality of students at entry and exit; in the effectiveness of whole institutions and sub-sectors; in provisions for liberal education, professional training, research, and criticism. Quality is a crucial criterion in the rewards of scientific fields, and 'best-science' is on the minds of government officials and business executives as well as senior scientists. Basic to the preference for competence is the robust fact that fields of study are structures of knowledge that have to be mastered by those who teach and those who learn. The general framework of education cannot take any shape at all that will fit other values but must be constrained by the relatively fixed forms constructed in the many fields as ways of organizing knowledge (Annan 1975). There is science, mathematics, languages; grammar and logic, induction and deduction.

Much has been said in recent years about equality and excellence in higher education, particulary about some of their more apparent conflicts and contradications, but little attention has been paid to juxtaposing an insistent set of values that we may call freedom or liberty: freedom of action as the basic condition for exercising choice, encouraging initative, engaging in innovative behaviour, allowing criticism, and inducing variety. Liberties are sought by groups and institutions as well as by individuals. Departments seek self-determination within the university; the university presses for autonomy from the state and outside groups. This set of values includes the powerful academic ideologies of freedom of research, freedom of teaching, and freedom of learning. And basic is the spreading desire for individual self-expression that comes to more people as democratic values raise expectations of individuality and economic progress provides time and resources for something beyond dawn-to-dusk routine labour. Linked to the desire for self-expression is a desire for variety and even for eccentricity — the latter, I understand, has deep roots in Britain. The future will be full of people thinking that higher education can help them be creative; and creative people, in myth and in fact, have long modelled to the world how richly rewarding it is to be inconsistent and eccentric.

And then nearly everywhere we have state-defined virtues and requirements operating as a fourth broad set of values, aside from and often counter to equality, excellence, and liberty. Sheer loyalty to the central political regime is at the heart of the higher education question in one country after another, coupled with associated moral virtues that are defined by public officials — 'virtuocracy,' as conceived by Susan Shirk (1982) in a study of education in Communist China. Virtuocracy is a particularly intense form of regime loyalty that centres on the moral transformation of individuals and society, and possesses such boomerang effects as alienation, sycophancy, and cadre privilege. More widespread are the efforts of central officials to have academics commit themselves to nation-building, as centrally defined, from the infrastructure for transportation and communication — do engineering, not classics! — to the social integration of tribes and factions and the cultural integration of singular identities. On down the continuum of less severe mandates lies the accountability thrust that has developed in the most advanced systems as the costs of higher education have moved it up the governmental agenda. In short, the state, in the form of specific bureaus and officials, comes at higher education with many preferences and priorities, guidelines and commands, that run on a different axis of value from equality, excellence, or liberty.

Merely to identify four such broad legitimate orientations is to suggest the confusion that must necessarily follow, since the conflicting values press behaviour in contradictory directions and encourage antithetical forms and procedures. Social justice presses towards open-door admission, mass passage, and uniform graduation. But competence argues for selection at the outset, willingness to fail and weed out, and for graded certification that labels some persons as more capable than others. Liberty plays at times against both equity and competence, toward a maximizing of choice and celebrating of variety, away from fair shares and the uniformities that we call standards. And when regimes are preoccupied with the virtues of faculty and students, little heed is given to equal treatment or competent training or freedom of choice. Even those possessed merely by visions of cost containment and accountability can in the name of financial exigency, knowingly or unknowingly, lead a system into a stage where the other values are submerged.

Then, too, analysts of these primary orientations are increasingly stressing their internal complexities and contradictions. Equality becomes *equalities*, and, in practice, a bundle of contradicting impulses (Rae 1981). The demands of the state for 'relevance' to national development prod the university in conflicting directions: a practical socio-economic relevance stresses technology, natural science, and specific professional training; a cultural relevance, pointing often to cultural revival and national identity, hinges on support for the humanities and the social sciences, with particular focus on one's own country; and the imperatives of political relevance stress conformity, uniformity, and discipline. As noted by James S. Coleman (the political scientist) in the case of African universities: 'The ideology of relevance applied to frail new universities imposes upon them a heavy overload which is patently compounded when the demands upon them are so inherently contradictory' (Coleman 1981).

If such disparate primary values are each to be expressed, the understructure must be full of inconsistencies and contradictions. Then, system organization becomes compromise written large. The elemental strains and dilemmas widen and deepen as we expect more of higher education and work harder to embody these and other values.

To the great and growing complexity of the operating structure we can add the great and growing complexity of the normative side of academia.[3]

THE GOVERNANCE FIT[4]

At least we have now started in the right places. We have turned our backs on the mind-softening platitudes of the stated purposes of systems of higher education. Instead we have concentrated on the nature of academic tasks and the ways in which academic workers become grouped around the primary operations. We have also reviewed four sets of values (there are more, of course) that will inescapably affect how we organize higher education. Now we can turn directly to the many ways in which influence is distributed and applied in the system, remaining as much as possible at the system level of governance. But the perspective applied here remains bottom-up rather than top-down and more inside-out than outside-in. Centring attention on the work mandates and other internal logics of the system, we can ask: What governance arrangements are 'naturally' generated? What structures of governance help this or that function to operate well? What governance 'fits'?

The answers are considerably removed from the simple slogans of modern political ideologies as well as traditional managerial doctrines. The research of the last decade allows us to sort out some of the complications. We can: (a) grasp the basic forms of authority active in the system; (b) explore major means by which disciplines and enterprises are concerted and thereby turned into a system; (c) identify structural differentiation as the key problem of academic governance and point to the biases of alternative forms of differentiation; and (d) speculate about the respective merits and demerits of unitary academic government and more decentralized or federal-like arrangements of systematic influence. As we do so, we shall see that 'fit' is a matter of balance among alternative forms for effecting national governance. Too much emphasis in any one direction, for example upon state command, produces an imbalance that leads to a 'fit' in a different meaning of the term! — a sudden and violent attack of a disorder, a convulsion, an exacerbation of troubles perhaps leading to prolonged sickness.

In exploring the complexities of academic governance, we will not find any assistance in the type of political science of the last quarter century that reduced questions of power to the amount of influence that Person A has over Person B. Rather, conceptual sustenance is found in the growing amount of macro political analysis that seeks the specific structural location of legitimate influence, approaches that when combined point to three faces of power: the power of groups to prevail in overt conflict over explicit issues; the power of groups to keep issues off the agendas of action; and the power of groups to shape conceptions of what can and ought to be done.

Multiple Forms of Authority

As noted earlier, much authority in academic systems is discipline-rooted. Scholarly expertise confers a crucial and distinctive kind of authority. One aspect of that authority is personal: individual professors exercise extensive supervision over the work of students, and senior professors often do so over the work of junior faculty, with their decisions typically not closely circumscribed by bureaucratic rules or by collegial norms that foreclose individual discretion. 'Personal rulership' is an operative form, with age-old roots in the dominance of the master in the early academic guilds and strong ideological supports in the ideas of freedom of research and freedom of teaching.

The other main branch of knowledge-rooted authority is collegial rule, a classic form of traditional authority in which a body of masters or near-equals comes together on an essentially one-person-one-vote basis to decide matters and often to elect presiding officials. Collegial authority is so common in department meetings, faculty meetings, university senates and councils, and increasingly in the peer-review operations of national bodies, as to be virtually an assumption of the higher education system — a far cry from traditional business management. Its legitimacy is virtually unquestioned.

When personal and collegial authority are blended, the result is a guild arrangement in which the individual master has a personal domain within which he controls subordinates while the masters come together to exercise control over a larger territory of work: the field of study, the interdisciplinary programme, the college. This combination is often also known as professional authority, in juxtaposition to bureaucratic and political forms, but the term 'guild' remains the more precise of the two (Clark 1977 Chapter 5, 'Guild'). In practice, professionals exercise authority in a host of ways, through bureaucratic position and political struggle as well as by means of personal and collegial dominance.

In any event, we can assert confidently that guild (professional) authority is the bedrock of authority in academic systems due to its virtually 'natural' possession of subject-area operations. All other forms of legitimate power in the system have to take it into account and adjust to it. It has been there from the beginning, and it is widespread today. Marjorie Reeves (1970 p.64) speaks of the development of the guild form from the medieval period 'right down to the present age' and comments: 'The astonishing thing is that the medieval-guild model has served the Western universities so long and has shaped so powerfully the thinking of so many academic generations' in comparisonn to 'the industrial-plant concept' and other modern models. The guild understructure of the higher education system will bulk ever larger in the future. It springs directly from high knowledge that steadily increases and the esoteric expertise of academic workers that widens and deepens.

And then there is much creeping decentralization in modern systems that pushes authority back toward the levels where this form is strongest. Neil Smelser (1974 p.129) generalized well from a study of public higher education in California that 'as a system grows and becomes more complex, it becomes progressively unmanageable if day-to-day authority continues to rest with the central agency; although ultimate authority may still continue to reside in that agency, it becomes imperative to delegate operative authority to lower levels.' However, he also went on to say that often 'the decentralization lags behind the realities of growth'! More widely, Rune Premfors (1981) noted at the end of the 1970s that decentralization of operative authority had been considerable during that decade in Continental systems of higher education as national policies became increasingly comprehensive and ambitious. In the expanded, elaborated system, the centre cannot hold to the integrated control it might exercise over a smaller, simpler system. Planned or otherwise, authority slips toward operating units. If it does not, due to the resistance of accumulated rigidities or opposition of central governors, the system is likely to become 'progressively unmanageable.'

Directly above this bedrock authority in levels of organization there appear several forms that are more enterprise-based. One is trustee authority, prominent in Anglo-Saxon higher education historically and transferred internationally to many countries influenced by British and American models, in which there is some supervision by outsiders who are part-time, unpaid, and have primary commitments elsewhere. Trusteeship is a form of public influence effected without going through governmental channels. Most systems, emphasizing those channels, have managed to do without it, leaving specific and general publics to proceed through the legislature and the executive to influence policy, usually on a more system-wide basis. Thus trusteeship localizes such participation and influence, tying it to specific institutions. It then serves as an instrument of institutional aggrandizement, linking the interests of some outsiders to the welfare of the individual college or university.

The other major form of authority that is enterprise-based is the bureaucratic type. Most noticeable in the business side of the university, where there are hierarchies of bosses and clerks, an 'administration' also forms on the more academic side as the scale of organization increases. Bureaucracy at this level has been weak historically in the systems of the European Continent, but after the expansion of the 1960s such weak administration became seriously dysfunctional, generating a flow of reforms to strengthen it. Institutional bureaucracy has been modest in Britain, organized around the vice-chancellorship, and extremely strong in the United States where campus-level administration of a major sort is virtually a century old. Notably, the location of bureaucracy at this level produces another set of institutional boosters, since, even more than in the case of professors, job rewards and career successes depend directly on the apparent success of the enterprise. The perspectives and interests of local bureaucrats can then be fundamentally different from those of officials in central offices of regional and national systems.

Finally, at the system level, legitimate power attaches to bureaucrats, specifically to those in the ministry or department of education; to political figures, specifically to those debating educational matters in the political parties, the legislature, and the top positions in the executive; and to academic oligarchs, specifically to those serving on research councils, superior councils of public instruction, and such mediating institutions as the University Grants Committee. All are legitimate; all have a definite place. Everywhere, the interactions of the several central groups are complicated. And the underlying trend is towards greater complexity at the top, as well as at the bottom and middle levels, in the many forms of authority.

In any given system, there is a swirling mixture of at least a half-dozen major ways by which some persons legitimately acquire and exercise systematic influence over others. The odds are high that we will add more forms and related groups than we subtract, as we work to reform and improve our systems.

Multiple Means of National Integration

At the third seminar of the SRHE Leverhulme programme a year ago, devoted to the topic of change, I made brief mention of four pathways of co-ordination, alternative ways in which parts are linked together to form what we call a national system: the bureaucratic, the political, the oligarchic, and the market (1982). The first three are forms of authority, as identified above, in which efforts are made to take charge, to aggregate, to steer. The market form is qualitatively different, a type of interaction in which, in pure form, no one is in charge and matters are disaggregated. That action may be competitive or not, divergent or convergent. Market-type interaction may release energies and produce rapid change. But it may also become a great stationary force when institutions settle into a mutually-acceptable division of labour, or voluntarily become fixated on one rewarding model and thereby produce academic drift as the main form of change. And, of course, in real life the pure model is often overriden by monopoly and oligopoly, with one or two institutions sitting astride the entire institutional market. But whatever their specific nature in a given country, market-type interactions provide important elements of co-ordination, thereby substituting for governance. We will find all four pathways of co-ordination in any national system — at lease *some* political influence, *some* bureaucratic persuasion, *some* oligarchial dictate, *some* steering by various types of markets — but in quite different combinations.

The main point of my argument a year ago was that all four pathways of co-ordination were necessary, and needed to be studied and judged as a matter of balance in relation to one another, particularly over time. Each one can produce disasterous results, such as stagnation and failure of response. Each can facilitate change in one period, constrain it in another. Hence these forms tend to compensate for and stimulate one another — 'market failure' inducing state intervention, 'state failure' causing actors to seek market-like interactions — as in the growth of private sectors of higher education in recent years in many Latin American countries (Levy, unpublished manuscript). The rigidities of strong academic oligarchies on the European Continent helped to stimulate a host of political and bureaucratic intervention in the last two decades. Here too one must be impressed with the importance of multiple ways; a variety, even a redundancy, of pathways of system integration. That variety seems increasingly a required part of the territory, one rooted in the complexity of tasks we find on the factory floor and the plurality of values and interests the system must seek to implement. The means of co-ordination become ever more various.

Biases of Differentiation [5]

If support of variety is the name of the game, then much co-ordination and governance needs to put differentiation rather than integration at the centre of attention. How can we create more major parts? How can the parts be best related to one another in order to carry out particular functions or implement basic values? Several ideas can guide our vision.

First, conflict among basic tasks and values in higher education is accommodated better by diverse than by simple structures.[6]   The more diverse national systems are more capable of reconciliation than the simple ones. A composite of unlike segments and procedures: (a) permits better immediate response to different known demands; (b) allows varied later adjustment to the unknown and un-anticipated; and (c) provides a more ambiguous total space within which conflicting actions taken in the name of justice, competence, liberty, and loyalty can be played out. The sunk costs of each of the values are not so directly challenged because true believers get at least some territory of their own, are able to work their way around others, and find it difficult to determine who is doing what to whom. Those who are capable of holding several values in the mind at the same time find some structural supports for each and manoeuvre by shifting priorities over time.

Within their institutions, systems can and do generate more fields and programmes side by side at any level of training and more levels arranged in a progression of increasingly advanced tiers. Among their institutions, systems can and do proliferate institutional types, arrange the types in functional and status hierarchies, and make permeable the boundaries between the sectors so that students can move from one to another in search of different types and levels of training. Diversification is the key to how higher education systems effect compromises among a plurality of insistent tasks and values. Simplicity demands confrontation.

Second, in the service of competence, in a wide range of tasks, the crucial form of diversification in modern advanced systems is status differentiation among institutions. A moderate degree of hierarchy allows status to be awarded to institutions and sectors on grounds of perceived quality and encourages them to compete on this basis. One might immediately object and say that competence can be better achieved by administrative controls that seek to establish minimal standards and to reward for outstanding performance. But given the complexity of tasks and the compelling need for many parts to be semi-autonomous, it becomes virtually impossible, even self-defeating, to attempt to ensure competent effort in most of the system by top-down oversight, planning, and administration. Formal co-ordinators are in a steady state of frustration, as critics demand they improve the system and rulers send down commands from on high, while the levers of basic change remain remote to the touch if not hidden completely. The problem becomes sociological: namely, to find the ways to hook group and institutional self-interests to chariots of ambition. There must be something to be won by working harder to be better, by all those who man the understructure. The something is higher status and its associated rewards.

The question of balance in hierarchical arrangements immediately occurs. A middle-ground provides the openness and the incentives, the grounds for hope. Institutions can compete for better personnel, and hence young scholars can flow from one institution to another in search of better conditions of work. Institutions can shift their clienteles towards the higher-quality inputs of their betters. There are many reasons for worrying about academic drift, but competence as it is understood in the system and society at large is not one of them. Drift is towards 'better'; it is a standards-serving process because it pursues status, and status is linked to perceived standards. This is a prime reason why status hierarchies are not as bad as they are normally seen through the lens of modern interpretations of democracy. Where they do not exist, there will be strong pressure to create them in order to guarantee a bottom-up search for competence.

The importance of institutional status hierarchies in promoting competence has been stressed by 'best-science' advocates. Modern science at its best requires concentration of talent and resources. It can hardly be promoted by equalizing and thereby scattering talent and funds across institutions and programmes. France in the West and the Communist nations in general have tried to assist 'best-science' by putting it into a separate research structure — the national academy approach. The Federal Republic of Germany has used the many institutes of the Max Planck shelter. But if best-science, best scholarship more broadly, is to have protective and supportive locations within the higher education system itself, then there must be concentrations, some favourable treatment within and especially among institutions.

The problem is to couple some hierarchy with some openness, pluralism, and peer review, a problem noted in classic form by Henry A. Rowland, an American scientist and exponent of best-science élitism, who attempted to specify in the 1880s what needed to be done to improve the science of physics in the United States (Kevles 1979 pp.43—44, 375). The existing system of four hundred institutions he likened to a cloud of mosquitoes: hardly any could be compared with the 'great academies' found in Europe that provided 'models of all that is considered excellent' and thereby stimulated physicists to their 'highest effort.' There had to be some concentration of talent in physics in a few first-class universities. Best-science required an institutional pyramid, commanded at the heights by a best-science élite and open to talent at the bottom. All levels of the hierarchy would need to be pluralistic, with groups of physicists divided along the lines of specialty, training, and geography and having access to many journals and granting agencies. The US system, especially after World War II, did indeed evolve in the direction that Rowland had advocated.

Institutional hierarchy can be and often is a form of quality control. It apportions status, respect, and rewards on grounds of perceived competence, utilizing both public opinion and peer assessment. It can and often does concentrate resources efficiently for the carrying out of expensive tasks, from the forming of bureaucratic élites to the staffing of research laboratories. The problem is how thereby to preserve high standards while allowing for institutional and individual mobility.

Third, in the service of liberty, the most essential form of diversification is the creation and maintenance of different sectors and sub-sectors, down to the point of allowing institutions to be individually distinctive. Within the general system, enterprises need the freedom to initiate on their own and thereby choose a line of development. Much choice, we may note, can be made available within universities and colleges that are highly diverse within themselves, such as the 'educational city' that we call the American state university. But there are limits to the size and complexity of the individual enterprise which, when exceeded, cause severe problems of overload in work and management and confusion in organizational character. Institutions that try to do it all, replicating within their structures all that is found within the system at large — superinstitutions, we might call them — suffer some of the same problems of overload and characterological confusion as persons who try to be superwomen or supermen. Critically, certain bona fide interests will be resisted or suppressed. No matter how extensive its internal diversity, an institution will still have some dominating points of view that will cause it to handle some activities badly if not to prohibit them entirely.

The classic case in one country after another in recent years has been the resistance of university professors and administrators to short-cycle education, recurrent education, and various so-called 'nonformal' approaches. The resistance has a host of reasons that need not be explored here, but it has clearly weakened these forms of education. The groups that wish to carry the new values and work them up in operations need the freedom to choose for themselves. Hence a separate institutional form is usually preferable, rather than any attempt to implement the newer emphasis in the older settings where they are not congruent with controlling values and are not profitable for controlling groups (Levine 1980; Cerych and Sabatier, unpublished manuscript). The new institutions can bypass, in part, the resistance of the old ones, reducing the self-interest costs of change.

It is increasingly necessary to divide up work among institutions and types thereof so that different units can wholeheartedly devote themselves to different tasks. Professional training at many levels, general education of different types and for different kinds of students, research of quite different complexity that ranges from the most basic to the heavily applied — all can be assumed by different supporting structures, sorted out by planning or unplanned evolution or a combination of the two.

Notably, separate institutions are typically less coupled than the parts of a single organization and hence can reap the benefits of flexibility that inhere in loose coupling. We can extend to whole sets of universities and colleges the suggestive findings of recent analysis of coupling within organizations (Aldrich 1979 pp.83—84):

1   Loose coupling allows portions of the organization (or system) to persist and evolve independently of other parts. This is advantageous for change.
2   Loose coupling allows 'local adaptation of organizational (or system) sub-units facing environments that in the aggregate pose conflicting demands . Components can adapt without affecting or disrupting the overall adaptation of the whole.'
3   'Loosely coupled systems permit the retention of a greater number of mutations and novel solutions than do tightly coupled systems, as they survive in out-of-the-way units or rarely invoked practices.' These new or little used practices are cultural insurance or cultural capital, kept alive for possible later use.
4   'Loose coupling permits the confinement of a breakdown in one part so that it doesn't affect the rest of the organization.' As we have already noted, academic systems need ways of segregating failures, chiefly by means of low interdependence within academic enterprises and especially among them.
5   'Loose coupling may permit greater self-determination by persons in organizational sub-units, thus raising levels of involvement and generating a greater sense of efficacy among them.'

In short, a prime reason why undifferentiated national systems cannot handle modern higher education so well as complex ones is that they do not provide as much liberty for a range of ideas, activities, and supporting groups. Despite the confusion, duplication, and overlap thereby produced, a vast complex of institutional types and marginally differentiated institutions is the name of the game for liberty and innovation in modern higher education. But the problem is how to maintain a high level of institutional liberty and individual choice without limiting equality too severely and weakening standards too much. Permeable boundaries are crucial. Diversity becomes more acceptable to those with their eyes on equality if the diverse channels of participation are void of dead ends. Having second and third chances and the possibility of transferring from one sector to another, one institution to another, diminishes the disagreeable effects.

Similarly, diversity and a high degree of individual choice become more acceptable to those with their eyes on competence and consumer protection if some academic surveillance, such as accreditation, operates across sectoral and institutional lines, maintaining some minimal standards and reigning in the roguish behaviour of institutions and their staffs that amounts to consumer fraud.

Fourth, justice in higher education is most effectively implemented if it is institutionally disaggregated instead of applied in a blanket fashion across a system. As we have seen, competence and liberty require sectors and hierarchies; merit and choice entail differences and rankings, unlike segments seen as relatively high and low, noble and less noble, even as systems strain to blur the perceptions of the differences. Hence, if these two values are to be served even modestly well, system-wide equal access, treatment, and outcome are not possible.

The idea of disaggregating justice is not a popular one, since equity issues loom large on the national agenda in many countries, attracting parents, students, politicians, and administrators alike to the promise that inequities can be wiped out by sweeping measures. But system-wide attacks on equity issues in higher education have great potential for boomerang effects as they try to flatten institutional differences and to command a system to be unitary, thereby undercutting the grounds for competence and liberty. Since the system cannot be made operationally unitary and differences are maintained and enlarged, high expectations on equality are inevitably frustrated. Sooner or later, the vision of equity has to centre on fairness in segments of the whole and even possibly at the level of the individual institution.

Systems may thereby help contain the self-defeating tendency of the pursuit of equality. As Ralf Dahrendorf (1979) has noted, equality has a built-in frustration effect. Behind the demand for equality is the wish to extend opportunity: how can more people come to enjoy more life chances? But many life chances defy continuous extension, since to increase them past a certain point is to destroy them. The acquiring of a degree increases one's chances in life as long as the degree has some special value in the eyes of others. To be valuable, it cannot be had by all. As soon as most persons can have it, it adds little or nothing to life chances; take for example the declining value of such degrees as the high school degree, the associate in arts degree, and the bachelors degree in the American system. It is a bitter irony for those who vigorously pursue the equalization of access, treatment, and outcome in higher education, that the end results, if achieved, would be relatively worthless. Everyone would have the same thing but be worse off.

A more sophisticated concept of extension of opportunity apparently must be rooted in differentiation rather than integration, pluralities rather unities. Justice in academic systems will necessarily have to be varied and specific, attached to contexts that promote different competencies and, in their aggregate, widen the play of liberty.

Fifth, state control of higher education works better by long-run rewards than by short-run sanctions. States can have intervention strategies that respect the peculiarities of institutions organized around multiple fields of knowledge and where the values of justice, competence, and liberty must be exercised. But governments are inclined to reach for direct controls, rules that reduce day-to-day discretion. The imagery is: do this job in the following manner, do not deviate from this procedure — make sure every professor teaches twelve hours a week and reports periodically on how he spends his time. Negative sanctions are emphasized, generating defensive strategies by those to whom they are applied (Benveniste 1980). Then, too, when goals are not easily measured and compliance can only at best be partially evaluated, such sanctions soon lose effectiveness, frustrating those who try to apply them.

In contrast, governmental guidance can be effective over the long-run where governments concentrate on setting broad directions of development, maintaining the quality of the professional personnel, and supervising system in a mediated form in which the balance of control shifts from government to academics at sucessively lower levels. Key to this is the attractiveness of higher education as an area of employment (Is talent attracted or repelled?) and the quality of professional socialization (Are controls internalized in the individual academic and the operating group that make for responsible behaviour?) The state can have its 'accountability' in the form of general oversight alone, if professional controls within the system hold academics accountable to one another and to general norms of objectivity and fairness. Enlightened oversight is the way to go, since no matter how precisely governmental officials attempt to define objectives, the outcome will largely depend upon the co-operation of those in the system. And if we seek them out we may find many of the necessary mechanisms of efficiency embedded in the system. Reflecting on the growth of the disciplinary perspective in the nineteenth century in Germany, R. Steven Turner (1971 p.159) noted that 'appointive procedures which subordinate institutional to disciplinary values' are collectively a 'universal characteristic of the modern professoriate which underlies its unparalleled efficiency as an instrument of science and scholarship.'

Sixth, value ambivalence in higher education is mirrored in structural ambivalence. Modern complex higher education systems are mixed in character, rather than tending to one pole or the other: eg public or private, equity or excellence, liberty or loyalty. Like individuals, collectivities can be fanatical for a time, but the costs of pursuing only one set of values soon become too high and counter-reforms set in to restore the place of other values. The inherent contradictions of these systems in effecting basic social values lead to mixed structures.

Compromised systems also require modest expectations. Failure is often a shortfall against high expectations about how much we get done, how fast it will happen, and how superior will be the results. Many persons and groups, beginning with politicians, have a vested interest in promising large and quick results as they struggle competitively for favour in political and bureaucratic arenas. But systems that must intepret, embody, and implement a wide range of contradictory values need modest expectations on the possible realization of any one. And such realistic hope goes hand in hand with the growing uncertainty that attaches to policy and action. Organizational theory has come to emphasize the uncertainties produced within modern organizations by environments that change more rapidly than in the past. But it is not merely rapid change that is at work. There are also the pressures, within and without, of heavily-bearing values that have grown more numerous. Uncertainty comes from facing equalities *and* excellence *and* liberty *and* loyalty more fully than before. Modest expectations are an accommodation to this ambivalence of situation and response.

Unitary Bind versus Federal Pandora's Box

In the paper presented at the SRHE Leverhulme conference on change, in Bristol a year ago, I concluded with two points by way of advocating federal conceptions of academic organization. The first was that the university itself can be seen as a federal system, due to the way that the semi-autonomous, discipline-centred departments pursue interests and possess authority that are different from the interests and authority of the whole. This conception was particularly raised in recent analyses by Halsey and Trow (1971 pp.111—112) in their study of British academics, and by Moodie and Eustace in their study of British academic governance (1974 p.61), the latter concluding that 'whatever the precise boundaries of departmental autonomy, its existence makes of every university [in Britain!] a "federal" structure rather than a strongly centralized system.' The second point I made was to push the federal principle to the level of the entire system, not to advocate any particular division of powers among national government, provincial or state government, and institutions, but to point to the necessity of agency pluralism at each level of government as an instrument of checks and balances and the need to have bodies mediating between the centre and the periphery. This is clearly not the direction in which reform moves in most countries at this time in history. Rather, the main thrust is toward unitary system — sweeping post-secondary institutions as much as possible into a single formal system, consolidating educational activities at each level of government into one agency as fully as possible, and reducing further the operational independence of such buffering units as the British University Grants Committee.

In which direction is it safer to err? Surely what scares us about the federal approach — linked to the above analyses of matrices, redundancies, and loose coupling — is that we leave so much to chance. We let go; we raise the lid on an academic Pandora's box, not knowing what will come out, but suspecting we will be flooded with ills. To change the metaphor: we imagine a ship adrift, if we do not have purpose-designed rudders and stabilizers and a commanding staff on the bridge to keep a steady grip on the wheel. Numerous groups and individuals quite naturally do not want to take those kinds of chances. Spontaneous action seems too risky. Besides, others will steer if we do not. In addition, we know the way. Better to bind up the system, for there is too much mischief in disciplines and academic enterprises 'doing their own thing' — the analogue of the 'mischief of factions' in federalist theorizing.

Surely what we fear most about the unitary approach is the way it cramps a multiplicity of approaches and increases the likelihood of the arbitrary dictate and the large error. Nearly every time we plan centrally we eliminate some options of the operators. In each reform, we add structures that constrain future choices. If we do not want things to escape our eyes, we systematize some more, generating a rule book that clogs formal channels and in turn stimulates underground activity for getting things done. We no longer need to go to the European continent to observe such tendencies to bind a system: we can find them at home, in your system and in mine. And we can say by now that we are having some experience in Britain and America with arbitrary dictates that sweep across academic systems, without much trial-and-error to clear the way, and hence increase the likelihood that errors will be written large. Such errors naturally follow when the national centre assertively attempts to reshape the system and has accumulated the power to do so. And future generations will find the mistakes difficult to undo, since institutions of a particular character will have been closed, others deliberately weakened, high-quality personnel dispersed, power resolidified in an altered state, and alterations written down in central legislation and central administration rules.

The thrust of this chapter, of course, is heavily toward the federal side, basing the argument not on age-old principles but on the internal nature of the higher education system in the last decades of the twentieth century. It is functional to be federal. It is dysfunctional for the understructure of academic activities when the superstructure tapers to a peak and an hierarchy of encompassing control is thereby established.

SIX COMMANDMENTS FOR ACADEMIC GOVERNORS

Those who scoff at traditional principles of organization and management — as I did at the outset — and then go on to offer complex and even contradictory descriptions and explanations surely can benefit from occasional effort to put matters as bluntly as possible. If old principles of hierarchy of command and accountability are deficient, what are the precepts to take their place? If top-down thinking is particularly inappropriate for the higher education sector, what simple ideas help us grasp a bottom-up logic?

I suggest six points, enunciated as commandments in the hope that gall will concentrate the mind and provoke response. The commandments are intended for those who are positioned to govern higher education in its higher reaches, located at one of the levels of co-ordination that stretches from the campus to the national centre: multi-campus administrations, state and regional co-ordinating bodies, state and regional political institutions, national bureaus and national political channels, and voluntary associations that aggregate academic interests and press them upon government. In most countries, most of the time, the key figures in this superstructure are the civil servants who attend to higher education.

Commandment One: Thou shall conceive of higher education as bottom-heavy. Authoritativeness properly resides far down the line. Along the lower operational levels, it is radically fragmented and diffused, located in dozens, even hundreds, of groups and even in the activities of particular individuals. If much influence is not allowed to locate in this manner, the system is likely to malfunction. Trickle-up is more important than trickle-down.

Commandment Two: Thou shall understand disciplines as well as institutions. The discipline is the equal of the enterprise as a primary form of academic organization and a centre of production. The disciplines are intrinsically different from one another. They must be treated differently. Therefore they must be studied for their crucial differences. The sophisticated academic governor reads the history, sociology, and economics of science or asks staff to do so. A working knowledge of how the operations of physics differs from those of biology is as important as a grasp of student enrolments and projected capital expenditures.

Commandment Three: Thou shall divide power and otherwise seek to differentiate. Never seek to base higher education on one source of support, for then one encourages a monopoly of power. Never rely on one mechanism of allocation and governance, for when that nail is bent the battle is lost. If higher education must depend heavily on national government, then dependence should be on many bureaus rather than on one, that is, on an array of sources of funds rather than a single channel. Multiple sources of support permit the play of multiple interests, the expression of various values, and, through warranted redundancy, guard against heart failure from the clogging of a single artery. Much horizontal and vertical dispersion of influence is required. Those who press hard to neat up a system in the name of coherence and economy are probably damaging its long-run capacity to operate effectively. Centralization *and* formalization *and* the search for simplicity and efficiency reduce flexibility and diminish the capacity to change.

Commandment Four: Thou shall legitimate variety and ambiguity. One must help institutions and institutional sectors to develop and stabilize different roles, different mixtures of tasks. One must put an attractive gloss on ambiguity in purpose, procedure, and outcome. Appropriate doctrines need to be worked up and constantly used that justify unplanned variety. One should glorify muddling-through, redundancy, pluralism, organized anarchy, decision accretion, mixed systems. Justify trial and error, and tentative steps. Seek comfort in the benefits of disorder. Beliefs to the contrary will lead you and your colleagues into unintended and un-anticipated brinkmanship, even unknowingly creating revolutionary situations, as you seek to be clear and consistent and to offer stability and happiness.

Commandment Five. Thou shall build and support institutional initiative. Because of its bottom-heavy construction, higher education is peculiarly dependent on the release of energies at lower levels. A key level is that of the institutions as a whole. Due to the fragmenting strength of the disciplines, institutions need assistance in pulling their parts together. Forces operating from above, as in the case of segmental budgeting, also slash the university and college into segments and weaken the roles of those whose commitments are campus-wide. Institutional integrity has been weakened in many national systems during the 1960s and the 1970s, first by greater governmental involvement attendant upon expansion and then from the top-down efforts to contract and consolidate that we have witnessed in the late 1970s and early 1980s.

Academic governors should place high on their agendas the problem of strengthening the capacity of institutions to cope and develop. Governors should be worrying more about leadership at this level than about how to make institutions into co-ordinated units in an administered system.

Commandment Six: Thou shall support operational initiative. Over-exertion at the department level is the surest means of productivity. That exertion is best promoted by strengthening the conditions of independent judgement in such core activities as student admission, curriculum development, and faculty selection. Accountability has to depend on professional self and small-group control, with heavy dependence on the incentives of the disciplines for good work. More in this sector of society than in others effort will be discouraged by top-down command and system-wide routine. As severe as it may be, the boredom of workers in industry will be light compared with the problem of boredom among academics when political and bureaucratic controls preclude local choice in the performance of the many activities of the many different academic clusters. Much self-determination is a functional requirement.

Reducing lower initiative is one of the favourite routes by which modern nation-states manage to get it wrong in relation to higher education. In at least a moderate degree, all state systems have this problem. Wise governors worry constantly about how to contain this tendency.

The question for Monday morning is: how can we liberate initiative at the institutional and operation levels?

CONCLUSION
Systems of higher education survive and produce effectively by an

extraordinary combination of inflexibility and flexibility. In their totality, they are indeed stubborn, often in the past persisting over decades and even centuries solely on the basis of a few fields of study, notably law, outliving political regimes, returning to vigour, much like other natural communities, after being laid low by war, famine, plague, depression, hostility, and simple neglect. There is always a common core that continues over centuries and that can be perceived under the various guises that it takes. That core contains a fixation on high knowledge, even a devotion to the idea that knowledge is an end in itself.

But then the variations on the basic forms of higher education are many and are destined to increase. Fields of study are added according to local and national will, private and public intentions, and virtually without limit. Since there is no way to stop the division of labour in society, there is no way to halt the division of knowledge in the academic sector. More of the population want in, interests thereby multiply, and over the long run inputs and outputs become more heterogeneous. The structure stretches, and then stretches some more. As we lift our eyes from the immediate administrative problems, what strikes the eye is increasing variety.

In any major country, the universe of intersects of academic enterprises and disciplines will be ever-more inexhaustible in quantity and type. In the diversity of the system lies its constant attraction and promise. Governance then becomes a word for how we attempt collectively to cope with that diversity: to steer, just a little, the many ways, most of them unplanned, by which the system elaborates itself, thereby exhibiting flexibility in settings of growing uncertainty.

NOTES

1 This section draws upon Burton R. Clark (forthcoming 1983) *The Higher Education System: Academic Organization in Cross-National Perspective* Chapter 1 'Knowledge', Chapter 2 'Work'. Berkeley and Los Angeles: University of California Press
2 This section draws upon Burton R. Clark *op. cit.* Chapter 3 'Beliefs', Chapter 7 'Values'.
3 For an instructive, systematic analysis of the British system of higher education that distinguishes the normative from the operational at four levels of organization, see Becher and Kogan (1980).
4 This section draws upon Burton R. Clark *op. cit.* Chapter 8 'Preferences'.
5 This section draws upon Burton R. Clark *op. cit.* Chapter 7 'Values'.
6 A similar argument may be found in Joseph Ben-David's study of the higher education systems of Germany, France, Great Britain, and the United States, from which he concluded that 'the feeling of crisis and anomie that prevails in many academic circles... derives mainly from internal causes, namely, the difficulties of systems of higher education to accommodate within their existing structures their new and extended functions' (Ben-David 1977 pp.180—181).

REFERENCES

Aldrich, Howard E. (1979) *Organizations and Environments* Englewood Cliffs, NJ: Prentice-Hall

Annan, Noël (1975) Equality in the schools. In John Vaizey (Editor) *Whatever Happened to Equality?* pp. 89—102. London: British Broadcasting Corporation

Becher, Tony (1981) *Physicists on Physics: The Aristocracy of the Intellect* Unpublished paper

Becher, Tony and Kogan, Maurice (1980) *Process and Structure in Higher Education* London: Heinemann

Ben-David, Joseph (1977) *Centres of Learning: Britain, France, Germany, United States* An Essay prepared for the Carnegie Commission on Higher Education. New York: McGraw-Hill

Ben-David, Joseph and Zloczower, Abraham (1962) Universities and academic systems in modern societies *European Journal of Sociology* 3, 45—84

Benveniste, Guy (1980) *Implementation and Intervention Strategies: The Case of PL 94—142* Unpublished Paper, Stanford — Berkeley Seminar on Law, Governance and Education, October 1980

Biglan, Anthony (1973) Relationships between subject matter characteristics and the structure and output of university departments *Journal of Applied Psychology* 57, 204—213

Cerych, Ladislav and Sabatier, Paul (Editors) *Implementation of Higher Education Reforms* Unpublished MS. Paris: Institute of Education, European Cultural Foundation

Clark, Burton R. (forthcoming 1983) *The Higher Education System: Academic Organization in Cross-National Perspective* Berkeley and Los Angeles: University of California Press

Clark, Burton R. (1977) *Academic Power in Italy: Bureaucracy and Oligarchy in a National University System* Chicago: University of Chicago Press

Clark, Burton R. (1982) A cross-national view. In Wagner, Leslie (Editor) *Agenda for Institutional Change in Higher Education* Guildford: The Society for Research into Higher Education

Coleman, James S. (1981) *The State and the University in the Republic of Zaire* Paper prepared for Conferences on Politics and Education, University of California, Santa Barbara

Dahrendorf, Ralf (1979) *Life Chances* Chicago: The University of Chicago Press

Fleck, Ludwik (1979) *Genesis and Development of a Scientific Fact* Chicago: University of Chicago Press

Halsey, A.H. and Trow, M.A. (1971) *The British Academics* Cambridge: Harvard University Press

Kerr, C., Millett, J., Clark, Burton R., MacArthur, B. and Bowen, H. (1978) *12 Systems of Higher Education: 6 Decisive Issues* New York: International Council for Educational Development

Kevles, Daniel J. (1979) *The Physicists: The History of a Scientific Community in Modern America* New York: Vintage Books

Levine, Arthur (1980) *Why Innovation Fails* Albany: State University of New York Press

Levy, Daniel *The State and Higher Education in Latin America: Private-Public Patterns* Unpublished MS.

Lodahl, Janice B. and Gordon, Gerald (1972) The structure of scientific fields and the functioning of university graduate departments *American Sociological Review* 37, 57—72

Moodie, Graeme C. and Eustace, Rowland (1974) *Power and Authority in British Universities* Montreal: McGill-Queen's University Press

Premfors, Rune (1981) *New Patterns of Authority in Higher Education* Paper prepared for Conference on Higher Education in the 1980s. Paris: Organisation for Economic Co-operation and Development (OECD)

Rae, Douglas (1981) *Equalities* Cambridge, Mass: Harvard University Press

Reeves, Marjorie (1970) The European university from medieval times. In Niblett, W.R. (Editor) *Higher Education: Demand and Response* San Francisco: Jossey-Bass

Shirk, Susan L. (1982) *Competitive Comrades: Career Incentives and Student Strategies in China* Berkeley and Los Angeles: University of California Press

Smelser, Neil (1974) Growth, structural change, and conflict in California public higher education, 1950 — 1970. In Smelser, N. and Almond, G. (Editors) *Public Higher Education in California* Berkeley and Los Angeles: University of California Press

Turner, R. Steven (1971) The growth of professorial research in Prussia 1818 to 1848 — causes and context *Historical Studies in the Physical Sciences* 3, 137—182

DISCUSSION AND COMMENT

Discussion centred around the role of the state in the governance of higher education. Was the chief problem to find ways of controlling state control? Or was it to find ways whereby higher education could be made to reflect more accurately the public interest, as interpreted by the government?

Perhaps not surprisingly the SRHE Leverhulme seminar opted on the whole for discussing the first. US experience suggested that the solution was to create multiple and cross cutting instruments of control, rather than allowing control to rest with one body, and to diversify as much as possible the range of funding agencies. In the US, it was argued, institutions and departments thrived best when governance was dispersed and lacked a coherent decision-making structure. In Britain, however, although funding was dispersed the ultimate source, whether for recurrent grant, fee income or research council grants, was the DES. Most speakers wanted this diversity of funding preserved and, if possible, increased. There was also general agreement that the range of patronage needed to be extended beyond government sources.

The argument for pluralist funding arrangements was put in several different ways. First, some saw it as simply a means of avoiding or minimizing state control. But it was also argued that governments found a heterogeneous funding system preferable. It was politically more defensible because there would always be some parts performing well, and it offered more scope for intervention than a single funding approach. A third and complementary argument was that governments are never omnicompetent and are liable to take decisions on an ideological basis. A pluralist funding system offered protection against governments' mistakes.

These arguments, however, all approached the problem putting the higher education interest first. Two contrary views were expressed. The first was that there was widespread concern in government that higher education was in a sense unmanageable: it was slow to adapt, it accepted uncritically a balance of teaching and research, it was broken down into departmental units that bore no relation to the problems outside, and it was run in such a democratic or participative manner that decision making was over-concerned to protect existing interests. The second was that it was not governments that created resources but society. Why should society be deprived of its legitimate role in the governance of higher education? How did higher education decide that it was satisfying society needs?

These views prompted a number of responses. Universities should concentrate their defence on what they were truly authorities on, the advancement of academic disciplines, rather than the broader canvas of societal needs, which was the responsibility of government. A distinction should be drawn between political and financial controls. The former should be resisted because they led to intervention in curricula, appointments and eventually research. Financial controls were a lesser evil. One speaker drew attention to the situation in France where the élite institutions were subject to more controls than the rest on the grounds of their greater importance to the state. This was the reverse of the situation in Britain. In most states, however, governments were not unified bodies and power was divided between different departments and ministries. This tended to benefit higher education, which could then play the system, seeking support for projects and programmes from a variety of different government sources. The seminar was broadly agreed that:

a It is important to encourage diversity amongst institutions and governance systems need to encourage institutional initiative.
b The existence of multiple sources of funding is an encouragement to institutional autonomy.
c A balance has to be struck in any system of higher education between the legitimate interests of the state and the professional expertise of the academic in the pursuit of his own field of study.
d External controls need to be differentiated between institutions serving different functions.

3

POLICY MAKING AND ACCOUNTABILITY IN HIGHER EDUCATION

by Lord Crowther-Hunt

This paper has a triple remit. The first is to consider how the central government in Britain makes and develops higher education policy; it suggests ways in which the policy-making process might be improved. The second is to consider the requirements of political accountability in both the formulation and the implementation of higher education policy. The third is to outline two alternative institutional models to give practical effect to the differing requirements of the principle of political accountability.

POLICY MAKING

Nowadays the accepted wisdom is that the election manifesto of the winning party sets the main policies of the new government. The pledges therein contained, the late R.H.S. Crossman argued, could be forced through any government department by a determined minister in the face of any degree of bureaucratic resistance. So, for Dick Crossman, the party manifesto was 'the battering ram of change'.[1]

There may be some truth in this general proposition — but, as far as higher education policy making is concerned, recent manifestos have hardly been clarion calls to specific action. Thus the Conservative 1979 manifesto simply said this about higher education:

'Much of our higher education in Britain has a world-wide reputation for its quality. We shall seek to ensure that this excellence is maintained. We are aware of the special problems associated with the need to increase the number of high-quality entrants to the engineering professions. We shall review the relationship between school, further education and training to see how better use can be made of existing resources.'[2]

Hardly any indication there of what has actually happened in higher education these last three years — unless actual higher education policy was foreshadowed in an earlier, non-specific, part of the manifesto which said:

'The state takes too much of the nation's income; its share must be steadily reduced. When it spends and borrows too much, taxes, interest rates, prices and unemployment rise so that in the long run there is less wealth with which to improve our standard of living and our social services.' [3]

This lack of specific commitment to specific higher education policies was also a characteristic of the Labour Party's manifestos of 1974. Thus in the manifesto of February 1974, the Labour Party simply pledged itself to:

'a big expansion of educational facilities for 16—18 year olds.' [4]

And its one specific pledge that 'All forms of tax relief and charitable status for public schools will be withdrawn' was, of course, implemented neither then nor later.

Nor did Labour's manifesto for the General Election of October 1974 set out much of a blue print for higher education policy — even though it devoted much more space to the subject than in the preceding February. Thus the relevant sections stated that:

'The Labour Party believes that full opportunities for the education of our children, our young people and students of all ages are an essential part of a fair society and indispensable to the social contract....'

'As in all our plans economic restraints are bound to influence timing. But the next Labour Government will:

"Stop the present system of direct grant schools and withdraw tax relief and charitable status from the public schools, as a first step towards our long-term aims of phasing out fee paying in schools;
Continue to move towards a fairer system of student grants;
Provide increased opportunities for further education and training including compulsory paid day release, especially for young people who leave school early; legislate for an annual review and an annual report to Parliament on youth services....
We will support the further development of the Open University which was founded by a Labour Government and which has enriched the lives of thousands of people of all ages." '

No doubt this absence of clear party policy commitments in the sphere of higher education is one reason why in recent years the main policy initiatives seem to have come from departmental officials. This was certainly what I found when I became Minister of State for Higher and Further Education after the election of October 1974. To my surprise the Prime Minister gave me no general guidance about the government's higher education policy nor any indication of what he hoped I might achieve in the department when he offered me the job. Nor did the Secretary of State for Education, Reg Prentice, when I reported to him during my first day at the Ministry. So I was left to do what I could with the department's higher education policies which I then inherited.

Primarily, at that time, the department was concerned with cutting back the number of teacher training places in England and Wales from 120,000 to 60,000 — the policy decision to do so having already been taken. Secondly, the department was concerned with forecasting the number of places to be provided in the future in the advanced sector of higher education to give continuing effect to the Robbins principle of providing enough places in higher education for those qualified and willing to take them up. Both these main policy questions were having to be considered in the climate of enormous pressure from the Treasury to restrain or cut back public expenditure. It was then that I became aware of the inadequacies of the department's approach to these particular problems and to policy making in general in higher education. These inadequacies are best illustrated first by considering the department's concept of educational planning and policy making at that time. Secondly, I want to show how these inadequacies were reflected in the department's policy of matching the output of teacher training colleges to the likely number of teaching jobs in the schools, and in the way the department was planning the longer-term provision of places in higher education.

The DES Concept of Planning and Policy Making

At that time (1974-5) the department very much prided itself on its own internal arrangements for long-term policy making. In particular there was 'Policy Group A' whose terms of reference were 'to review developments and consider future policy in relation to higher, further and adult education'. It was chaired by the Deputy Secretary for Higher and Further Education — and its members were the under-secretaries who headed the relevant operational branches (eg the under-secretary heading the universities branch and the under-secretaries heading each of the other three further and higher education branches) together with representatives (also at under-secretary level) from Finance Branch, Statistics Branch, HM Inspectorate, and Planning and Programmes Branch.

'Policy Group A' was responsible (as was its counterpart on the schools side — 'Policy Group B') to the 'Policy Steering Group' which was chaired by the permanent secretary and consisted of the two deputy secretaries, the Senior Chief Inspector, the director of Establishments, the Accountant General, the director of Statistics and the head of Planning and Programmes Branch. The Policy and Planning organization was serviced by the Planning Unit which had a sort of secretariat, co-ordinating and supporting role.

These institutional arrangements for long-range policy making were themselves inadequate in a number of ways (which the recent changes have done little to remedy). But more important than the institutional inadequacies was the department's whole approach to long-term planning and policy making. In essence, the department's concept of planning was far too limited. This was well set out in the OECD's highly critical study of the department's activities.[5]   The OECD report made, in effect, three main criticisms of the department's planning activities. All of them seemed to me, from my experience in the department, to be well-founded. Indeed, I had reached the same conclusions myself (and committed them to paper) after I had been in the department three months and before the OECD report was published.

The first of the OECD's criticisms is the by now well-known one that too much of the department's planning was done in secret — and was not, therefore, open enough to public gaze and scrutiny. This had at least two serious consequences as the OECD report pointed out:

'One is that in certain cases policy is less likely to be understood and therefore less likely to be whole-heartedly accepted when the processes that lead up to it are guarded as arcane secrets. The second is that goals and priorities, once established, may go on being taken for granted and hence escape the regular scrutiny which may be necessary for an appropriate re-alignment of policy.'

And to those criticisms could be added the further point that a number of outside bodies had a lot of expertise and experience to offer on education issues — the universities, the polytechnics, the local authorities and so on — and it was obviously to everyone's advantage that they should be able to make their contributions to long-term policy making while the departmental thinking was in its formative stage. Clearly, they could hardly begin to do this when the formative stage was conducted behind firmly closed doors.

The second, and to my mind more fundamental OECD criticism was of the department's concept of planning. And, broadly speaking, what the report is saying here is that the department saw its planning function as 'identifying existing trends' and then seeking to cater for them as best it could in the future. This is, of course, an essentially passive concept of planning — reacting to events. But the underlying assumption of the OECD report was that a much more positive concept of planning was needed. Planning in the OECD view should have been much more than a mere reaction to likely trends and demands. They took the view that trends and demands were not all god-given, immutable or natural. There was no worthwhile figure, for example, of likely 'natural' demand for places in our universities and other institutions of higher education in, say, the year 1981 (which was then very much the focus of attention) — though the department had talked a lot about such figures as 750,000 and 640,000 for that year. But the fact was (and the department's planning concept failed to recognize this) that we could have influenced any given figure for that year upwards or downwards depending on what was done about the level of student grants and other variables under the goverment's control.

Accordingly, long-range planning should have included considerations of where existing demands and trends were taking us — and, if they were taking us in the wrong direction, then we ought to have set about identifying new goals and sought to influence demand and trends accordingly. In other words planning should have taken a view of where we ought to have been going in the longer term and not simply seeking to provide educational facilities to cope with long-term projections based on existing trends. And the department's failure to include this more positive concept of planning into its work led the OECD investigators to conclude that 'there is no attempt at a new identification and formulation of educational goals in a world where the traditional canons of knowledge, values, attitudes and skills are continually questioned'.

The third major criticism of the department's attitude to planning was that it was too purely educationally oriented. Here the main point was that it was not sufficiently concerned with considering educational problems in the context of their relationship to the problems which other government departments were facing. And from this it concluded that the department was not sufficiently concerned with the role of education in meeting the needs of a modern industrial society.

The DES Concept in Action: Teacher Output

The department had done an enormous amount of work in developing its planning techniques to ensure that our national resources were not wasted by producing more teachers than could actually be employed in our schools. It took great pride in its achievement here. So when I moved in in October 1974 it was already agreed policy that to match the output of teachers to the likely requirement for them involved reducing by the early 1980s the number of teacher training places in England and Wales from 120,000 to 60,000. But the whole basis on which that planning was based was in my view inadequate. It illustrated very clearly the essentially passive nature of the department's concept of planning.

Naturally, the obvious starting point for planning the future supply of school-teachers were the estimates of the number of children to be taught in the 1980s. Here, it was clearly right to start with the likely number of children within the ages of compulsory school attendance; and there could, in my view, be no serious criticism of the department's work in this respect — based as it is on sophisticated projections about the birthrate trends. But the inadequacy of the department's concept of planning becomes clear when we consider how it calculated the number of those over the age of 16 to be taught in the schools in the 1980s.

Here, two factors were obviously important in trying to estimate the likely number of the over-16s in our schools in 1986. The first was the size of the age groups concerned; and we could be reasonably certain about that since the children concerned had already been born. The second factor was the likely 'staying-on' rate. And here the department did its best to base its future estimates on projections of past and current trends. Thus it produced in 1975 a highest hypothetical projection for 1986 of 569,000 over-16s in our schools, a lowest hypothetical projection of 283,000, and a suggested planning figure of 387,000[6] — whereas the 1972 white paper had produced a planning figure of 543,000.

Now I am not concerned whether the 1975 planning figure of 387,000 was more likely to be right than the much higher 1972 planning figure of 543,000 — even though the 1975 planning figure involved a reduction in the estimated 1986 requirement of teachers of some 17,000 compared with the 1972 planning figure. My essential criticism was that this concept of planning was entirely based on reacting to existing trends in the staying-on rate. But the staying-on rate then, or in the future, was not something which was god-given and immutable. It was something which governments could influence upwards or downwards by a whole series of variables under their control — by what they did about education maintenance allowances, for example. So the crucial factor in long-range planning here should have been whether, as a matter of educational and national policy, it was desirable for a higher proportion of young people to stay on at school beyond the age of 16, or not. If it was, then the government should have done what was necessary to encourage such an expansion; and if it was not, then places should have been limited or cut back accordingly. But the department had no view on this question — and, as far as I know, had done no work which would have enabled ministers to take a decision one way or the other.

In this general connection, it is just worth pointing out that both regional comparisons within the UK and international comparisons between the UK and other European countries could have been a useful starting point in working out a positive long-term policy instead of simply reacting to events. Thus, we already knew that within the UK there were significantly different staying-on rates in the different regions. In January 1974, for example, the staying-on rate in the North Region was 18.5 per cent of the relevant age group, 17.9 per cent in the North West, and 20.4 per cent in Yorkshire and Humberside — compared with 33.2 per cent for Greater London and 27.5 per cent for Wales. So either we were wasting natural talent in the North by accepting the low staying-on rate — or we were wasting educational resources in the South and Greater London — unless, of course, the level of natural ability was higher in the South than in the North, or we needed a more lumpen and ill-educated workforce in the North than in the South. Similarly, we knew that the staying-on rates for the 16 to 18-year-old groups in other European countries already outstripped our own very substantially. So should we have sought to emulate our European neighbours or not? But neither this question nor questions about regional comparisons entered into the departmental planning of teacher supply — which was so heavily based on reacting to trends rather than seeking to influence them.

There were a number of other questions, too, to be considered if we were to have a more positive approach to the long-term planning of the number of teacher training places in our colleges of education — and certainly before deciding to cut back teaching training places from 120,000 to 60,000 with the consequent physical closure of a number of colleges of education and the not inconsiderable staff redundancies. For example:

a   Was teacher training (or could it be with certain modifications) a better and more useful form of higher education (even if a substantial proportion of its products did not subsequently go into teaching jobs) than some of the more irrelevant courses that the department was ready to approve to fill some of the abandoned teacher-training places?

b   Would not the cut-back in teacher training significantly restrict the number of girls going into higher education — and was it in the national interest so to do?

c   Would not the cut-back in teacher-training places significantly reduce a traditional avenue into higher education for boys and girls from working-class homes?

d   If we were to cut back the number of teacher-training places would it not be in everybody's interest to phase it with a commensurate expansion in the vocational training facilities we needed to provide for those who leave school at 16 for full-time employment? At that time only about 20 per cent of these got any further education and training through day release, etc. — compared with some 80 per cent of their counterparts in Western Germany and Sweden.

e   What was the most efficient class size to aim at and what were the best teaching methods to be employed if we were to get the best 'value for money' in our schools?

f   Would it have been to our advantage as a country greatly to expand the number of under-5s in nursery classes (existing plans envisaged full-time provision for less than 15 per cent of the age group) at the expense, if need be, of the provision we made for those between 5 and 16 or for the post-16s?

But issues like those I have just raised had not received any significant attention. This was, however, perhaps hardly surprising when the departmental planning operation was entirely and narrowly concerned with trying to match the output of teachers to the likely number of children to be taught — and which, even within that narrow confine, restricted itself still further simply to reacting to current trends rather than seeking to influence at least some of them.

The DES Concept in Action: Provision of Places

Long-term planning designed to produce the 'right' number of places in the advanced sector of higher education was perhaps even more important than any other single aspect of the department's work. For one thing those places were extremely expensive — very much more expensive than places in the schools (just over half our education spend of nearly £6,000 million a year went to the schools while about one-third went to the very much smaller number of individuals in full-time advanced higher education and research). Secondly, this was the area which supplied the highly trained and highly educated manpower which was so obviously crucial to the country's social, cultural and economic prosperity. Yet it was here, it seemed to me, that the department's planning was at its worst — and fully merited the harsh criticisms which the OECD report directed at this part of its activities.

In the department's planning of higher education places its essentially passive concept of planning came out most clearly. It was here, par excellence, that it saw its job as 'identifying existing trends' and then seeking to cater for them as best it could.

The OECD report had noted that as far as students in higher education were concerned the department had gradually cut back its estimates of the number of places required by 1981 in our universities and polytechnics from 835,000 to 750,000 — and then in 1975 to 640,000 (and in the 1976 white paper on public expenditure the figure was put at 600,000). And it noted, too, that the department was planning for a pretty even split of these numbers between the university sector on the one hand, and, on the other, the polytechnic and public sector.

Now, the departmental estimates of the total number of places needed were based on the department's estimates of likely student demand — thus implementing the Robbins principle and planning on the basis of elaborate calculations and projections about the numbers in the different relevant age groups and estimates, in the light of current and recent trends, of those who would be 'qualified' for higher education places in 1981 *and* willing to take them up. Essentially, therefore, planning was making forecasts about likely 'natural demand'.

What the department failed to recognize was that there was no such things as 'natural demand' — or, more precisely, that 'natural demand' could be moved substantially upwards or downwards by various actions and influences very much under the government's control. For example, the relationship at any given time between student grants, the cost of living, and the wages and salaries of 18 to 21-year-olds in full-time employment clearly had an impact on the likely demand for places in full-time higher education. Thus, doubling the level of the student grant would have been likely to increase student demand — just as replacing the existing system of student support by a parsimonious loan scheme would have been likely to decrease demand. So if the government decided as a matter of policy that it wanted to achieve a significant increase in demand for places in higher education, then it could influence events accordingly — just as it could achieve a substantial reduction of demand and provision if it wanted to.

Clearly, then, an essential ingredient in planning the number of places in higher education in the future should have been a policy decision on the proportion of the relevant age groups for which such places should be provided. And to plan on that sort of basis inevitably involved considering a whole range of problems together which the department either neglected completely or considered piecemeal. For example, more positive planning of this kind meant that we needed to consider such questions as the proportion of the relevant age groups for which other major industrial countries would be providing advanced educational opportunities, the overall likely demands of industry and the professions for highly trained and highly educated manpower, the proportions of the relevant age groups who were likely to have the capacity to benefit from, and successfully cope with, the forms of higher education which were going to be provided (and what those forms were going to be) — together with such priority questions as whether more resources should go to increasing the proportion of the 18 to 22-year-olds in full-time advanced higher education at the expense, say, of the resources to be made available for research, or for further vocational training for the 16 to 19-year-olds in full-time employment, or for recurrent education for adult students, etc. In other words, it was quite simply wrong to plan our provision of places in higher education on estimates of so-called 'natural demand'.

Moreover, there was a further major criticism of the department's planning of higher education which was also echoed in the OECD report. This was on the point to which I have already referred — the fact that the department was planning for a pretty even split between the university sector in the number of higher education places to be provided. Here the report commented simply and pointedly:

'There appears in this even split in higher education between the university and the polytechnic sectors more of elegance and formal parity than of rational estimation of social demand or of long-term projections for highly qualified personnel in the State, the economy and society. The reasons given to us include the apparent coincidence of organic expansion estimates and the wishes of existing universities.'

But clearly, any positive long-term planning for the apportionment of students between the two sides of the binary line (and the department needed to reconsider the justification for the binary system) should have been based on such questions as the comparative cost on each side of the line of developing and running institutions to cope with whatever expansion of numbers the government in the end decided to provide for, the relative quality of their respective end products, and an assessment of the need for the different sorts of education they were providing — if, in fact, they were providing significantly different kinds of education. Clearly, concepts of 'elegance and formal parity' were not enough. And if the department's policy of building up the polytechnics was based on more than concepts of 'elegance and formal parity' — perhaps in the belief that somehow or other the polytechnics were making or could make a more relevant contribution (and more economically) to the needs of the country than the universities were making or could make, then this needed to be proclaimed publicly so that it could be publicly discussed and challenged. Furthermore, long-term policies for apportioning students between the universities and the polytechnics should have been the subject of detailed discussions with those on both sides of the binary line before decisions were taken. And to make such discussions meaningful the department needed to make available very much more information than it was ready to reveal during the time I was there.

Finally, in its long-term planning of student numbers and how they should be distributed between the different types of institution, the department should have paid heed to another of the OECD report's pertinent criticisms. For besides being highly critical of the essentially passive nature of the department's planning, it was also critical of the fact that in its planning the 'role of the educational system is not reviewed or related to the functions of different departments'. In other words the department's educational planning did not sufficiently consider the role of education in relation to the major 'non-educational' problems the government and the country was facing. Instead, 'the education service is identified institutionally and equated with the services provided by DES, in spite of the fact that the branches of this service cannot be taken as a static and stable phenomena.'

So, then, planning the longer-term provision of advanced higher education places was and is in urgent need of reform. It was and is too passive, too narrowly conceived, too secret and too little based on a comparative assessment of priorities. The necessary spring-cleaning will have to start with the Department of Education itself.

Reflections on Policy Making in the DES

Unless a minister comes into the department with clear and well thought-out plans for what he wants to achieve, nothing much will happen. And even if he has clear plans, he probably will not remain in the department long enough to implement anything of significance. Thus, for example, since 1944 we have had twenty-one ministers of education — which means that, on average, they have lasted just under two years each. In recent years, ministers of state for higher and further education have lasted about seventeen months. So ministers are not usually in the department long enough to have full consultations with all the groups concerned with higher education and then work out with them the necessary changes that should be made.

The problems which arise from short tenure are compounded by the day-to-day low-level activity which absorbs so much of a minister's time. In his early days in the job there will be a plethora of meetings with all the educational pressure groups who are anxious to get his ear. Thus there are sessions with the university vice-chancellors, the polytechnic directors, the Open University, Cranfield, the Association of University Teachers (AUT), etc. — all slowly and painfully setting out once again all the issues they have only recently explained to his predecessor. The educational journalists want a look in too. But all this has to be done amidst the massive burden of low-level casework which constantly crosses the minister's desk. Thus, for example, I had to deal with at least forty letters a week from MPs and others raising individual student grant questions (where the minister is the last forum for appeals) and questions about departmental approvals (or non-approvals) of particular courses at particular institutions, etc. If you are a minister in the House of Commons, you have your local constituency casework to deal with. If you are a minister in the Lords — you don't, of course, have a constituency burden — but you will have to be present in the Lords each day, reinforcing the small ministerial team there on the government front bench. There are numerous delegations of foreign visitors to be received — and you are expected to visit as many colleges and universities as you can. If you are a Cabinet minister you have to spend an enormous amount of time at Cabinet or Cabinet committee meetings which have nothing to do with education at all. All in all, ministers of education and their ministers of state have far too little time for discussion of, and thought about, major policy questions. In this context the new House of Commons Select Committee on Education, Science and Arts welcome as it is from so many other points of view, must have added considerably to ministerial burdens and reading.

To get higher education policy making on the right lines, the following basic changes have to be made:

a   The department's planning machinery needs reforming.
b   The department's attitude to long-term policy making must seek to determine objectives (taking into account our national manpower needs rather than reacting to trends).
c   The day-to-day burden on education ministers must be reduced so they have time to concentrate on major long-term policy questions. This will involve a major decentralization of much of the decision making, which at present is done in the department.
d   Ministers should stay long enough in the department to work out (in open discussion with the interests affected) the necessary major policies and strategies — and long enough, too, to implement those policies.
e   Parties out of power should have ready, on assuming office,

detailed policy blue prints worked out in discussion with all the groups affected by them.

POLITICAL ACCOUNTABILITY

In any democratic state the decision-making processes should be organized in such a way that the government's decisions elicit the maximum degree of consent from those particularly affected by them. This may mean that the will of *majorities* may have to be restrained in the interests of *minorities*. In other words the decision-making structures in a state need to be so organized that the various acts and decisions of government must be based on the maximum degree of willing consent from the governed. One way of bringing this about is to ensure that those particularly affected by the decisions of government are given full opportunity to participate in the government's policy-formulation processes. And where this means building into the process the representatives of the various interests particularly concerned, it is much better that those representatives should be nominated or elected by the interests themselves rather than selected by the government. If they are nominated by the interests themselves they can then be held politically accountable by their 'constituents' for their actions or views.

These considerations have obvious implications for bodies like the University Grants Committee (UGC) and the National Advisory Board for Local Authority Higher Education (NAB). If we are to have organizations such as these concerned in the future with the formulation of higher education policy, it follows that they must not be *nominated* bodies. Their composition should *not* be determined by the Secretary of State for Education, but by the different interests they are supposed to represent in the policy-making process. It also follows that the advice they give should be public advice. Secret submissions behind closed doors are a violation of the basic requirements of political accountability.

The considerations set out above (this page) also apply to subordinate policy making at the local government level and, even, within the individual higher education institutions themselves. Which could mean that individual higher education institutions would be required not only to provide full representation on their governing bodies for all who are affected by their decisions but also to have at least a proportion of their governing bodies drawn from among those elected by the people to run our national or local affairs. The representatives of the people have an inalienable right to be part of any decision-making process which might affect them.

Any democratic system also demands that those who spend public money should be politically accountable. But there can be different degrees of, and different mechanisms for, political accountability. At the very least political accountability means, as far as higher education finance is concerned, that the central government must determine the total amount of money to be spent. But should the actual spending of the money be done by the Department of Education (DES) in direct relationship with each university, polytechnic, etc. or should the money be handed over to some other organization or organizations (like the UGC or NAB)? If the latter alternative is the preferred road, does political accountability require the central government to set objectives for the bodies charged with disbursing the public money allocated to them? In the present political climate and given the virtually insatiable demands for public expenditure of all kinds (health, defence, roads, investment in the nationalized industries, etc., etc.) the answer must surely be 'Yes'. Alternatively, of course, the spending of *all* higher education money could be handed over to existing democratically elected assemblies (ie the different local authorities). If the responsibility for *all* higher educational expenditure were handed over to existing local authorities, the concept of political accountability might require the local authorities to operate within tight objectives and constraints set by central government, or be left to operate without any such constraints or centrally specified objectives.

Whatever institutional structures are devised to give effect to the maximum degree of participation in the policy-making process, it is also necessary in any democracy to devise mechanisms through which the representatives of the people can examine the effect or efficiency of the policies that have been formulated and carried out in their name. This is clearly when bodies like the Select Committee on Education, Science and Arts have an important role to play. But their post-mortems can hardly be fully effective if they are denied access to what happens in individual institutions of higher education. And if these central bodies are not to have such access, then democratic accountability means that local or regionally elected bodies should take on the local or regional post-mortem role. Regular democratic post-mortems are the sine qua non of healthy and effective democratic policy making.

Against these differing degrees and facets of political accountability must be set the views of many of the academics who work in the various institutions of higher education. They start by believing they know more about higher education, its potentialities, and limitations, than any general purpose, part-time or full-time politicians who, in the cause of democracy and political accountability might seek to interfere in what they do not really understand. For academics, therefore, politicians must be kept at arms length — so the less the degree of democracy and political accountability, the better. This view is old-fashioned and short-sighted. Certainly, it can hardly be maintained in today's climate. Much better recognize that politicians need to be educated in the values and practices of higher education. If, as academics, we cannot defend successfully what we do before politicians (most of whom, anyway, are intelligent men and women of good will) then we need to question very seriously indeed whether we should actually be doing it.

DIFFERENT INSTITUTIONAL MODELS

This third part of the chapter puts forward for consideration two contrasting institutional models through which higher education policy can be made and implemented. These take into account the various issues raised in the first two parts as well as the different higher education policies of our main political parties (in so far as these are known). For it is clear that any institutional structure we might wish to recommend must be capable of being the vehicle for the educational policies of whichever party, or combination of parties, wins political power and of serving successive governments of different political complexions.

The first model is a decentralized structure; it would be part of any regional system of government which might be developed in Britain. The second is a highly centralized decision-making structure and would fit in well with the way we run our affairs at present. From a purely political point of view either is within the realm of the possible. There are, of course, any number of permutations and combinations of both. But, among other things, this outlining of the two political and constitutional extremes should throw some further light on the problems of higher education policy making and implementation.

A Decentralized Model

The Social Democrat-Liberal Alliance is committed to a regional structure of government for the United Kingdom. The final details have not been worked out or agreed. The Social Democrats have put forward for discussion a scheme which would involve creating a directly elected assembly for Scotland and another for Wales; and there would be similar, directly elected assemblies and governments for each of eleven English regions.[7] The scheme is broadly that set out in Volume II of the *Royal Commission on the Constitution*.[8] The Labour Party has already committed itself to a directly elected assembly for Scotland and is considering the possibility of similar assemblies for the English regions. The following paragraphs set out what the powers of such assemblies might be as far as higher education is concerned.

The Scottish assembly and government would have the power to enact primary legislation. In other words, in certain specified fields like health, housing, education, agriculture, social welfare, transport, etc., the Westminster parliament would cease to legislate for Scotland; legislation in these specified subjects would be the responsibility of a Scottish assembly and its associated government. This was broadly the scheme that was approved by the Westminster parliament in the Scotland Act 1978. However, the act excluded from the legislative competence of the Scottish assembly universities, university staff, and grants to universities; they were to remain under the control of the Westminster parliament and government. Under the model here presented the Scottish universities would come under the control of the Scottish assembly and government which would then have complete legislative power and authority over the whole of higher and further education in Scotland. Thus, for example, it would be for a Scottish assembly and government to decide whether or not it wished to maintain a binary system; and it would be for a Scottish government and assembly to decide the amount of money to be channelled to the universities and to higher and further education generally. It would also be for the Scottish assembly and government to decide how research should be carried out in Scotland — whether in the universities, or in other institutes of higher education, or in special establishments set up for the purpose; and the Scottish assembly would be able to determine how much money should be devoted to research.

As far as finance is concerned, this model for Scotland envisages that the Scottish assembly would have some taxing power of its own. But most of its income would come from a block grant from the United Kingdom parliament in accordance with a complex formula which would take account of Scottish needs and resources; it would be along the lines of the old Rate Support Grant system. A crucial feature of this block grant system would be that it would, as the name implies, be a block grant. In other words the Westminster parliament and government would *not* be able to earmark any of the money so granted to be spent on higher education or the universities, or research, or roads, or schools, etc. The allocation of public money in Scotland to health, education, roads, etc. would be done by the Scottish assembly and government.

The broad scheme for Scotland outlined above certainly satisfies one of the essential requirements of political accountability. It would be clear that a democratically elected Scottish assembly and government had complete power over Scottish higher education and could, therefore, be held politically accountable by Scottish voters. After that, though, the waters of political accountability could become muddied. The Scottish assembly and government might decide to share the functions of running higher education in Scotland either with some Scottish version of the UGC and/or some Scottish version of NAB or with the Scottish local authorities themselves in such a way that it was not really clear who, in practice, was really responsible for what. Still, if it did that, the Scottish assembly and government would still have to accept full responsibility to the Scottish electorate for what it had done. And so it would, too, if it decided that each of the various institutions of higher education in Scotland including the universities was to be run by a board of management elected by all the members of the institution concerned or was to be run in any other way.

As far as England and Wales are concerned the regional model here outlined is different from the Scottish one. England would be divided into, say, eleven regions and each region would have its own directly elected assembly. There would also be a directly elected assembly for Wales. These twelve assemblies would all have the same amount of power, but, except in the most limited sense, they would (unlike the Scottish assembly) *not* have the power of primary legislation. In other words, the Westminster parliament and government would still legislate on all subjects for England and Wales. But there would be institutional and constitutional devices to inhibit the central government from legislating in so much detail that the different regions would have no scope for subordinate policy making. In other words, the situation would be broadly as in West Germany where, in practice, the federal government makes broad policy on all matters, but it is left to the different Länder governments to administer those policies and adapt them to their own special needs. Each regional assembly would take over the existing regional ad hoc authorities in its area (eg the regional health or water authorities); and it would also take over the existing offices and outposts of central government which have been given administrative functions in its region.

This would mean, as far as higher education is concerned, that the UGC and the NAB would be abolished. The responsibility for running higher education would be handed over to the regional assemblies and their associated governments. The central government in Whitehall and Westminster would be able to make broad policy (see page 63 below), including whether or not the binary line should continue, but it would be for each region to co-ordinate the courses, etc. run by the different higher education institutions in its area. And, of paramount importance, it would be for each regionally elected assembly and government to decide the total amount of money to be spent on higher education in its region and how it should be allocated between its different higher education institutions.

Each regional government and assembly would have, like its Scottish counterpart, a limited taxing power. But the great bulk of its income would come from a block grant from the United Kingdom parliament which would be distributed by Whitehall in accordance with a formula which would take account of each region's needs and resources; again it would be along the lines of the old Rate Support Grant system. And it would be crucial to the success of the scheme as a whole that the central government should not operate through any system of earmarked grants. Thus, it would be for each region to determine the balance of spend within the region as between hospitals, schools, roads, universities, polytechnics, etc. The following paragraphs set out in some detail how the financial side might operate.

Each year each regional level government would carry out its own public expenditure survey (on the lines of the present United Kingdom PESC exercise). Thus, for example, the education committee of a regional government would estimate the expenditure it needed in the next year for its educational policies — with provisional estimates for the succeeding four years. These estimates (as with PESC) would include both current and capital expenditure. In the course of producing them the chairman of the education committee would, of course, have detailed discussions with the local authorities in the area and become fully aware of their needs. Naturally, the chairman would also have discussions with the DES in London, but it is important that the United Kingdom minister of education should not normally have the power to impose views on the chairman of any regional level education committee. All the other regional chairmen of the different functional committees would build up their estimates in a similar way. The regional government would then consider the estimates of its functional committees and finally agree on the total proposed expenditure and its provisional allocation between the different functional committees.

The regional government would then submit its estimates to the UK Treasury indicating what proportion of the forecast expenditure would be met by:

a   the income derived from the UK government by way of the block grant;
b   the income derived from the independently levied taxes;
c   loans.

In finally approving the estimates of the regional level governments the UK government would need to satisfy itself that:

a   the aggregate demand on real resources was acceptable;
b   there was no objection to the broad distribution of that demand among the different economic categories (eg that it would not put an impossible strain on the UK road-making industry),
c   that the proposed functional spending pattern would enable a regional level government to carry out the various responsibilities placed on it by the United Kingdom government.

The UK government would have the power to:

a   impose a global percentage cut on a regional level government's estimate of expenditure;
b   insist that a greater proportion of proposed expenditure be met from revenue.

It would then be for the regional level government to make its own decision as to how this should be reflected in the pattern of its functional expenditure and in the taxes under its own control. The central government would not normally be expected to seek to alter the pattern of functional expenditure proposed by a regional level government.

In this regional model, then, each region would determine the size and funding of its own higher education sector and also the allocation of funds for research. It would all be done as part of a comprehensive regional plan.

It might well be thought that in the national interest certain universities should be excluded from this regional pattern. Thus, for example, the Open University, Oxford, Cambridge and London might be considered to be national rather than regional institutions. So, provided their number were kept small, they could come directly under the DES — as the Open University now does.

In this regional model it is important to recognize that very many of the existing functions of the DES would be handed over to the various regional governments. Thus, for example, local authority school closure or reorganization schemes or school building schemes or buildings for higher and university education would not need the approval of the DES — but would be determined at the regional level. And, of course, the DES would no longer be concerned with the approval of higher education courses; that, too, would be done at regional level. For the future the DES would be concerned with broad policy making which might include deciding whether there should be grants or loans for students in higher education and what size they should be. It could also include setting upper limits on the numbers admitted to higher education at any given time; if that were done, each region would be allocated an overall quota — with the region being left to determine its allocation between the different higher education institutions and the different courses. Westminster might want to lay down a prescribed pattern for the governing body of each institution (eg a certain number of local authority representatives, university staff, students, etc.) and the precise powers to be vested in each governing body; alternatively, that might be left to the by-law making power of each regional government. Equally, the central government might well want to prescribe that each regional education committee (out of each regional assembly a number of functional committees would be formed to run the regional services — on the existing local government pattern — so each region would have a functional committee for health, another for education and so on) should co-opt a prescribed number of people from the various higher education institutions in the region to assist them in their work. Central government, too, might want to create special 'national' research institutions.

Provided that national policy making in the DES is in future handled as suggested in the first part of this chapter — and that subordinate policy making in the regions is similarly handled — this decentralized structure could meet both our national and our regional needs as far as the formulation and implementation of higher education policy is concerned.

A Centralized Model

The centralized model for running higher education starts with the assumption that the Westminster government should be able to determine and implement whatever higher education policies it believes to be in the national interest. Thus it must be able to determine not only the total amount of money to be spent on higher education as a whole, but, if need be, the total spend of each higher education institution. It must be able to set effective limits on the number of places to be provided at all levels. It must be able, if it wants to go down the manpower planning road, to set targets or limits for the places to be provided for the study of different subjects — and it must be able to secure the allocation of those places to particular institutions. If the central government considers it to be in the national interest that there should be more places for mature adult students, or for part-time students or for ethnic minorities it must have the power to ensure that individual higher education institutions take any quotas of these, or of other special category students, that the government proposes to set. If the central government believes that the formal qualifications for entry into higher education should be raised, lowered or otherwise altered, it must have the capacity to impose that policy on whatever higher education institutions it chooses. It must be able to determine the numbers of places to be provided for foreign students and the proportions taken by any individual institution. It must be able to insist, if it so wishes, that all or most home students should be educated only in the area in which they live. It should have the capacity to determine the sort of research it wants to encourage or provide for — and which institutions should undertake that research. If the central government takes the view that non-advanced courses should be provided alongside advanced courses in the same institution, then it must have the capacity to achieve that end.

But while a centralized model must provide for the most detailed central government control of higher education as indicated above (this page), it does not necessarily follow that a particular government would want to exercise its powers in such a detailed way. On the contrary, a government might want, for example, to do no more than set a limit on the total amount of state money to be provided for higher education — and leave all else to 'free competition' between the individual institutions in the higher education sector. So any centralized model should make that possible as well. The paragraphs that follow therefore outline a centralized model which would make possible the most detailed controls as indicated above or the minimum degree of government intervention outlined in this paragraph. The model is also designed to meet as many as possible of the requirements of political accountability.

While this centralized model assumes that all power would be concentrated in the DES, one of the requirements of political accountability is that there must be at least token representation in the ultimate decision-making process of the institutions and interests ultimately affected by those decisions. Thus, there would need to be a national advisory council for higher education. But it would be advisory only. In no sense would it be an executive body as well.

A national advisory council for higher education would consist of the representatives of all bodies concerned with higher education provision: thus representatives of the universities, the polytechnics, and the local authorities — all nominated *not* by the Minister, but by the different interests themselves. The council would also contain representatives of those who employ the output of our higher education system — business, the professions and the trades unions. The council would be chaired by someone nominated by the Secretary of State and include representatives of the DES and of other interested government departments — eg Employment, Trade and Industry. No doubt it would break down into a number of committees for detailed working purposes.

It would be the minimum job of the national advisory council to advise the government on the total amount of financial provision to be made for higher education. Its maximum job would be to advise in whatever way it believed to be necessary on such issues and details as illustrated on page 64. It is important that its advice should be published.

It would be for the government to reach whatever decisions it thinks proper in the light of the advice tendered by the national advisory council. The detailed implementations of those decisions, though, would be the responsibility of two new bodies, a university sector committee and a public sector higher education committee — that is, as long as the government chooses to maintain the binary system. Each of these bodies would be composed of representatives of the institutions in their sphere of authority — and the representatives would be nominated *not* by the minister, but by the institutions themselves. There would be some overlapping memberships with the national advisory council.

The precise functions of the university sector committee and the public sector committee would depend on whether the govenment of the day chose to act in accordance with the centralized model described on pages 63 and 64. The fundamental characteristic of the committees, though, is that they would be *executive* bodies. They would have complete power over their respective sectors. The extent to which they chose to operate that power would depend on the policies of the government of the day.

The clear implication of the paragraph above is that, as far as the public sector of higher education is concerned, the polytechnics, etc. would be removed from local authority control and come directly under the 'command' of the public sector committee. This is an important ingredient of the model. To leave local authorities with any powers over these institutions would unduly muddy the waters of political accountability.

In a model with such a centralized concentration of power the whole scheme would be more acceptable to the various higher education institutions if their day-to-day operations were completely under their own control. So an important ingredient of this model is that the governing body of each higher education institution should be predominantly or exclusively composed of the academic members of the institution itself and appointed by the institution. This extra degree of 'participation' would make its contribution to producing the greatest possible degree of consent by the governed to the acts of government.

Clearly, the centralist model outlined above could be varied in a number of ways. But as it stands in its stark form it could be an effective model for higher education policy making and implementation. It assumes that the DES would reform its own internal policy making along the lines indicated on pages 56ff. Its major disadvantage is that it would impose still further burdens on the DES. On the other hand it would make possible the implementation of a more uniform higher education policy in all parts of Britain.

NOTES

1   R.H.S. Crossman *Inside View* pp.83 et seq.
2   The Conservative Party Manifesto 1979.
3   Ibid.
4   The Labour Party Manifesto *Let us Work Together* February, 1974.
5   *Education Development Strategy in England and Wales* Published by the OECD in Paris at the end of 1975.
6   DES *Reports on Education* No.82, March 1975.
7   *A New Deal for Britain: Decentralising Government* Green Paper No.3.
8   *Royal Commission on the Constitution, 1969—73. Vol. II.* Memorandum of Dissent by Lord Crowther-Hunt and Professor A.T. Peacock. October 1973.

DISCUSSION AND COMMENT

The seminar was attended by several present or past DES officials as well as a former minister (Lord Crowther-Hunt), the Labour shadow spokesman for higher education (Phillip Whitehead), the chairman of the Select Committee for Education, Science and Arts (Christopher Price), the chairman of the Committee of Chairmen of Regional Advisory Councils (Peter Lister), and a number of academics and others who had taken part in policy formulation over the years. There was comparatively little comment on Lord Crowther-Hunt's analysis of the short-comings in the performance of the DES, but a great deal on where the burden of responsibility lay. One strongly argued position was that the fault lay with the politicians:

it was the responsibility of political parties to develop policies for publication in party manifestos, it was the responsibility of ministers to be active and give leadership in policy matters, and the only reason that officials became influential in policy formulation was to fill the vacuum which existed because politicians did not exercise the leadership that was required of them. The remedy in some people's minds was for government to be more strongly committed to making policy, for there to be much greater use of political advisers, and for civil servants to be forced to argue out policies more publicly than is presently the practice. In defence of DES planning it was agreed that one effect of Robbins had been to hand over policy making to the demographers and to give low priority to discussion about the objectives of higher education.

It was agreed that an important constraint on policy making was the lack of public interest in higher education. This affected party involvement in the subject, ministerial attitudes and the standing of the DES within the government. It was possible that this was changing as a result of the publicity engendered by the cuts in student numbers and the well publicized Labour Party policy document on higher and further education. It was also suggested that the politics of education was becoming more pluralist: the activities of the Select Committee, the *THES,* leaked DES and CPRS memoranda had all contributed to discussion about policy and ultimately to policy making. More open policy making would lead to greater public accountability. There was not much evidence that the public wanted a great deal of central direction in educational policy but public discussion stimulated participation and improved the quality of decision making.

Lord Crowther-Hunt's main criticism of DES planning was that it was based on existing trends and was not sufficiently sensitive to alternative scenarios and to the impact entirely new policy initiatives could have on problem areas. One answer to this, it was agreed, would be to give a much higher priority to policy analysis and to the creation of a strong policy studies centre for higher education which could provide ministers and the DES with a better and more informed analysis of policy options than is currently available.

4

CO-ORDINATING STRUCTURES:
THE UGC AND US STATE CO-ORDINATING AGENCIES

by Robert Berdahl

INTRODUCTION

The problems in proving cause-and-effect patterns in social relationships with multiple variables are immensely complex and this complexity is obviously made greater when the relationships are examined against different backgrounds. It has now nearly become obligatory for American political scientists undertaking comparative analyses of even US state and local governmental activities to warn that the different historical, social, political and economic conditions in the various states and localities may seriously limit the value of any policy findings. If this is considered to be true in domestic American comparisons, how much greater is the problem when one compares across national boundaries? Notwithstanding such difficulties, this chapter will attempt a comparative look at the University Grants Committee (UGC) and at American state co-ordinating boards, the closest parallel to the UGC in the US federal system.

Definitions

Comparative analysis requires early handling of definitions. If terms do not have the same meaning across the boundaries involved, no subsequent generalizations are safe. I have limited myself here to two clusters of three terms each, all crucial to the understanding of later observations.

The first cluster of three related concepts which require definition refers to the terms governance, co-ordination, co-operation. When one conceives of universities and colleges acting together as a system, it would be possible for them to do so under several different mantles.

Governance here means the legal power literally to impose binding decisions on a college or university throughout the scope of its management domains.

Co-ordination here refers to a legally-constituted power to attempt harmonious or coherent or balanced development of the institutions under the same jurisdiction. Such efforts, as will be discussed below, can be based on advisory powers, or de facto regulatory powers, or de jure regulatory powers — but in each such case, the powers in question apply only to limited areas of institutional operations and do not supersede the governing systems in place at the constituent institutions or segments.

Co-operation here means a voluntary process by which institutions try to co-ordinate their activities without a government-sponsored legal structure.

There is a blurring of these three functions in real life, as, for example, while co-ordinating agencies do not govern, governing boards with jurisdiction over multiple campuses must not only govern but also co-ordinate. Similarly, there is nothing to stop institutions falling under either governing systems or co-ordinating systems from continuing to promote voluntary co-operative activities. Nevertheless, analysis will be aided by keeping these functions conceptually distinct.

The second cluster of related concepts is that of academic freedom, substantive autonomy and procedural autonomy. The Carnegie Commission on Higher Education used different words for the same concepts: intellectual, academic and administrative independence respectively. Whichever words are actually used, the concepts are distinguished from each other as follows.

Academic freedom is that freedom of the individual scholar in his/her teaching and research to pursue truth wherever it seems to lead without fear of punishment or termination of employment for having offended some political, religious or social orthodoxy.

Substantive autonomy is the power of the university or college in its corporate form to determine its own goals and programmes — if you will, the *what* of Academe.

Procedural autonomy is the power of the university or college in its corporate form to determine the means by which its goals and programmes will be pursued — the *how* of Academe.

These three terms are obviously also interrelated; for example, a college enjoying greater autonomy would seem more able to protect the academic freedom of its faculty (although autonomous Oxford in the early nineteenth century itself denied academic freedom to its faculty); or along another dimension, a government could impose such a heavy set of procedural controls that they have serious impact on a college's ability to achieve its self-chosen substantive goals. Notwithstanding such blurring of categories in real life, it will be helpful in analysing the relations between higher education and government to keep also these second three terms conceptually distinct (for greater elaboration on these terms, see Ashby 1966; Berdahl 1971; Carnegie Commission 1973; Dressel 1980).

With the above rough definitions in mind, let us now re-examine the assigned topic: 'Co-ordinating Structures: the UGC and US State Co-ordinating Agencies.' It should first be clear that we are dealing primarily with the phenomenon of co-ordination, rather than with that of governance or that of co-operation. This means that I will concentrate, for comparative purposes, on those twenty-seven state boards of the co-ordinating variety, largely omitting from further attention the twenty which combine co-ordination with governance. The UGC partakes of no powers of governance and even its impressive spectrum of co-ordinating activities is based on de facto rather than de jure regulatory powers.

The second point to follow from the definitions is that within the phenomenon of co-ordination we shall be looking primarily at its impact on substantive autonomy. This is not because it is more important than academic freedom; it reflects rather the fact that to the extent that academic freedom issues (as here defined) have surfaced, they have not been connected with the operations of either the UGC or the US state co-ordinating agencies. While the same cannot be said regarding issues of procedural autonomy, where co-ordinating structures on both sides of the Atlantic have been known to impose procedural controls, this chapter's emphasis on substantive autonomy issues reflects my belief that the crucial decisions relating to 'the future of higher education' will be made or not made in the substantive domain.

Having stated that belief rather dogmatically, let me back off a little by acknowledging a valid criticism from Burton Clark, who has warned against treating the co-ordination process too narrowly as a bilateral government-institutional relationship. In an insightful article entitled 'The many pathways of academic co-ordination' he urges that, to the political and bureaucratic modes of co-ordination which we all recognize as traditional, we add those coming by academic profession and by the market:

> 'All national systems involve all four of the major forms specified here and all four are apparently required for effectiveness. The special function of political co-ordination is to articulate a variety of public interests. . . as these are defined by prevailing groups within the outside of government. The special function of bureaucratic coordination is to compose a formal system out of fragmented parts and to provide fair administration. The function of academic oligarchy is to protect professional self-rule, to lodge the control of academic work, including its standards, in the hands of those permanently involved and most intimately connected with it. And the special function of the market is to enhance and protect freedom of choice, for personnel, clientele, and institutions, and thereby indirectly promote system flexibility and adaptability.' (Clark 1979 pp. 265—66)

Clark does not argue that each system has equal shares of the four different modes of co-ordination, but rather that the proportions of each vary markedly from one system to another. For example, behind the formal facade of the British Secretary of State for Education and Science and the civil servants in that department and the UGC, Clark points to the pervasive role of British academics in making the system function. Similarly, alongside the various state structures for co-ordinating and governing American higher education, Clark underlines the primary role played by market forces based on student choice fortified by institutional, state and national student financial aid programmes.

I want to incorporate Clark's valuable insights into the analysis by offering the following propositions:

1   That the US state systems, heavily driven by market forces in a context of enrolment decline and fiscal austerity, will come under heavier political and bureaucratic co-ordinating pressures to correct the possible abuses of institutions cutting corners to compete for survival. What will be needed if the necessary retrenchment and reallocation processes are to enhance rather than threaten academic quality will be a greater active participation in these processes by the academic profession. In other words, the US state systems could well profit from the British practice of heavy reliance on co-ordinating modes wherein the academic profession plays a larger role.

2   That the UGC, heavily influenced, as just noted, by the professoriate, will come under increasing political and bureaucratic co-ordinating pressures to avoid excessive rigidities in protecting the status quo stemming from faculty reluctance to accept the need for selective (uneven) retrenchment. Thus, the traditional subject rationalization processes, so traumatic for the professional participants in the process, will need to be supplemented by a greater (though not primary) reliance on student choice and market forces. In this regard (and the Select Committee on Education, Science and Arts has already said it), the British system could well profit from US state systems' efforts (in conjunction with federal programmes of student aid) to use the planning process to encourage rather than inhibit the operation of market forces.

THE EVOLUTION OF US STATE SYSTEMS

The Bases of State Primacy in the US Federal System

Before the nation were the states, and before the states were the colonies. Although the first state university was not founded until 1785, some colonies and states had rendered steady aid to private colleges in their jurisdiction well before that time. Harvard, Yale, Bowdoin, Williams and Columbia, for example, received grants of funds; Dartmouth benefited from a state land-grant; and Princeton, Union and Williams profited from state-authorized lotteries. However, Whitehead (1973) has argued that these early colleges were not thought of as 'private' in the contemporary sense of the term, and that the colonies/states which chartered these institutions felt no compunctions about placing some public figures ex officio on the governing boards or later changing the size and nature of these boards by state legislation. According to Whitehead, such actions did not stem from any state desire to 'control' the colleges but merely to ensure their general harmony with surrounding society and to guarantee probity in the administration of any public funds received. The colleges were considered to be serving a public purpose by virtue of furnishing society with its educated leaders.

The enactment of the federal Constitution in 1789 did nothing to alter this primary state role. Under the residual powers clause of the Tenth Amendment, all powers not delegated to the national government nor forbidden to the states were reserved to the states and to the people. Education is nowhere mentioned in the Constitution and is thus juridically a state concern.

This basic constitutional fact did not, however, prevent the federal government from very early on passing laws setting aside public lands in certain territories about to become states for the endowment of 'literary institutions'; however, in terms of the early nineteenth century the federal role was minimal and the primary state concern was relating to the many non-state colleges which dominated the scene. This task was made more complicated by virtue of the Supreme Court decision in the 1819 Dartmouth College case. Here Chief Justice Marshall struck down New Hampshire's efforts to alter the governance structure at Dartmouth on the grounds that such an action would impair the contract between the state and a private entity. Traditionally this decision has been interepreted to signal (1) the proliferation of private colleges, especially church-controlled institutions, since both philanthropy and sectarian influences were thereafter presumed to be protected from state control; and (2) the need for states to establish *public* institutions which *would* operate subject to state jurisdiction. Whitehead, however, provides caveats concerning both parts of the generalization about a sharp private/public dichotomy following the 1819 case. Against the notion of a separated and autonomous private sector, he provides evidence of continued private college requests (including some from Dartmouth itself) for various forms of state aid, and he cites the following factors not directly related to the Dartmouth College case which explain why such aid was later not often forthcoming and why state links with private institutional governing boards were ultimately ended:

'1) the falling popularity of small, élitist institutions clinging to a classical curriculum in the face of state legislatures which were increasingly taken with concerns for common schools and welfare activities like insane asylums and institutes for the deaf and dumb; 2) an increase in religious divisiveness among the numerous sectarian colleges which led both to a termination of most state subsidies and increasing prohibitions written into state constitutions against state aid to religious, and even in some cases, merely private, institutions; 3) replacement of state ex officio membership on some private college governing boards with elected alumni representatives; 4) a vigorous national advocacy by President Charles William Elliot at Harvard of the notion of "the compleat private university" supported entirely by the American voluntary system.' (Whitehead 1973)

Whitehead's central thesis, then, is that a really distinct notion of a private sector of higher education emerged only during the last quarter of the nineteenth century, and that any assumption of a permanent wall between states and their private colleges is historical myth. On the other hand, it is no historical myth that for about the next hundred years, there was very little interaction between state systems and private higher education. Again, one of the post-1945 issues on the state board agendas has been to develop explicit state policies toward private sector institutions within the state. This topic will be examined again below.

Concerning the caveat on the other half of the Dartmouth case conventional wisdom, the notion of a distinctively 'public' state sector after 1819, Whitehead shows that most state universities founded before 1867 received relatively little state funding (Virginia and South Carolina being two exceptions) and that most were established along corporate lines not too dissimilar from private institutions and enjoyed many of their same operating freedoms. Normally instrumentalities of state governments were required to operate under fairly tight fiscal controls in order to ensure that their activities and expenditures were in strict conformity with their established legal base. When the states began to found public universities, however, they turned not to their normal models of public accountability but rather to the private sector precedents wherein charters had been granted to legal entities known as boards of trustees (or some variation of this term) who thereby gained the power to govern the institutions largely free of state public sector controls. Of course, the exact powers granted to the public institutions varied somewhat from state to state, and as time passed and more colleges were established, they varied even within a state from one type of institution to another. But the following summary provides a picture of some dimensions of what has been called a self-denying ordinance (Carnegie Commission on Higher Education 1971 pp.100—101):

'— Twenty-three states give some form of constitutional recognition to higher education whereas few state departments, other than constitutional offices, are so recognized.
— Forty states confer corporate powers on their highest educational boards (few other departments have them).
— Elections or appointments of board members are for a longer period than for most public offices, and it is often specified that selection of board members be on a nonpolitical basis.
— Many boards have been given direct borrowing power rarely given to state divisions.
— Many are given power to appoint treasurers and select their own depositories and disburse funds, especially institutional funds, directly — a condition very rare in other state agencies.
— Many higher education boards are given wide discretion and in many instances complete autonomy on policy matters, such as admission requirements, graduation requirements, programs, courses, and

degrees to be offered.
— Almost all states leave to the higher education boards full authority over all matters relating to academic and professional personnel.
— Most states require more or less complete personnel reporting in connection with the budget but leave final determination to the boards after the appropriation is made. Few boards are given complete authority over administrative and clerical personnel other than the highest administrative position.'

Except for those cases where such legal arrangements were put into state constitutions (Glenny and Dalglish 1973), state grants of power to public institution governing boards could later be altered by mere state legislation, a major difference from the private sector after the Dartmouth case. And, of course, even state constitution provisions could be amended, albeit with greater difficulty. The impressive thing is that, given the pressures which later emerged, so many essentials of the self-denying ordinance survived as long as they did in as many states as they did.

Complexity in State Systems

When, in a given state, there was only one state university, its lay board of trustees could advise the governor and state legislators on what programmatic and fiscal policies they considered to be in the best interests of both the university and the state. Student numbers were so low, the costs involved were so relatively modest and curriculum issues in the early days of classical studies were so straightforward that most problems emerging between the early university and state government could be worked out on a direct bilateral basis. The trustees, after all, had been appointed partly on the basis of their ability to include a concern for the public interest in their deliberations. Furthermore, such trustees often had strong political connections with which to back up their advice.

But the century following the Civil War witnessed basic changes in several aspects of American life which were ultimately to have major impact on higher educaiton. The economy gradually shifted from agricultural to industrial; society similarly moved from rural to urban; state governments abandoned laissez faire for extensive regulatory and welfare activities; and the national government grew in power and functions even more than the states. Responding to these changes, higher education developed from an élite to a mass system with accompanying increases in number and diversity of institutions, in costs, and in complexity of curriculum. The public sector ultimately grew so large as to contain over three-quarters of the students enrolled.

These additional layers of complexity can be examined one by one. First, following the federal Morrill Act of 1862, a number of states established separate land-grant institutions to teach agriculture and mechanical arts, although in some cases these functions were simply assumed by the existing state university or contracted to private colleges. In any case, the curriculum was broadened, more students were attracted and both diversity and costs increased.

Next, the traditional offerings of the state university were joined by increased interest in graduate education and research, heavily influenced by German science, and by new programmes in public service, a distinctly American contribution to higher education, exemplified by the practice of the 'Wisconsin idea' at Madison by President Van Hise.

Another layer of complexity resulted from the spread of normal schools, speeded by state moves to compulsory secondary education. Soon many of these institutions became state teachers colleges; then some became state colleges with programmes through the Masters degree in liberal arts and business administration as well as education; and finally, an increasing minority have even been designated as state universities, with expansion into doctoral level work occasionally permitted.

Another major source of growth and diversity has been the American community college movement. Catering at first to urban areas relatively neglected by earlier established universities and colleges, the junior colleges widened access to large new groups of young people. As time passed, these institutions broadened their functions and became 'community colleges', where college transfer, two-year technical and adult education programmes were all combined. Although these institutions began as products of local government, problems of funding, planning and co-ordination gradually brought them more and more into the statewide orbit as well.

State problems with higher education were not confined to appropriating adequate funds to provide the necessary facilities for broadened student access, as difficult as even this probably was. In addition, thorny questions arose about the desirability of the state university and the land-grant college beginning to overlap in programmes, about the wisdom of normal schools evolving toward university status, about the educational rationale for two-year institutions becoming four-year ones.

In these various issues, the device of traditional lay trustees was something less than totally effective in helping the state to resolve them. The same 'boosting' spirit that made each local chamber of commerce work to put its city larger on the map also operated in most governing boards to cause them to push aggressively for bigger and better facilities and programmes. Often such requests were justified but sometimes they were not. While governors and state legislators had considerable practice in working through budgetary fights — even bitter ones — they lacked any frame of reference by which to judge the increasingly complex questions relating to allocations of new programmes and changed institutional missions.

The problem of responding to competing and contradictory lay trustee advice was compounded by the fact that state governments were expanding many of their other functions at the same time: agriculture, highways, police protection and prisons, public health and hospitals, parks and recreation, welfare and industrial regulation — all these and others demanded time, attention and state funds.

During the years when early state legislative suspicions of excessive gubernatorial power still lingered, the part-time legislators would tend to adopt piecemeal, ad hoc responses to these various pressures — and a maze of overlapping boards, commissions and agencies were created, each with its own goals and budget needs. Relative political strength rather than relative state needs more often than not determined the results.

It gradually became evident that only a greatly strengthened state executive office could bring some coherence out of this haphazard crazyquilt mode of operations. Starting with Illinois in 1917, state after state undertook a comprehensive reorganization and consolidation of government.

The consequences of such reorganization were to centre state policy-making power in the executive budget process. The overall idea (often imperfectly realized) was for the governor to be given both the power and the responsibility to run a coherent administration and a tight ship.

To retain some degree of legislative check on this burgeoning executive power, most states provided for a post-audit to be conducted under legislative supervision, and an increasing number of state legislative bodies have created their own review and research agencies, with substantial staff to provide careful analysis of executive fiscal and programme proposals. State activities, then, would often receive rigorous examination from both executive and legislative branches.

State Responses to Increased Complexity and Cost

At a time, then, when many other independent and quasi-independent state activities were being brought under more direct executive control and legislative scrutiny, did the self-denying ordinance relationship survive the general weakening in the lay trustee pattern of coping with increased costs and complexity in higher education?

The answer varies from state to state, and from period to period, but a safe generalization is that by the 1980s all states except three had moved to replace the original bilateral relationship involving great institutional freedom of action with some type of formal, statewide board of higher education, dealing with the institutions on a multilateral basis and narrowing, sometimes more, sometimes less, their former freedom of action. It is nevertheless also true that the creation of these statewide boards with their special status (several are even established on a constitutional basis) represents a distinct continuing concession from state government, often still exempting higher education operations from the controls normally imposed on other state activities.

Although as early as the late nineteenth century normal schools and teachers colleges in some states were administered by one governing board (frequently the state board of education because of its interest in teacher education), the first truly statewide boards for all senior institutions in a multiple-unit system were created in the early twentieth century. Superseding any existing institutional or sub-system governing structures, consolidated governing boards were established in Florida in 1905, in Iowa in 1906 and in some fourteen other states (including Alaska and Hawaii, later added to the Union) by the end of World War II.

In the other thirty-four states, however, state government continued to deal directly with separate institutional or sub-system boards, notwithstanding increased strain in doing so. In eleven of the states, between 1945 and 1970, presidents sensed the increasing danger of state modification of the bilateral patterns and moved to set up more or less formal channels for voluntary inter-institutional co-ordination. However, none of those eleven voluntary associations still survives as the major organ of institutional co-ordination within a state although several still operate alongside a co-ordinating board.

In twenty-seven states a statutory board has been created on the co-ordinating model wherein institutional and/or sub-system governing boards continue to function, but within the multilateral planning and co-ordinating guidelines laid down by the co-ordinating board. Unlike the consolidated model, which universally has strong governing powers, or the voluntary association, which universally lacked any binding powers, the co-ordinating boards differ markedly from state to state, ranging from purely advisory functions to powers of lump-sum appropriations protected by constitutional status. Table 4.1 indicates the pattern of statewide boards in the various states as of 1982.

Consolidation and Co-ordination

The above flash picture of the types of state boards of higher education currently existing in the various states does not adequately reflect the considerable movement from one type of board to another which has occurred over the past twenty years. Clearly this is a field of operations in flux, and it is safe to state that no single national model has emerged which seems able to satisfy the various expectations placed upon it by the widely divergent constituencies with which it has to work.

The major problem contributing to the pervasive instability is one of 'role ambiguity'. Persons on the higher education side expect that the state board will act as an advocate, helping to advance the institutions' needs with the state decision-makers, while those associated with state government usually expect that the board will act as an arm of the state, applying appropriate forms of acccountability to the functions of universities and colleges.

The consolidated governing board model is best equipped to handle this role ambiguity, since it normally identifies first and foremost with the universities and/or colleges which it directly governs. Thus, its role as advocate is usually (but not always) well anchored. Some state officials will

TABLE 4.1
A classification of the 50 states by pattern of state-level co-ordination and
governance of higher education, 1982 (1202 Commissions excluded)

Pattern			States with Pattern		
A	No board	(3)	Delaware	Vermont	Wyoming
B	Voluntary association	(0)			
C	Advisory co-ordinating agency	(8)	Arkansas California Michigan	Minnesota Nebraska New Hampshire	Oregon Washington
D	Co-ordinating agency with regulatory powers	(19)	Alabama Colorado Connecticut Illinois Indiana Kentucky Louisiana	Maryland Missouri New Jersey New Mexico New York Ohio Oklahoma	Pennsylvania South Carolina Tennessee Texas Virginia
E	Consolidated governing board	(20)	Alaska Arizona Florida Georgia Hawaii Idaho Iowa	Kansas Maine Massachusetts Mississippi Montana Nevada North Carolina	North Dakota Rhode Island South Dakota Utah West Virginia Wisconsin

accept this board departure from an arm-of-the-state role because they
see a different value maximized: that of centralized responsibility for the
whole system. State officials have sometimes expressed impatience in
co-ordinating board states with the agency's disclaimer that it cannot
intervene in certain types of problems because they fall under the jurisdiction
of the different governing boards operating under the co-ordinating
umbrella.

Support from the institutional side for a consolidated board as advocate,
and from the state side for a consolidated board as the single location
for system responsibility, has meant that four states in the past fifteen
years have changed from co-ordinating boards to consolidated governing
boards, and several more have come close to doing the same. However,
weaknesses of the consolidated model apart from obvious span of control
and centralization problems in states with large numbers of institutions have
caused other analysts to continue to support the co-ordinating model,

whatever its problems with role ambiguity.

The co-ordinating board model continues to function in twenty-seven states, among them some of the largest: California, New York, Texas, Michigan, Pennsylvania, Illinois and Ohio. Although some of the following material will apply to both types of boards, the focus during the remainder of this part of the chapter will be on the co-ordinating board model most relevant to the UGC.

Co-ordinating Board Functions
Co-ordinating board functions are generally those of planning, budget review, programme review, capital outlay review and sometimes administration of student aid programmes and federal programmes which are channelled through the states. The early boards tended to pay most attention to budget review, in many instances having to develop elaborate systems of formula budgeting. These formula systems were efforts to move the higher education budgeting process toward concepts of institutional equity and data-based objectivity in place of the fairly crude inter-institutional political fights that had sometimes led to demands for creation of the co-ordinating board in the first place (Conant 1964).

While boards continued to develop and refine such budget techniques as programme budgeting, zero-based budgeting and performance budgeting (Caruthers and Orwig 1979), by the 1960s state master planning seemed to become the dominant function of many boards. Using the California Master Plan of 1960 as a model, board after board produced comprehensive long-range plans for the expansion and development of higher education in its state, usually allocating role and mission assignments to the public sector institutions which would sustain or enhance the diversity of institutional types within the state. Usually these plans emerged out of complex and expensive participatory modes, in which numerous parties from the constituent institutions were involved. However, when it was found that demographic, economic and social conditions were changing so fast, the emphasis shifted from infrequent master plans to continuous or rolling or tactical planning, in which specific problems would be studied without re-opening the whole strategic framework.

With the rapid growth of enrolments by the later 1960s, many boards found that they needed to give more attention to developing programme review procedures both to consider issues of unnecessary duplication of high cost academic programmes and to monitor institutional conformity with assigned role and mission. These procedures sometimes involved use of out-of-state consultants, sometimes inter-institutional committees and sometimes staff-produced programme indicators. The early efforts were to evaluate proposals for new academic programmes; by the mid-1970s when enrolment decline and state fiscal austerity began to become problems, the process in some states was extended to the review of existing programmes, with a few boards (eg New York and Louisiana) exercising the power to terminate existing programmes judged either inadequate in quality or not needed by the state.

Co-ordinating Board Structures
While four of the early advisory co-ordinating boards contained majorities drawn from institutional representatives (often presidents, sometimes, trustees, practically never faculty), as time passed the institutional majorities were dropped in favour either of minority representation or none at all, and board powers were strengthened.

Now the more prevalent model is of a group of twelve to fifteen non-institutional members to operate a board with limited regulatory powers, defined here to possess final approval powers over academic programmes.

Co-ordinating Board Staffing
Because co-ordinating boards often operate in no-man's land between the institutions and state government, they often draw critical fire from both sides. Board leadership has no constituencies to whom to turn for support in time of crisis: neither students, alumni nor football teams on the one side, or strong groups of voters on the other. Thus, not too surprisingly, there is considerable turn-over in senior staff positions.

It is rare for institutional presidents to become directors of co-ordinating boards, though less rare for co-ordinating board directors to later become university or college presidents. The directors normally turn to the institutions to recruit their senior deputies for academic affairs and for budgeting. There are national networks for each of these operational areas, and serious efforts are made to improve the professionalism of board performance through periodic conferences and workshops.

In perhaps a quarter of the boards they have received exemption from state civil service personnel rules; in a few more only the top policy positions are exempt. Thus, the larger number of boards find that they must recruit, pay and retrain staff under rules not of their own making.

Current Issues
The biggest issue presently facing co-ordinating boards is which strategies to adopt to face the following combination of conditions: possible enrolment decline; state fiscal austerity; increasing state pressures for performance evaluations; and reductions in federal programmes in higher education.

There are those who argue that the state systems should not overreact to forthcoming adversity by trying to prescribe desired outcomes and then use the planning, budget and programme review processes to force the issues. Rather, a group like the Carnegie Council on Policy Studies in Higher Education would propose continued major reliance on student choice and the free market; the very title of its final report *Three Thousand Futures: the Next Twenty Years for Higher Education* (1980) points to a preference for less state co-ordination and more autonomy for the three thousand plus institutions now in existence.

However, Breneman, an economist, has pointed to the bad fit between current conditions in higher education and those which would be necessary for a pure market relationship to exist:

'1 The "firms" in this industry are not seeking to maximize profits or to minimize costs for a given level of activity. ...

2 The educational services produced by colleges and universities are not priced to the student at marginal cost, average cost, or even full cost. ...

3 The information available to students about colleges can hardly be considered complete (or even adequate) in many cases. ...

4 Some firms in this industry (the state institutions) receive substantial public subsidies, whereas comparable firms (the independent institutions) do not. ...' (1981 p. 25)

Breneman then predicts that most state systems will follow a mixed pattern of responses, combining some state planning, budget review and programme evaluation with large doses of student aid funds to maintain student access and choice. Planning activities in this context will probably focus on re-examination of institutional role and mission, to see if the desired diversity is being sustained in the face of pressures for most institutions to move towards the popular student programmes of study. Budget activities will probably grapple with problems of funding institutions during a period of enrolment decline by means other than (or in addition to) enrolment-driven formulas. The special value which formulas based on average costs bring to institutions during a time of expansion (when their additional costs are marginal) has the exact opposite effect on the way down when budgets are reduced by average costs and the institutions are saving only marginal costs by reduced enrolments.

Programme review activities are increasingly turning to evaluations of existing academic programmes with the thought that retrenchment calls for the elimination of weaker programmes and the protection of stronger ones. This is clearly a more traumatic experience for the institutions than merely being told they cannot introduce a new programme. But if the state board role in evaluating existing programmes is rejected, there may be worse fates waiting in the wings. As mentioned earlier, there have arisen over the past fifteen years developments within the state post-adult functions which go beyond traditional concerns with the legality or efficiency of expenditures of public funds to an effort to assess the *effectiveness* of programmes so funded. This requires the state audit staff to develop indicators of programme quality, and they have proceeded to do this for a wide variety of state functions. So far this Legislative Program Evaluation movement (LPE) has looked only passingly at higher education functions;

but it has developed its own sub-unit within the National Council of State Legislatures, holds workshops on improving the state of the art; and bids fair to extend its performance auditing even to the sacred groves of Academe if, in the meantime, the institutions, the regional accrediting associations and the state boards of higher education do not arrive at agreed procedures for publicly validating the quality of academic programmes.

In the areas of state student aid programmes, state boards will face the problem of meshing state programmes with the changing nature of federal student aid. If the present cut-back in federal programmes is limited to a one-term Reagan presidency, the difficulty will not be acute. But if a reduced federal role in promoting access and choice becomes a more permanent feature, then state boards must grope for creative ways to use overly-strained state treasuries to try to maintain the dynamism of the student market. Also relevant to this issue will be state policies relating to tuition levels, admission standards and state aid, direct or indirect, to private higher education.

This last topic, state policies toward private higher education, will take on particular importance during a period of retrenchment — for political pressures will be acute to push state policies toward favouring one sector or the other. Breneman and Finn argued for a policy of conscious state board intervention both to safeguard programme quality and to buffer the private sector from the effects of a laissez faire approach:

'If substantial overall contraction does occur in a state's postsecondary system, and if the state does not intervene in that process, then (1) the 'wrong' programs and institutions will survive through their skill at political manipulation, (2) the private sector will suffer a disproportionate and possibly undesirable retrenchment, and (3) randomized, piecemeal erosion will occur, resulting in a large number of crippled institutions rather than a smaller complement of healthy ones.' (1978 p.51)

However, here one must recognize the political attractiveness of the market approach, for there are no invidious choices to be made about which institutions or programmes to close down. Students vote with their feet, and Adam Smith's invisible hand will operate to see that the results are for the best. State boards that recommend policies of selective, rather than across-the-board cuts may find themselves increasingly unpopular with state political leaders who seem to develop an instinct for conflict avoidance. Will state boards learn to be persuasive in the face of these political realities?

THE UNIVERSITY GRANTS COMMITTEE

Origin and Early Operation: 1919—1946

As early as 1889 the British Treasury had created an ad hoc Committee on Grants to University Colleges which was instructed to distribute the grants in such a way as 'appreciably to strengthen the financial position, especially of the newer and poorer colleges, in the beginning of their struggle for existence, and to stimulate local munificence to renewed and greater efforts' (Berdahl 1959 p. 51).

Several more ad hoc grants committees functioned up to 1906 when one was made into a continuing body and then in 1910 transferred to the jurisdiction of the Board of Education. By World War I all institutions in the United Kingdom except Oxford and Cambridge Universities were receiving some form of modest governmental subsidy.

The impact of World War I on the universities was so severe in terms of inflation, deferred maintenance, and drops in student numbers that even Oxford and Cambridge joined the delegation which in 1918 was invited to meet with the President of the Board of Education and the Chancellor of the Exchequer. At this meeting the university heads indicated their need for a greatly increased grant, but insisted that they were unwilling to accept ordinary governmental controls as a condition of its appropriation: 'No one but ourselves can have any idea of how that money can best be spent from time to time. The doors are open, and if we make fools of ourselves, you can take it away. Inspect freely, but there must be absolutely no control' (Hopkinson 1927 p. 27).

The government evidently agreed with this position, for when the University Grants Committee was created in 1919, with the terms of reference 'to enquire into the financial needs of University education in the United Kingdom and to advise the Government as to the application of any grants that may be made by Parliament to meet them,' it was placed not under the Board of Education, but under the Treasury.

The original University Grants Committee consisted of a part-time chairman, Sir William McCormick, and ten distinguished academics not in the active service of any of the institutions which might be claimants for grants. Members of the UGC were appointed by the Chancellor of the Exchequer after consultation with the President of the Board of Education and the Secretary of State for Scotland. The committee was served by a full-time secretary drawn from the Treasury and some clerical assistants. An observer later remarked on the symbolic significance of the administrative pattern: 'An academic Chairman, and a civil servant (usually of the Treasury) as Secretary; the one as it were facing to the Universities, the other to the Treasury' (Hetherington 1954 p. 6).

This new grants committee adopted the practice of its predecessors of visiting each recipient institution at least once each five years; but the quinquennial grants were not begun until 1925, reflecting postwar fiscal uncertainties. Government funds were literally allocated by the Treasury but it was de facto guided by UGC advice. And the funds arrived at the institutions as block grants, with local managerial discretion as to their use within the very broad guidelines earlier discussed with the UGC.

In its early reports the UGC examined nearly all facets of university life and offered suggestions for many improvements, but went no further in pursuing actual national co-ordination of university policies than to praise the practice of voluntary inter-university consultations such as had taken place in 1921 on the question of the raising of fees.

The UGC did, however, urge each university to address itself to 'the formulation of a definite policy, in the light of which the many problems of its future development over a period of years can be considered and decided, in due relation to its financial position and prospects.' In the same report the UGC made clear that this exhortation for universities to engage in advance planning did not include the prospect of national policy guidelines: '...even if we thought we could propound, as we are sure we cannot, an ideal common policy for all universities, we should not feel the slightest wish to press its adoption' (UGC 1925 p. 28).

In this benign context, there was very little early criticism of the UGC and its operations. In fact, by the mid-1930s the editor of the *Universities Review* said that the UGC 'not only is trusted implicitly by university teachers but is coming to be regarded as the champion of our peculiar rights,' (October 1935 p. 1) and a head of a university college termed the UGC operations a 'miracle of self-effacement' (Murray 1935 p. 21).

In 1936 the chairmanship was made full-time, reflecting the gradually increasing workload and a few years later the UGC became deeply involved in acting as a clearing house for all the plans for the use of the universities in the event of war. In this effort it was joined by a strengthened Committee of Vice-Chancellors and Principals (CVCP) and together these two bodies succeeded in getting the universities through World War II with less disruption than had been experienced in World War I.

Thanks to co-operation and joint planning between the CVCP and the UGC, the latter was able to present to the Treasury in 1945 outlines for a ten-year university development plan which would require substantially enlarged government grants. The Chancellor of the Exchequer agreed to an immediate doubling of these grants, and promised even more following the reports of a series of committees of inquiry appointed by various government departments to investigate the national need for certain types of professional specialists.

Enlarged Terms of Reference and Postwar Activism: 1946—1963
Building on the Education Act of 1944, which promised to increase greatly the number of students qualified for university matriculation, there were at least ten specialized manpower study committees which reported between 1943 and 1946, in each case recommending an expanded supply of

university-trained professionals (Berdahl 1959 pp. 72—73). The most influential of these bodies was the Barlow Committee on Scientific Manpower which, among other observations, noted: 'the State has perhaps been over-concerned lest there should be even a suggestion of interference with the independence of the Universities ... we think that circumstances demand that it should increasingly concern itself with positive University policy. It may be desirable for the purpose to revise the UGC's terms of reference and strengthen its machinery' (1946 p. 21).

In July 1946 the CVCP issued 'A Note on University Policy and Finance in the Decennium 1947—56' in order to present the collective views of its members on the issues arising out of the succession of committee reports dealing with university activities. In this very significant document, the vice-chancellors' committee stated (emphasis added):

'... the universities entirely accepted the view that the Government has not only the right, but also the duty, of satisfying itself that every field of study which in the national interest ought to be cultivated in Great Britain is, in fact, being adequately cultivated in the university system, and that the resources which are placed at the disposal of the universities are being used with full regard both to efficiency and economy.... The universities may properly be expected not only individually to make proper use of the resources entrusted to them, but also collectively to devise and execute policies calculated to serve the national interest, and in that task, both individually and collectively, *they will be glad to have a greater measure of guidance from the Government than until quite recent days they have been accustomed to receive.*'

Soon thereafter, on 30 July 1946, the Chancellor of the Exchequer told parliament that since the universities had entered into a new phase of rapid expansion and of planned development, he was anxious that the UGC should serve a more positive and influential function than it had served in the past. He then announced the following new terms of reference (emphasis added):

'To enquire into the financial needs of university education in Great Britain; to advise the Government as to the application of any grants made by Parliament towards meeting them; to collect, examine, and make available information relating to university education throughout the United Kingdom...; *and to assist, in consultation with the universities and other bodies concerned, the preparation and execution of such plans for the development of the universities as may from time to time be required in order to ensure that they are fully adequate to national needs.*'

The UGC, for its part, envisaged its new relationship with the universities as a 'form of partnership,' and denied the view of some cynics that 'the principles of central planning and of academic autonomy are ... irreconcilable opposites' (1948 p. 82).

The grants committee had already in 1943 recognized that a membership of ten retired academics was too small to carry the increased wartime workload, so the government added five younger, practising academics and the average age dropped well below its previous level of seventy! Later three more members were appointed and persons from industry and commerce and secondary education henceforth constituted an important minority on the committee. A full-time deputy chairman and a strengthened and enlarged administrative and clerical staff completed the new orientation.

The change to appointment of active academics raised certain questions about representation of university interests and fairness among institutions. But the UGC chairman in 1955 insisted that:

> '...the members are not selected as representatives of any particular interest; the over-ruling consideration is that they should personally carry the confidence of the Chancellor of the Exchequer and of the Universities, though attention is also paid to achieving some balance in the academic membership both geographically and with reference to the most important interests in University teaching and research.' (Murray 1955 p. 254)

The strengthened grants committee was given jurisdiction over previously-separate national grants to education in agriculture, veterinary medicine and forestry; and several new colleges created in the postwar years were added to the grant list. The larger and busier UGC then found it necessary to create numerous specialist subcommittees to advise it on their respective fields. These subcommittees included both UGC members and co-opted outside experts.

This practice was particularly needed in conjunction with a brand new development in UGC grant procedures: for the quinquennium 1947—1952 nearly thirty per cent of the grants allocated by the UGC went in the form of funds earmarked to support special fields of study. These fields (medical and dental education, agricultural and veterinary studies, teacher education, the social sciences, Oriental and African studies, Slavonic and East European studies) had all been subjects of the specialized inquiries mentioned earlier, and the UGC justified their earmarked grants as a temporary expedient, on the grounds that:

> '...without some plain indication of the amount of the new money intended for the financing of such developments, it would be a difficult and invidious task for the universities to effect the rapid

readjustments in the proportionate rates of expenditure on different departments which national consideration may demand.' (1948 p. 78)

The UGC consoled itself somewhat with the thought that no institution would be forced to accept an earmarked grant against its will, but even this did not prevent some university grumbling. The vice-chancellor of Oxford University, for instance, noted in 1948:

'...we are in danger of being killed by kindness.... An embarrassing problem is created by the very large grant which the UGC is earmarking for Social Studies, the present popular emphasis upon which may or may not be temporary.
    '...the amount of earmarked money which can be absorbed by an institution without loss of independence depends largely upon how much free money there is to balance it.' (Oxford University Gazette October 1948)

It was therefore with obvious relief that the UGC announced in 1952 the end of the system of earmarked grants. Its sense of responsibility to the government prompted the committee to add a qualification to its decision — the hope that the specially aided fields of study would henceforth be treated no less favourably than other departments and that the UGC would be consulted before any major reductions concerning them were made.

However, with the return to all block grants in 1952, it should not be assumed that it was the status quo ante, for in the meantime UGC 'influence' over the uses of block grants had increased considerably. One Oxford college head had pointed out as early as 1948 that there was 'some humbug' in distinguishing too sharply between earmarked and block grants: 'Universities know quite well that if they use any part of their block grant for purposes which the UGC has not approved, they cannot expect further support for them. The UGC is paymaster and paymasters, like leopards, keep their spots' (Ogilvie 1948 p. 15).

From the paymaster side, quotes from the UGC chairman in 1947 hearings before the Select Committee on Estimates (SCE) and from the UGC secretary in hearings before the Public Accounts Committee (PAC) in 1952 tended to confirm the de facto control that goes implicitly with block grants (emphasis added):

'[Block grants] are not earmarked as regards particular things within the universities; that is to say, in making a grant to a particular university, we do not say, "Of this sum of £50,000, £10,000 is for chemistry and £10,000 for physics," but we do know in fact which is the programme the university wishes to follow, and the grant is fixed in relation to that programme, *so that the allocation is in fact very definitely in relation to a programme.* The university may vary that programme *very slightly* as time goes on. That leaves the university a certain freedom of choice as conditions may change, but beyond that the grant is made in relation to a quite clearly known programme.' (SCE 1947 Q. 1940)

'...there is always of course, the consideration that if, at the end of the quinquennium they have done things which they know the [Grants] Committee do not like or have refrained from doing things which they think the Committee might have wished them to do, that might affect the amount of grant that is allocated to them next time there is a distribution.' (PAC 1952 Q. 1977)

In some later SCE hearings of 1952 Mr Enoch Powell of that committee asked the vice-chancellors present how the UGC, furnishing only approximately two-thirds of any institution's funds, could still demand to control the objects of expenditure of the remaining third. Sir Hector Hetherington replied soothingly, 'I think demand is the wrong word. ... It is not a compulsion, it is an honourable engagement' (SCE 1952 Q. 438).

It was this very indeterminancy which gave rise to some parliamentary criticisms during the 1950s, with efforts made to alter UGC status and practices along several lines.

First, the Public Accounts Committee (PAC) in 1948 pushed the Treasury very hard to provide a statutory basis for the operations of the UGC, still operating from the Treasury Minute issued in 1919. The Treasury resisted, offering what it called 'strong reasons': '...It had never been the policy of any government that the universities should be subject to statutory regulations or that academic policy should be controlled by the state.' The PAC admitted being 'impressed by the arguments advanced by the Treasury' and withdrew its recommendation (PAC 1949 p. 1).

Secondly, both the PAC and the SCE complained that parliament was not receiving sufficient and timely information to help it judge how the proposed grant-in-aid to universities would be spent and whether such grants had been wisely used. On this issue the Treasury and the UGC gave ground, improving both the timing and quality of the information provided.

Thirdly, both the PAC and the SCE urged that the Comptroller and Auditor General (CAG) be given access to university records relating to non-recurrent capital grants. Noting that the annual sums involved had risen to over seven million pounds, each committee argued that no academic freedom issues would emerge from CAG efforts to improve efficiencies in the capital building process. Again the Treasury resisted, on the grounds that if the comptroller had such access, then the Treasury as the responsible accounting department would also have to seek access, and this development might upset the delicate balance that had prevailed for so long and so well. The Treasury and the UGC did, however, agree to appoint the Gater Committee to study administrative procedures relating to capital development, and in 1956 the UGC published and accepted the Gater Report, urging universities to comply with its recommendations on ways to improve the process.

Fourthly, the PAC also sought CAG access to the records of the UGC itself. The Treasury found this 'compromise' no better than the original proposal and instead instituted a series of changes in capital development programmes which went beyond even the Gater Committee recommendations. The PAC in 1957 agreed to put the issue aside for a while in order to give the new procedures a chance to work.

Finally, during this period the UGC also endorsed a major expansion in the number of universities serving the country. With strong UGC co-operation, and by-passing the tradition of starting life as university colleges granting London University degrees, new free-standing universities appeared in Sussex, Essex, Kent, Warwick, Lancaster, York and East Anglia. For those who later assumed that the major expansion of British higher education only followed the Robbins Committee Report in 1963, the above facts are worth remembering.

From Crypto-Dirigisme to the Real Thing: 1963—1982
After some seventeen years (1945—1963) during which time governments of both major political parties had remained essentially supportive of the UGC and the universities, the following two decades were to witness decisions by governments of both parties which indicated that government support for higher education and its specialized treatment would sometimes have to defer to other values and necessities.

The Conservative government in power in 1962 evidently felt its austerity and 'Pay Pause' programmes were more important than full-funding for the university expansion just described above. By itself a Treasury decision to cut the total level of grants available is nothing out of the ordinary. What was unusual was that Mr Henry Brooke, Chief Secretary to the Treasury, nevertheless insisted that, even with grants significantly reduced below recommended levels and with academic salary increases held to three per cent, the universities would still be held to proposed expansion targets with no expectations of lowered academic standards.

It had been the long-standing tradition until then that UGC advice to the government on university needs should be confidential, but in this case Mr Brooke felt obliged to add that:

'...considerations of economic policy, which are of course right outside the scope of the UGC's responsibility, have made it necessary to depart from the Committee's recommendations. This in no way alters the Government's confidence in the Committee's judgment in the whole field of university matters on which they are responsible for giving the advice.' (House of Commons 14 March 1962)

University and parliamentary opinion erupted in such a barrage of criticism (Berdahl 1963) that, according to a later report from Sir Edward (later Lord) Boyle, a Treasury minister alongside Mr Brooke in 1962, the government's guilty conscience led it not only to increase academic salaries and university recurrent grants within the next year, but also to give an immediate public acceptance to the Robbins Committee recommendation in 1963 for major university expansion during the remainder of the decade (Kogan 1971). While most of the fiscal damage had been made right within a year, the psychological scars were to linger much longer.

The Robbins Committee reported in October 1963. Although the Conservative government in power at the time accepted many of the committee's recommendations, one which it did not accept concerned the crucial matter of ministerial responsibility for the UGC. In spite of an explicit Robbins warning about the possible consequences of such a move (paras. 773—781), and in spite of the explicit opposition of the Committee of Vice-Chancellors and Principals (1968), the government accepted the view of the one committee dissentient and ultimately transferred the UGC from the Treasury to the Department of Education and Science (DES). It seems that the Treasury was increasingly uneasy at having such a large and specially treated spending unit inside its own department. But Robbins and others had hoped to put the UGC with the Lord President of the Council, who also had jurisdiction over government funding of research, rather than with the DES, where educational interests might begin to second-guess UGC advice. To make this more palatable a separate administrative section was created in the department for the universities and civil science, headed by its own minister of state and served by its own joint permanent under-secretary.

This new arrangement took effect on 1 April 1964; in October the Labour Party came to power and by the following February the office of joint permanent under secretary on the university side was dropped and the universities and science section merged with the main administrative apparatus. The government evidently considered that the experiment was not working. The vice-chancellors later cited this fairly abrupt change as evidence that their anxiety about the new ministerial arrangements had 'not been groundless' (1968). Sir John (later Lord) Fulton, Vice-Chancellor of the University of Sussex, offered one explanation of university misgivings:

'There should be two bureaucracies. They should then meet at a level at which there should be a political decision. If there is to be a conflict between the needs of the universities and the needs of parents and primary schools I want that decision to be taken politically. I have no right as a university person to say what that decision should be. I am entitled to say that it must not be taken anonymously by members of the civil service down the line but by people, responsible to the nation, who can be brought to account for it. This is what the machinery of the UGC used to ensure. This is in danger of being destroyed because half of it has been taken away.' (1966)

The CVCP was also publicly critical of the controversial Woolwich speech of 27 April 1965 in which Secretary of State for Education and Science Anthony Crosland laid out the binary system principles in terms contrasting the responsiveness of the public sector with the snobbery associated by him with the university sector and its autonomy under the UGC. It was not until eighteen months later, and just after the DES publication of a white paper on polytechnics that Mr Crosland requested a meeting with the CVCP to discuss the meaning of the binary policy. The CVCP later remarked (emphasis added):

'Meetings of this nature, which were almost all arranged ad hoc, were undoubtedly of value in a number of respects. They did not, however, offer a satisfactory alternative to a regular and accepted pattern of consultation whereby the Minister put himself in a position to ascertain the views of the universities on major issues *before* national policy was formulated, particularly on the broader questions concerning the development of the whole or any significant sector of the higher education system.' (1968)

It was also in 1966 that the Public Accounts Committee re-opened the issue of giving the Comptroller and Auditor General access to UGC and university records. After extended hearings Mr Crosland accepted the PAC proposal (PAC 1967), with comptroller audit to commence in January 1968. This result was no great surprise to informed university opinion, which understood that at least some of the spirited academic opposition testimony was a conscious means of getting firmly into the record the denial by the comptroller that he would ever raise questions about academic policies. Nevertheless, one could hardly see in the new policy a source of reassurance to the university community of the force of its expressed views in the eyes of parliament and government.

On 21 December 1966, Mr Crosland announced that university grants for the 1967—72 quinquennium would be based on the assumption that fees for overseas students not already embarked on full-time courses would be raised from an average of £80 to about £250, and that fees for home students would not be changed. The CVCP later noted:

'Academic opinion in the universities was sharply aroused, both by the unilateral action of the Government without prior consultation and by the discriminatory character of the increases proposed. These reactions were presented forcibly to the Minister by our Committee.' (1968)

No reversal of policy was obtained, however, and the universities were unable to maintain a united front in opposition since some with large foreign student enrolments would have been heavily hit by any effort to defy the 'suggestion'. (Legally, each university sets its own fee levels.) The CVCP ultimately recommended to its members compliance for at least one year while discussions on long-term fee policy could get underway with the DES. All but three universities then raised their fees for overseas students, and proposals from the National Union of Students (NUS) for joint opposition from themselves, the CVCP and the Association of University Teachers (AUT) were not followed.

As Mr Crosland himself later indicated, it was possible to tighten up on the university sector not only by policy decisions taken politically, but also by altered UGC administrative procedures. When asked if there had been a change in climate in the relationship between government and the universities while he had been secretary of state, he replied (emphasis added):

> 'Yes, a clear change. We rejected the notion of having two Permanent Secretaries in the Department, one specially to look after the universities. Then I insisted that the universities should be made accountable to the PAC. Lastly, *and most important*, the UGC itself was persuaded to take a much more positive line on productivity, specialization, concentration of subjects and control of building through cost limits. The type of letter reaching the universities from the University Grants Committee is now much more detailed in its guidelines for expansion.' (Kogan 1971)

One wonders how much 'persuasion' was necessary for the UGC to move in this direction, for, given the enormous growth in size, cost and complexity of the university sector, it is unthinkable that the UGC could have continued to act in its earlier informal fashion, whatever the minister's attitude.

In ten brief years student numbers had more than doubled, institutions on the grant list, with the creation of new universities and the transfer of the colleges of advanced technology to the university sector after Robbins, nearly doubled, and the amount of national grant expanded by a factor of five. Furthermore, this was accomplished by a generally acknowledged maintenance of high academic standards, at a time when the successive Conservative and Labour governments struggled with a most recalcitrant economy. Clearly, one needs to balance the earlier list of unpleasantries with a recognition of the government-UGC-universities partnership that brought off this remarkable achievement. Nor is this all: a reading of the two UGC quinquennial reports for the period (1957—62 and 1962—67) will reveal a host of interesting developments in curriculum, by no means all confined to the new universities.

However, all this development could have come only by paying a price — the price being a considerably more active UGC. A staff of 22 in 1953 had risen to 112 by 1968. The UGC expanded its system of expert advisory subcommittees, which increasingly took up the task of attempted rationalization of their subject fields. The normal UGC advice in this regard pertained to encouraging new developments in some areas and at some institutions, and discouraging them in others; in the field of agriculture, however, it went as far as 'discouraging' the continued existence of agriculture at three institutions.

Another important UGC innovation was to send a Memorandum of General Guidance to each university along with its individual letter announcing the quinquennial recurrent grant. Where, earlier, such general guidance had probably been given orally in meetings between the UGC and the individual vice-chancellor, now it was evidently judged right and proper to put it into writing and give it fairly wide circulation.

The memorandum sketched the general background of committee thinking in such areas as total student numbers, postgraduate numbers, unit costs, collaboration with industry, inter-university and inter-sector collaboration, fields covered by earmarked grants, and the various subject areas in which the committee was taking a particular interest (eg biological sciences: 'The Committee do not think that more Schools of Biological Sciences are desirable and would prefer to see further developments take place selectively in existing schools.').

The UGC said that it did not expect all universities to agree with all points raised in the memorandum, but then ended it with the following rather strong statement:

'The Committee hope that Universities will find it helpful to have the considerations mentioned in this memorandum before them when they come to decide their own development policies and priorities for the quinquennium. Each University is free to determine the distribution of its annual block grant in the light of the guidance, general and particular, which the Committee have given. It would, however, be in accordance with generally accepted convention that the Committee should be consulted before any major new developments, outside the framework set by the Universities' quinquennial submissions and the guidance contained in this general memorandum and in the individual allocation letters, are undertaken.' (1968)

In May 1970 the UGC took this one step further, by issuing a *preliminary* Memorandum of General Guidance and an individual university letter to use 'as a possible basis for the preparation of ... proposals' for the 1972—77 quinquennium. Later, when the actual quinquennial grants were announced, the final memorandum and letters of 'indication' were sent. The preliminary documents were evidently welcomed by the vice-chancellors as a means of channelling university quinquennial planning in realistic directions. The student numbers tentatively projected for each institution by 1976/77 were broken down into arts-based and science-based, with a further indication that, except for increases in part-time and short-course postgraduate work, postgraduate enrolments nationally should probably not rise above their 1969/70 level of eighteen per cent.

The UGC was obviously headed more and more toward quantitative analysis and greater specificity in its 'suggestions'. The UGC itself, in the last chapter of its 1962—67 quinquennial report, had analysed at length its necessary abandonment of the neutral buffer principle and its move toward what Sir Eric (later Lord) Ashby, a former UGC member, has termed 'crypto-dirigisme'.

With its procedures thus tightened, the UGC set about planning for the 1972—77 quinquennium. A government white paper in 1972 laid out *A Framework for Expansion* in which university growth of some twenty per cent was envisaged over the five years, with recurrent grants scheduled to involve a two per cent reduction in terms of grant per student. To compensate for the problem of rising prices, the government undertook to furnish an automatic supplementation of fifty per cent for non-salary increases in an agreed Brown Index of University Costs, and to negotiate about the other fifty per cent. The universities were expected to begin to move their staff/student ratios from 1:8 to 1:10 by 1982 and to reduce the proportion of postgraduate students (which had been rising rapidly) from nineteen per cent in 1971 to seventeen per cent in 1976.

Then the world economic crisis broke on the scene in the autumn of 1973 and the British national budget developments reflected its devastating impact. Higher education was not singled out for more extreme treatment than any other sector of the economy, but neither was it spared. First, even in the face of inflation running at twenty per cent per year, there was to be no supplementation in 1974/75. Second, even in the face of continued growth in student numbers, capital expenditures and equipment grants were severely cut. Third, the actual grants for each of the last two years of the quinquennium were not made known until six months before each was to be available, thus greatly complicating the universities' task in trying to work with the UGC in handling increased student numbers. Finally, while both of these last two annual grants included some anticipated impact of inflation, the 1976/77 grant was announced as a 'cash limit' with a warning that no further funds would be available for any reasons, including what had always been handled as a separate matter, supplementation for salary increases (Williams 1978 p. 36).

Fortunately for the universities, at about this same time there was a marked slow-down in student demand for university entry and within two years the 1972 estimate of 306,000 full-time students in universities by 1976-77 had to be reduced ten per cent. Notwithstanding such marginal easing of expansion pressures, the universities found themselves struggling badly to keep afloat. At the end of 1975 the CVCP issued a paper, *Universities in a Period of Economic Crisis*, which spoke of the universities' determination to continue to contribute to the nation's needs, despite reduced resources; but it also warned against the threats to academic quality from prolonged cuts, and urged an early return to some form of long-term funding. Clearly the old quinquennial grants were no longer acceptable unless automatic supplementation for inflation was included, but such built-in guarantees seemed too rigid for the government. It preferred instead to move towards the rolling process it used for all other public expenditures (PESC) wherein the Public Expenditure Survey Committee's five-year proposals are revised annually, and only the first two annual grants are firmly committed.

When it was time for the normal 1977—1982 quinquennium to commence, the government announced instead a change to a rolling triennium, with only the first-year funds firm (cash limit included) and provisional estimates for the next two years. Then, in the Spring of 1978, the DES published a discussion document, *Higher Education into the 1990s*, and it seemed to the higher education community that regardless of the substantive decisions which might follow public discussions of the document, the good news in terms of style of decision making was that the government was attempting to return to a longer perspective. There was also some movement on the public sector front, as the Oakes DES Working Group on the Management of Higher Education in the Maintained Sector reported (1978). A national body for the public sector was recommended which, if established, would presumably be able to work with the UGC to develop some long-missing trans-binary co-ordination.

However, longer perspectives for higher education planning and better trans-binary co-ordination were not to be the order of the day, for a national election in 1979 brought Mrs Thatcher's Conservative government to power, and its immediate priorities included neither of the above. Instead, it felt obliged to administer tough medicine to the whole economy, higher education grants included. Thus that same year the Secretary of State for Education and Science announced a policy of 'level funding' for higher education, later defined as grants for home students in 1981/82 and 1982/83 that would not be very different in real terms from those for 1980/81 (Shattock 1981 p. 3).

In that same first year in power, 1979, the Thatcher Cabinet also made another decision to save money by going to full-cost tuition fees for overseas students attending British post-secondary education. This re-opened the controversial issue of the government's role in setting university tuition fees. As mentioned earlier, in the context of Mr Crosland's first introducing differential fees for overseas students in 1966, in terms of strict law the government has no power to mandate such changes in university practices. But it can simply instruct the UGC to reduce the university block grants by an amount calculated to equal the value of the increased university income which the recommended higher fees would produce, and a university is free to defy such a recommendation only by giving up the fee income in question.

Earlier, in July 1976 a joint working party of the UGC and the CVCP had studied the whole tuition issue for both home and overseas students, and had recommended ending the differential charges and raising the common fee levels to about ten per cent of university income. The Labour secretary of state indicated a willingness to lessen the differential, but only by raising the revised home student fees far above what the working party had recommended. While extended negotiations were going on, the numbers of overseas students kept rising, each one still subsidized indirectly by government grant since even the higher fees did not cover their true economic costs. By 1978/79 the number of overseas students had reached over 58,000 (including 36,000 in universities) which constituted nearly twelve per cent of all students. The government subsidy involved was estimated to be about £102 million. When the Conservative government decided in 1979 to move steadily toward full-cost fees for overseas students a storm of protest arose. Procedurally, nearly every significant association in either the university or the public sector complained that there had not been advance consultation on a matter like this which would have such important impacts on both the financial and academic aspects of institutions in both sectors and on British relations with countries abroad. Substantively, no one seemed able to anticipate just what the differential financial and academic impacts might be on the various kinds of post-secondary institutions. What was certain was that the UGC was expected to reduce the universities' grant by some £65 million by 1982/83, a cut of 5 per cent, with cuts on individual university budgets ranging from 1 to 11 per cent. Their recovery was thus made dependent on fee income from overseas students (Education, Science and Arts Committee 1979—1980).

In the midst of such worries with cash limits, level funding and increased dependence on overseas students' fees, it would seem understandable if the UGC had done nothing beyond bailing out water to keep the university ships afloat. But in fact it continued with its usual pattern of letters of guidance in 1977 for the three years up to 1980/81. These letters contained general and specific advice concerning the development (or more often, the rejected development) of various fields of study, based usually on recommendations from the various UGC subject committees. Later UGC rationalization activities connected with efforts to reduce Russian studies and to control university library growth (the Atkinson Committee Report) produced angry university reactions from persons in the affected units. Positive efforts to encourage enriched engineering courses at four universities produced less criticism, although some persons at institutions not chosen grumbled about the criteria used.

Then, in a remarkably candid address to the CVCP in November 1980, Dr Edward Parkes, chairman of the UGC, spelled out the transition from crypto-dirigisme to the real thing. The speech accurately anticipated the selective retrenchment strategies of the next year.

'We want everyone to be good at some things, but we want you to concentrate on your strengths, and not support pallid growths which are now never likely to reach maturity. The excision of these feeble limbs is something where the committee can help, even it is only to lend you a financial pruning knife. ... There is going to be in the future a somewhat greater degree of direct intervention by the UGC in the affairs of individual universities than has been customary or necessary in the past. Before all your hackles rise and you start running to a council for civil liberties for protection, I should add that the committee is quite as staunch a defender of university autonomy as you are....

'The fact remains that the reconciling of what is desired *locally* with what is desirable *nationally* can be done almost covertly in an expanding system, where all the signs are positive, and the committee maintains steerage by selective addition, but in a system where some of the signs are going to be negative, where resources are going to be taken away as well as added, steerage necessarily becomes more overt.'

He said there was a risk that 'too many denizens of the groves of academe believe themselves to be immune from the changes taking place in the rest of society' and therefore resisted taking unpalatable action.

He said there were already too many people who thought the universities incapable of reform and had too cosy a relationship with the UGC. 'If those who think in this way are given evidence to support their view, you will not in future be involved in negotiation and argument with a UGC which, for all its many faults and fallibility of judgement, is at least composed largely of members who belong to your own world.'

Although he was not against public debate and dissent on genuine issues, 'I am opposed to a mulish opposition to any form of change based upon a sterile application of a concept of academic freedom, which may be the surest way to its destruction' (UGC October 1980).

Dr Parkes was correct that level funding would not survive; the government grants for the three years, 1981/82 to 1983/84, were scheduled to drop £71 million, or about eight and a half per cent. Added to the earlier uncertainties about possible drop-offs in overseas students' fees, the total loss of income estimated ranged from the UGC's eleven per cent to the CVCP's fifteen. What was certain was that the UGC was going to recommend a three to five per cent decline in student numbers by 1983/84.

The University Grants Committee, confronting this crisis, evidently considered five options:

1   The members could collectively or individually resign to protest the gross inadequacy of the government grants and/or the too-limited time period within which the proposed cuts were to be made.

2   The number of institutions on the grants list could be reduced (which in effect would mean closure of one or more institutions).
3   A tiered system, with the top tier funded for research and the other financed principally as teaching organizations, could be instituted.
4   Equal percentage cuts could be made for all institutions.
5   Selective retrenchment could be undertaken, with institutions affected on a differential basis according to aggregated UGC judgements about specific academic programmes.

The grants committee chose the fifth option, but obviously not without some temptations towards the other four, and not without some knowledge of the heavy price to be paid for choosing the fifth.

Dr Parkes was asked during a 1981 parliamentary committee hearing, 'If ... you could not discharge effectively the duties laid upon you, why did you not resign?' He replied that 'the Committee certainly did discuss the question of whether it should tackle a task which was being bounded by financial parameters which would necessarily produce not merely a good deal of anguish in the university system but a good deal of diseconomy. We concluded that we ought to continue with the task; that the Committee should not simply be a "fair weather" committee which was happy to play Father Christmas but the moment the weather turned rough it would resign, because we believed that ... we were the only group with sufficiently detailed knowledge of the system to take the best advantage of what was provided.'

This explanation did not satisfy everyone. Lord Robbins found the government cuts 'monstrous' and said that 'any self-respecting committee should have refused to impose them.'

UGC rejection of both the institutional closure and equal percentage cuts options was explained in a communication of 15 May 1981 to all British universities:

'It is not the Committee's intention to distribute the cut in resources equally between institutions and fields of study.... In order to maintain the vitality and responsiveness of universities, resources must continue to be made available for necessary new developments, as well as for new appointments in fields of special importance. The committee believes that this can and should be achieved without the closure of any whole university. Regrettably, however, savings of the order required must involve reducing the range of subjects taught at some universities, and this will involve recommendations for the closure or radical reduction of some departments with the likelihood of consequent redundancies of staff, both academic and non-academic. There will also be implications for the continued ability to conduct postgraduate teaching and research in some areas of study in some institutions.'

The emphasis given in the above statement to fields of study and departments explains the UGC's additional rejection of the two-tiered research and teaching university option. The committee obviously preferred to distribute recommended cuts on the basis of estimates of differential *departmental* strengths, with the institutional impacts an incidental aggregated result of departmental strengths and weaknesses. Dr Parkes explained during the parliamentary committee hearing that such departmental considerations were in fact fundamental, mitigated to a modest degree by aspects such as an abnormally high percentage of home-based students (eg Glasgow and Strathclyde), a unique responsibility such as the teaching of Welsh (eg Bangor and Aberystwyth) or issues connected with part-time education which tend to be localized in nature.

The resultant pattern of recommended cuts in student numbers was devastatingly unequal in terms of institutional impact: while London University received a cut near the national average of 17 per cent by 1983—84, York and Bath got off with relatively light 6 per cent and 7 per cent cuts respectively and three of the eight former colleges of advanced technology (which had been brought into the university system after the Robbins Report) reeled under recommended cuts of 44 per cent (Salford), 33 per cent (Bradford) and 31 per cent (Aston). In terms of subject area, engineering and technology were given small increases, while social studies, biological sciences, pharmacy, subjects allied to medicine and the arts generally were cut. It was reported that, in terms of relative costs, six places in the arts had to be sacrificed to save one in medicine.

Even-handed cuts would undoubtedly have produced some protests, but these differential or selective cuts led to assorted cries of outrage. Naturally each university that was to suffer more than the national average immediately challenged the process by which such decisions had been made. In particular, Labour members of parliament from the strong Labour constituencies around Salford, Bradford and Aston Universities pressed the government to justify the differential pattern of cuts. Sir Keith Joseph, Secretary of State for Education and Science, replied that the government, after determining the total amount of funds to be made available, had, as always, left it entirely to the UGC to determine the specific institutional grants. Since the UGC deliberations are private and its advice is considered confidential, no formal replies explained the details of the reasons behind the allocations.

Scottish Nationalists claimed that universities north of the border suffered more than their fair share, and renewed devolutionary demands that Scottish universities be removed from UGC jurisdiction to that of the Scottish Education Department.

Some members of the AUT compared UGC academic members and their selective retrenchment actions with the Jews at Dachau or Buchenwald who allegedly helped to choose each other as victims for the gas ovens. As a formal action, the AUT proposed a radical reorganization of the UGC to make it representative of the institutions themselves, open in its deliberations and directly accountable in the political process.

Even a Conservative organization, the Bow Group, published a pamphlet, *Learning for Change*, which was sharply critical of the UGC for its policy of fostering centres of academic excellence at the apparent expense of technology and vocational education. Industry should provide at least a third of UGC membership, the Bow Group suggested, with no more than a third from the universities themselves.

Critics professed to see a pattern of Oxbridge élitism dominating the UGC policy making and found a correlation between membership on the UGC and its subject committees and relative immunity from the most severe recommended cuts.

In mid-November 1981 unions representing 100,000 staff and 250,000 students held a massive political demonstration in Westminster in London. Over 10,000 faculty, staff and students were estimated to be in attendance, accompanied by 20 university vice-chancellors. Although the government gave no ground in the subsequent parliamentary debate and easily defeated the opposition motion through the operation of normal party discipline, three subsequent events seemed to indicate that some rethinking was going on. First, after considering university pleas for stretching out the contraction period from three to five years in order to allow more time for natural attrition to replace compulsory staff redundancies, the government instead added £50 million to the UGC grant to help the institutions finance the redundancies. Second, Sir Keith Joseph in a July 1981 public letter to Dr Parkes indicated that government will in the future, after dialogue with the UGC, wish to take responsibility for the very broad character of any distribution of recurrent grants. Third, according to Christopher Price, chairman of the Education, Science and Arts Select Committee, the UGC has been given a new right to make public its views which he hopes will help to clarify the necessary debate about objectives, needs and finance in higher education.

Separate government action relating to the non-university sector of higher education may ultimately go part of the way towards meeting another major objection which surfaced during the selective retrenchment process. Both Dr Parkes of the UGC and the chairman of the CVCP protested the inequity of having to make forced cuts in some university academic programmes which may in fact be superior in quality to counterpart programmes in polytechnics. In the absence of a public sector body with detailed knowledge of comparative programme costs and quality, the university sector retrenchment decisions had to be taken with only part of the relevant territory included.

The government has now created a national advisory body for local authority higher education, to co-ordinate the public sector institutions. Its board met for the first time in February 1982, and immediately moved to establish trans-binary links. The NAB and the UGC agreed to an exchange of senior observers and some joint working parties will undoubtedly be created.

Presumably, then, if the future brings the necessity for another round of severe budget cuts, the process of selective retrenchment next time will have been considerably improved. UGC membership will surely be chosen with a greater sensitivity; its subject committees will operate with increased awareness of the need for accurate and current knowledge; UGC criteria and formal positions will be more accessible to the public; university sector decisions will be taken within the broader context of knowledge of the entire binary system; and finally, government leaders will have been sufficiently involved in the broad scope of policy to feel ready to accept formal responsibility for the decisions, without, one hopes, getting so enmeshed in policy detail that the traditional arms-length university/state relationship breaks down.

COMPARATIVE COMMENTS

Nature of Agency Powers
UGC de facto powers appear to be much stronger than most US state co-ordinating agency de jure powers. While the Oklahoma board, with constitutional autonomy and lump sum appropriations, and the New York board with sweeping powers of programme registration and deregistration are both forces to be reckoned with, neither has yet undertaken anything as extensive as the selective retrenchment exercise of the UGC.

Whether it is 'good' or 'bad' to have and exercise such powers would seem to depend on the eye of the beholder. This beholder sees enrolment decline and fiscal austerity confronting systems in both countries, and it is his preference that persons with academic values should play strong roles in any painful decisions that have to be made. Therefore, the strength of the UGC, with its dominant role for academics, seems desirable — if not without some of the obvious costs of the divisiveness involved when academics try to do these things. (One remembers the Buchenwald analogies hurled at academics on the UGC.)

Shattock (1979), however, has speculated about the possible political costs of the cloistered UGC/DES/Treasury network, and has posited instead the potential value of the greater involvement of US institutions with lay persons and politicians in their local and state system governance and co-ordination patterns. Presumably the superior political effectiveness of the universities inside the US state co-ordinating systems might help avoid or lessen the imposition of severe retrenchment policies; but once such policies are launched, the political and market vulnerabilities of the American pattern may make it more difficult to protect the academic integrity of programmes and institutions.

For US state political leaders cannot disclaim responsibility for the actions of state co-ordinating boards in the way that the British Secretary of State for Education and Science can point to the UGC as the academic body which *in fact* made the operational decisions on retrenchment within the severe limits set by government policy. Thus, there are strong political pressures for the co-ordinating board to impose equal or proportionate cuts on all institutions, regardless of what this might do over time to the quality of academic offerings.

Another American force pushing in the same direction is that stemming from such heavy reliance on student choice and the market place as the keys to survival. An American humourist, Art Buchwald, has written about Desperate Tech U being driven to a hard sell: 'Our competitors are offering free cars to the kids, two-week paid vacations in Florida, and remedial rock music classes. If you expect to get a share of the freshman market, you're going to have to top them.'

On a more serious note, David Breneman, an economist, has written about the serious shortcomings of the market model when it applied to higher education (Mingle 1981 p. 25). What seems needed, then, is some appreciation of the way that the British system uses strong participation by the professional academics to protect programme quality.

Having said this, one can also recognize that the British system may be moving through the arrogance of expertise into overly rigid prescriptions of the shape of things to come. The UGC is now 'indicating' in more and more detail the desired breakdowns in student categories and the desired or rejected developments in academic curriculum. Here, then, the comparativist could agree with the Education, Science, and Arts Committee *Fifth Report* (1979—80) and its recommendations that the UGC obtain more general institutional role and mission statements and then allow more flexibility for institutional implementation and student choices. The US state co-ordinating agencies have a good deal of helpful experience to offer along these lines.

Nature of Agency Structures
Here the contrast between the two countries is strong: in the US, state agency membership has become almost totally that of lay persons; in Britain the UGC remains predominantly academic. The argument here parallels that made above: Shattock sees the US universities' political effectiveness enhanced by virtue of their greater contact with lay figures through such channels as state co-ordinating agencies; I see value in showing sceptical lay persons and politicians that good academics can transcend their disciplinary and institutional parochialism to act to protect both academic standards and the broader public interest.

Nature of Agency Staffing
As mentioned earlier, the US state co-ordinating agency's position 'in the middle' seems to have caused considerable turnover of intermediate and senior staff. Notwithstanding this fact, the agencies are able in a buyer's

market to be quite selective in drawing personnel with considerable experience in universities and colleges, and this, combined with several organizations developing professional networks and workshops, leads one to hope for even further improvement in staff quality.

While the British reliance on secondment of civil servants for most UGC staff softens the turnover problem (though even civil servants also come and go), the fact that most such persons (since the UGC stopped reporting through the Treasury in 1963) come from the Department of Education and Science raises other difficulties. Heclo and Wildavsky in their outstanding analysis of British government policy making, *The Private Government of Public Money* (1974), revealed the crucial importance of effective senior civil servants in a fairly tight informal network of policy analysts and advisers. With the best will for the individual DES civil servants who serve, or deal with, the UGC, one assumes that the modern personalities cannot reach the vital centres of power in the way that, in the old days, the UGC Secretary, Sir Edward Hale (formerly Treasury), could telephone his friend, Lord Bridges, Permanent Secretary at the Treasury, and get things moving with some dispatch.

I note here also that the same Education, Science and Arts *Fifth Report* endorsed the idea of procuring independent staff for the UGC. For the complex issues facing the UGC and the universities, it will no longer be sufficient to go to bat with the gifted amateur. A much more professional knowledge of higher education will be necessary, and here again the US experience has some relevance.

Nature of Agency Planning
The current crisis conditions are not a fair time in which to assess UGC planning, but even in earlier quinquennial periods its planning tended to be fairly short-run and numbers-oriented (Becher, Embling and Kogan 1971 p. 86). What seems missing is what is found in the better US state co-ordinating board planning: namely, a substantive focus on a broad examination of educational goals and values in society, and the appropriate diverse roles of the universities in meeting those goals; and a set of procedures which involve widespread participatory planning using accurate information.

While the SRHE Leverhulme seminars are an excellent exercise in certain aspects of planning, they cannot serve the purposes of the global stock-taking that is here recommended. As mentioned on page 79, most US state co-ordinating agencies are now moving towards rolling tactical planning on a smaller scale, but this is usually done in between periodic re-examinations of ends and means. It has now been nearly twenty years since the Robbins Committee Report, and it is time to regain perspective. After all, with the National Advisory Body now in place in the public sector, a new planning effort could plant one foot solidly there and the other on the sturdy, if weatherbeaten, University Grants Committee and then look to the needs of the country to the end of this century.

BIBLIOGRAPHY
Ashby, Sir Eric (1966) *Universities, British, Indian, African* Cambridge, Mass.: Harvard University Press

Barlow Committee on Scientific Manpower (1946) *Report* Cmnd 6824

Becher, Tony, Embling, Jack and Kogan, Maurice (1972) *Systems of Higher Education: United Kingdom* New York: International Council for Educational Development

Berdahl, Robert (1959) *British Universities and the State* Cambridge: Cambridge University Press

Berdahl, Robert (1959) *Statewide Coordination of Higher Education* Washington DC: American Council on Education

Berdahl, Robert (1982) Cutting the budget, resetting the priorities *Change* July/August

Bow Group (1981) *Learning for Change* London

Breneman, David (1981) Strategies for the 1980s. In Mingle, James *The Challenges of Retrenchment* San Francisco: Jossey-Bass

Breneman, David and Finn, Chester (1978) *Public Policy and Private Higher Education* Washington DC: The Brookings Institution

Carnegie Commission on Higher Education (1971) *The Capitol and the Campus* NY: McGraw-Hill

Carnegie Commission on Higher Education (1973) *Governance of Higher Education* NY: McGraw-Hill

Carnegie Council on Policy Studies in Higher Education (1980) *Three Thousand Futures: The Next Twenty Years for Higher Education* San Francisco: Jossey-Bass

Caruthers, J. Kent and Orwig, Melvin (1979) *Budgeting in Higher Education* ERIC/AAHE Higher Education Research Report 3. Washington DC: American Association of Higher Education

Clark, Burton (1979) The many pathways of academic co-ordination *Higher Education* 8 (3) May

Committee of Vice-Chancellors and Principals (1968) *Report on the Quinquennium 1962—67* London

Committee of Vice-Chancellors and Principals (1975) *Universities in a Period of Economic Crisis* London

Committee of Vice-Chancellors and Principals (1977) *Report on the Period 1972—76* London

Department of Education and Science (1972) *Education: A Framework for Expansion* Cmnd 5174

Department of Education and Science (1978) *Higher Education into the 1990s*

Department of Education and Science (1978) *Report of the Working Group on the Management of Higher Education in the Maintained Sector* Cmnd 7130

Dressel, Paul (1980) *The Autonomy of Public Colleges* San Francisco: Jossey-Bass

Education, Sciences and Arts Committee (1979—80) *First Report* Interim Report on Overseas Student Fees. HC 552

Education, Sciences and Arts Committee (1979—80) *Fifth Report: The Funding and Organisation of Courses in Higher Education* HC 787

Fulton, Lord (1966) In: Government and universities: a Cambridge discussion *Minerva* 4

Glenny, L.A. (1959) *Autonomy of Public Colleges* NY: McGraw-Hill

Glenny, L.A. and Dalglish, T.K. (1973) *Public Universities, State Agencies and the Law* Berkeley: Center for Research and Development in Higher Education

Heclo, Hugh and Wildavsky, Aaron (1974) *The Private Government of Public Money* Berkeley: University of California Press

Hetherington, Sir Hector (1954) *The British University System, 1914—1954* Aberdeen University Studies 113

Hopkinson, Sir Alfred (1926) Discussion in: The state and the university. In Third Congress of the Universities of the British Empire *Report of the Proceedings*

Kogan, Maurice (1971) *The Politics of Education* London: Penguin

Mingle, James (1981) *The Challenges of Retrenchment* San Francisco: Jossey-Bass

Murray, John (1935) Freedom in universities *Universities Review* 7 (1) October

Murray, Sir Keith (1955) The work of the University Grants Committee in Great Britain *Universiteit en Hogeschool* (Dutch) 1

Ogilvie, Sir Frederick (1948) *British Universities* Current Affairs Pamphlet 68. London: Carnegie House

Public Accounts Committee (PAC) (1949—50) *Fourth Report* HC 138

Public Accounts Committee (PAC) (1951—52) *Third Report* HC 253

Public Accounts Committee (PAC) *Parliament and Control of University Expenditures* 290

Select Committee on Estimates (SCE) (1946—47) *Third Report* HC 132

Select Committee on Estimates (SCE) (1951—52) *Fifth Report* HC 163

Shattock, Michael (1979) Retrenchment in US higher education *Educational Policy Bulletin* 7 (2) Autumn

Shattock, Michael (1981) *How Should British Universities Plan for the 1980s?* University of Lancaster 5th International Conference on Higher Education, 1—4 September

Universities Review October 1935

Universities Grants Committee (1925) *Report* February 5

University Grants Committee (1948) *University Development from 1935—47*

University Grants Committee (1964) *University Development 1957—62* Cmnd 2267

University Grants Committee (1968) *University Development 1962—67* Cmnd 3820

University Grants Committee Report of Chairman's address to the CVCP, October 1980

Whitehead, J.S. (1973) *The Separation of Church and State: Columbia, Dartmouth, Harvard and Yale, 1776—1876* New Haven: Yale University Press

Williams, Gareth (nd) *The Buffer under Pressure* University of Lancaster

DISCUSSION AND COMMENT

Comparisons between US models and the UGC are instructive in many ways. There is no national model in the US, but on the whole authority in the US tends to be more clearly located than in Britain though power is more diffused. In the US, co-ordinating board members are not drawn from the academic community, though they often have experience of higher education as trustees or regents, but on the other hand forward planning is more participative between the boards and the institutions. The quality of staff work for the boards is often very high while the current opinion is that this is not the case in the UGC. The administrative staffing in the UGC has now been reduced to fourteen.

A good deal of discussion centred on the role of the UGC in the changed political and financial climate and on the balance of powers between the UGC and the DES. It was agreed that the UGC would lose credibility with the government if it became merely a lobby for the universities. In any case the CVCP was the body constituted to represent universities. The UGC had suffered because over the years the government had become more powerful and the universities more fragmented so that the UGC's traditional role as 'go between' was difficult to maintain. The effect of the cuts had been to create a situation where the UGC and the CVCP were no longer on the same side. But there was really no sensible alternative to some kind of UGC-type body. If the UGC could be criticized for not knowing enough about individual universities, how competent could the DES possibly be in acting without the UGC as an intermediary? Moreover, the strength of the UGC lay in the prestige it had built up over the years. Any new body would have the greatest difficulty in carrying the same weight. In advising the government perhaps its chief fault had been its inability or unwillingness to embody more clearly a view about the relationship between universities and society.

A good deal of criticism was directed at the UGC's managerial skills. It was noted that the move from a quinquennial to an annual allocation system placed a great deal more strain on its twenty members. It was probably not possible to increase the membership and retain the present decision-making structure within the UGC. The committee was already stretched and any increase in the number of institutions, for instance if the polytechnics were transferred into the university sector, would require changes in the working arrangements. The general view expressed, however, was that the present staffing arrangements for the UGC were unsatisfactory. The officials looked to the DES for their promotion prospects and the turnover had recently been rapid. Moreover, they were not necessarily experienced or knowledgeable in higher education. A much more satisfactory situation would be if at least half the staff were drawn from the universities themselves, perhaps on secondment.

A subsidiary theme in the discussion was whether the UGC should have an advisory as well as a managerial role. One suggestion, not widely supported, was that the advisory functions should be passed over to a committee located in one or the other Houses of Parliament. Comparisons too were drawn with NAB whose financial controls seemed to be weaker but whose planning controls over courses were stronger if the secretary of state chose to use them. Relations between the UGC and NAB were likely to be crucial in the future co-ordination of higher education. It was agreed that the dialogue between the two bodies needed extending.

Speakers from both sides of the Atlantic drew attention to the importance of institutional role definition. The Select Committee had recommended the creation of US-style institutional 'mission statements' as a means of improving the planning of higher education. If one looked at higher education as a whole what one saw was a continuum of institutions rather than a binary line. Institutions could be administered as clusters rather than in rigid sectoral divisions. Giving institutions more freedom within an approved 'mission statement' would contribute to institutional autonomy as well as relieving the UGC of some element of its managerial work load. There was general agreement, however, that the advisory and managerial roles of the UGC should not be separated off from one another: to do so would be to weaken the UGC fatally at a time when, for political reasons, it was important for higher education to give it support. But on the managerial side the UGC needed to consider much more carefully how the system should be administered and what tests of quality and social or economic usefulness should be applied in exercising its semi-judicial role of judging between institutions for resource allocation purposes.

5

CO-ORDINATION IN THE PUBLIC SECTOR
NAB — AN INTERIM SOLUTION?

by John Bevan

INTRODUCTION

Immediately upon its establishment, the National Advisory Body for Local Authority Higher Education (NAB) became responsible for advising the Secretary of State for Education and Science on the provision of higher education, and the central allocation of resources in respect of that provision, for more students in more colleges than any body then or previously existing. The figures are summarized in Table 5.1. Although its remit is restricted to England it covers about one third of a million students in over three hundred and fifty colleges. The majority of the colleges have relatively few advanced students, and only about half the students are on full-time (or sandwich) courses; relatively few are studying at postgraduate level, and well over half are on courses leading to higher technician, rather than degree level, qualifications. In all these respects, including its variety, the local authority higher education system differs from the university one,

TABLE 5.1

Student numbers by mode and level for local authority polytechnics and colleges: England: 1980 (thousands)

Mode/Level	Polytechnics*	Other Colleges*	Total
Full-time and sandwich	117.9	45.5	163.4
PT day	45.7	67.6	113.3
Evening only	17.9	21.8	39.6
All modes/levels	181.4	134.8	316.2
Postgraduate	10.4	2.8	13.2
First degree	85.4	14.5	100.0
Teacher training**	14.4	17.4	31.8
Technician and other advanced	71.2	100.1	171.2

* 29 polytechnics and 330 other colleges are included. 30 of the largest providers are identified in Table 5.2

**Mostly at first degree level (BEd and PGCE)

and yet the futures of the UGC and of NAB are now inextricably bound up together. Against this background, this chapter seeks to examine the present and potential future place of NAB in the country's provision of higher education.

PRIMARY FUNDERS
It is useful first to consider briefly the notion of primary funders. By this I mean the body, or group of bodies, which in relation to an institution or class of institutions has the primary responsibility for deciding (or advising) on funding. Thus the UGC is the primary funder, in this sense, of the universities. The list appears to be as follows:

Universities	UGC
Direct grant institutions (OU, Cranfield)	DES
Voluntary (mainly church) colleges	DES
Local authority HE colleges, England	NAB
Local authority HE colleges, Wales	WAB (Welsh Advisory Body)
Central institutions, Scotland	SED
Local authority HE colleges, Scotland	Regional Councils, Scotland
HE, Northern Ireland	DENI*

There are thus seven primary funders in the UK. Their areas of responsibility are not in any real sense self-contained — although, of course, constitutionally distinct — as can be seen by considering, for instance, the competition for students on virtually identical courses, the mobility of some at least of those students, and the 'territoriality' of the mandatory student award provisions. One by no means insignificant consequence of the present distribution of responsibilities is that the government (UK), although having, it is to be presumed, a national view about higher education, does not express any overall view nor publish overall planning figures. The current public expenditure white paper (HMSO 1982) contains no relevant overall financial forecast and displays student figures which are limited to the aggregate of university students GB and advanced course students England.

NAB, for its part, is enjoined to liaise with the university and voluntary sectors, and has established cordial relationships with both. WAB, having been established even more recently than NAB, is required to liaise with it. Trans-binary is becoming, of necessity, trans-trinary, trans-Cheviot and trans-Offa.

There are, no doubt, cogent arguments why the provision of higher education, and *possibly* even the financial arrangements for it, should differ

---

* If the Area Education and Library Boards are regarded as distinct from DENI, then they should appear in the list as a separate entry. This does not affect the argument.

as between the provinces of the kingdom. The arguments do not appear to have been looked at in the same way on both sides of the binary line, nor is it apparent that the arguments in relation to provinces differ in kind from those that can be adduced in relation to the major regions of England. There is also a powerful general argument to the effect that a plurality of primary funders is a good thing, on the constitutional ground that a distribution of central powers is always wise, if only because it is a safeguard against major errors affecting the totality of the system.

Without, however, widening the scope of this chapter to consider the differing educational and legal cultures of the provinces, or embarking on a reconsideration of the rights and wrongs of devolution, it is plainly apparent that the present arrangement of primary funders is neither logical nor related to the patterns of student need/demand. Even *within* England, and considering only one aspect of the system to which NAB is already being asked to give attention, teacher training provision — particularly at the institutional level — cannot currently be planned without considering the provision in an area as a whole, whether offered by a university, an HE college, or a voluntary institution.

POWERS AND INSTITUTIONAL 'AUTONOMY'
The disparity in the distribution of powers between the institution and the centre, even though it may in practice be more apparent than real, is also of some interest. At least as seen from the vantage point of NAB the centre of power in a typical university lies in its senate; neither vice-chancellor nor council can effectively stand against it. Funding allocations from the UGC certainly constrain it, but subject to that significant influence, a senate can vary the university's programme without either external approval or external validation. Its college counterpart, on the other hand, is in a very different position. The academic board of a polytechnic knows that principal, governing body, and LEA all have their powers, and that — in general — the college needs both external approval and external validation before it can mount a new course. The coming of NAB is most unlikely to have any major impact on the position of the academic board in this sense, save in respect of external course approval, which now seems likely progressively to give way to a programme approval approach. External validation (quite outside the remit of NAB) will continue — though other forces may modify it in operation — and principal and governing body seem certain to retain their powers. The LEA's role will however be varied, if only in relation to the system by which AFE pool allocations will be made to and through it for the college.

The debate about institutional autonomy is neither new, nor talked out: it featured significantly in the Oakes report (HMSO 1978) and I have expressed my own view on some aspects of it on a previous occasion (Bevan 1980). It is now highlighted by an almost parallel difference at the centre: the nearest analogue within NAB to the committee of the UGC is not the committee, but the board. The UGC has no analogue of NAB's committee, composed as it is almost exclusively of politicians, and chaired by a minister. Moreover, despite close co-operation and structured cross-linkages, the operating methods and styles of the UGC and NAB are quite different. This is by no means simply a function of NAB's newness, but rather of a complex of conventions, traditions and (some) specific decisions.

These admittedly over-simplified descriptions of institution and of funding body do not lead one readily to suppose that the present distribution of powers, or the present state of institutional 'autonomy', are either logical or even necessarily appropriate to the system of universities and colleges as it now is. It is a reasonable assumption that if a system of higher education for some half million students were now being established, it would not feature two such radically different control systems in respect of institutions whose size, student populations, and range of provision are in many respects similar. The thought naturally occurs that a reaction to the earlier established sector has conditioned the setting up of a markedly different set of procedures for the newer institutions, whereas a more logical approach might have been to try to operate the whole system nearer to the balance point between self-government and wholly external control. On this model senates would have less effective power, and academic boards more; the existing course control for LEA colleges would disappear, but universities would receive a real external input into planning and validation. The alternative argument is, of course, that it is extremely difficult to operate effectively at or near an inherently unstable balance point, and that it is both sensible and desirable to choose to work with parts of the system deliberately differing one from another in their control mechanisms: this argument contains the proposition that the university and polytechnic models are equally valid in their own ways, albeit different, and that the country should have some of each. In this respect, the analysis mirrors that referred to in the discussion of primary funders, and necessarily gives rise to the same problems of articulation.

NAB's 'SHORT-TERM' PLAN

There are a number of distinct signals in the system that mark a series of possible responses to the problems and questions identified in the previous section. One — which it is not the purpose to discuss here — is the proposals current for the reform and restructuring of the provision of higher education in Northern Ireland. Apart from the very establishing of NAB itself, a second is the direction in which NAB is already moving in respect of institutional freedom of planning and action. Within three months of coming into existence, NAB had declared itself in favour of a move from individual course control towards programme planning (it has no responsibilities in respect of validation), in favour of an extended planning horizon, and in favour of the primary input into the overall plan being the college's own plan for itself. It had at the same time, however, assumed the continued existence of validation external to the institution, and of responsibilities for the planning of provision outside the college both at the local and regional level, and also at the centre, in a way not paralleled, so far as one can tell, by the UGC. In a process of transition towards its forward plan, NAB has also advised the secretary of state, both on the withdrawal by him of approval for some courses, and on the issuing of Circular 5/82, which provides through an accelerated approval and validation system for some new course starts in 1983.

In addition to working on the difficult question of the appropriate regional component for its planning, NAB has also spent considerable time looking at data base problems with colleagues from the universities and voluntary colleges. To put it at its lowest, it does not help the system that basic returns of key data have different reference dates, definitions and — in some significant respects — contents. It is an accepted fact that statistics that are both accurate and also truly comparable between different parts of the system are not available. Yet such comparisons are made, and the need for them is undeniable. In consequence one of NAB's priorities must be the improvement of the information available to it, even at the possible expense of a discontinuity in the time series of available data.

NAB AND THE COLLEGES

A major problem for NAB is the form of its relationship with the colleges for which it is responsible: indeed, even the phrase is an inaccurate shorthand for the colleges for advice on whose AFE provision and funding from the AFE Pool it is responsible. As I sought to make clear above (page 108), the variety is considerable, and ranges from the very large colleges, almost all of whose work is within scope (but which nevertheless undertake some lower level work), via medium sized colleges whose proportion of advanced work ranges from 100 per cent to less than 5 per cent, to colleges which are small by any count, containing at most a few tens of students in scope. For some colleges the advice offered by NAB goes to the whole essence of the institution; for others, however significant to those directly involved, it is, in overall terms, at the margin of the college's activity. Taken together with the number of colleges, and with the established fact that — despite NAB's formal terms of reference — some aspects of AFE provision cannot be intelligently examined without taking proper account of the associated NAFE provision, the facts lead almost inescapably to the conclusion that the principle of relating equally to all colleges in scope, though desirable, is incapable of effective realization in practice. The problem was recognized by the Oakes Committee, and led for it to the three models of funding (programme, course, and per capita). One is led inexorably to consider grouping colleges (one list of major providers that has been used is shown in Table 5.2), and even to consider *not* relating

TABLE 5.2

Colleges having *either* 50 per cent or more AFE students and 500 or more AFE students (FTE) *or* 30 per cent or more AFE students and 750 or more AFE students (FTE): England: 1980

College*	LEA	%AFE FTE	AFE FTE	NAFE FTE	All FTE	Full-time and sandwich AFE
100% AFE						
Bulmershe CHE	Berkshire	100	967	0	967	919
Bath CHE	Avon	100	781	0	781	732
West Midlands CHE	Walsall	100	568	0	568	531
City of Liverpool CHE	Liverpool	100	1,062	0	1,062	1,014
Garnett College	ILEA	100	719	0	719	462
90–99.9% AFE						
Crewe & Alsager CHE	Cheshire	99	1,253	7	1,260	1,196
Hertfordshire CHE	Herts	99	633	8	641	547
Worcester CHE	Here & Worcs	99	924	14	938	984
City of Manchester CHE	Manchester	98	838	18	856	783
Edge Hill CHE	Lancs	97	1,263	29	1,292	1,188
Rolle College	Devon	96	543	18	561	494
West Sussex IHE	W Sussex	96	671	27	698	656
Bretton Hall College	Wakefield	95	547	26	573	517
Avery Hill College	ILEA	91	726	66	792	647
Dorset IHE	Dorset	91	1,851	174	2,025	1,496
70–89.9%AFE						
W London IHE	Hounslow	86	1,774	270	2,044	1,546
Bolton Inst of Tech	Bolton	82	1,345	302	1,647	1,066
Hull CHE	Humberside	76	2,169	682	2,851	1,722
Ealing CHE	Ealing	73	1,524	554	2,078	1,270
50–69.9% AFE						
Derby Lonsdale CHE	Derbyshire	69	1,497	654	2,151	1,110
Chelmer Inst of HE	Essex	66	1,584	787	2,371	984
Slough CHE	Berkshire	60	1,147	752	1,899	513
Southampton CHE	Hampshire	53	1,308	1,157	2,465	669
Nene College	Northants	52	1,290	1,163	2,453	955
30–49.9% AFE						
SW London College	ILEA	38	1,132	1,802	2,934	848
Salford Collg of Tech	Salford	37	1,331	2,221	3,552	757
Cambs Cllg of Arts & Tech	Cambs	37	1,116	1,856	2,972	858
Luton CHE	Beds	36	888	1,569	2,457	452
N Gloucs Cllg of Tech	Gloucs	34	891	1,676	2,567	700
Buckinghamshire CHE	Bucks	33	818	1,660	2,458	672

* The variety in type and role of college is apparent.

directly from the centre to some minority providers. The arguments were all rehearsed, albeit imperfectly, at the time of the debate about Models A and B (DES 1981; CLEA 1981).

The perception of the centre held by the institutions is also of very considerable importance. At a time of relative plenty in resource allocations, the precise nature of what is going on at the centre is not examined at all closely by most of those universities and colleges. When reductions are made, however, the examination extends into unexpected areas, whether it is to the alleged educational philosophy of the centre, the backgrounds of those operating there, or even their presumed allegiances. It is suddenly perceived to be important that the UGC is staffed by civil servants, and the NAB, at least primarily, by local government employees. The fact that these staffing situations both flow — though differently — from imperfections in the nature of these two primary funders, both being un-incorporated associations, is overlooked. It ought not to be but it is; and it argues that if any changes are made in the first-order matters of the powers and responsibilities of the primary funders, then the opportunity to improve and correct second-order matters ought not to be overlooked. Ethos is important, and the more so when it impacts through perceptions on relationships.

THE FUTURE

This chapter set out to examine NAB's place in the country's provision of higher education. It has sought to do so both descriptively and comparatively, with such implications for the future as seemed relevant emerging consequentially from that examination.

The speed with which NAB has set itself to impact on the system owes much, of course, to the radical restructuring inevitably consequent upon the government's marked reduction in funding. However, it undoubtedly owes a certain amount also to the fact that NAB was, and is, seen by some as an interim solution only; there is a clear understanding that it has about three years before its operation is to be the subject of review. The issues identified in the paper lead one to suggest that some evolution of structure must take place. In particular, it would seem that:

a There are too many separate primary funders.
b There must be some resolution of the autonomy question as it affects approval and validation.
c The planning horizon needs to be the same for the entire system, and the planning input from different sectors consonant one with another.
d The interfaces within and between colleges, and between AFE and NAFE are unstable.
e The status of the primary funders needs changing.

It is, of course, easier to make the diagnosis than to offer prescription; (c) and (e) seem capable, given the will, of fairly straightforward solutions, but (a), (b) and (d), being more fundamental, are less amenable to simple recipes for acceptable change. It is natural to look to other countries for possible solutions, and many in the UK have examined, or even advocated, evolution towards the Australian model. So many national parameters differ (population density and distribution, explicit federal status, attitudes to the status of higher education institutions to name but three) that, as is often the case, one must question how well the model could transfer. Nevertheless, solutions to (a), (b) and (d) are all clearly structured in the Australian system of four statutory councils operating in an integrated way within a clear legislative framework. Tensions and conflicts have by no means been eliminated, but it may be that they have been reduced as far as any nationally structured system is capable of reducing them.

In the medium to long term, therefore, the possibility of a truly 'all UK' post-school education council, operating above evolved versions of the existing primary funders, cannot be ruled out. In the short term, there is so much of pressing urgency for those primary funders to get on with, and such a low probability of finding legislative time to enact a primary statute dealing with AFE and/or NAFE, that any early change of significance seems most unlikely.

REFERENCES
Bevan (1980) *The Role of the Governing Body* ACFHE
CLEA (1981) *The Future of Higher Education in the Maintained Sector*
DES (1981) *Higher Education in England outside the Universities: Policy, Funding and Management*
IIMSO (1978) *Report of the Working Group on the Management of Higher Education in the Maintained Sector*

6

CO-ORDINATION IN THE PUBLIC SECTOR
THE COUNCIL FOR NATIONAL ACADEMIC AWARDS

by John Pratt

INTRODUCTION

The Council for National Academic Awards (CNAA) has been one of the most distinctive features of British higher education over the last two decades. The Council has been called 'a unique and peculiar body, in the proper sense of those terms' (Lane 1975), established by charter with the object of ... 'the advancement ... of education, learning, knowledge and the arts'. The Council itself consists of a chairman and twenty-five members appointed by the secretaries of state for education and science and Scotland, plus co-opted members and assessors from the Department of Education and Science (DES) and the Scottish Education Department (SED). It awards degrees and other qualifications to students who successfully complete courses it has approved in non-university institututions of higher education in the United Kingdom. It is now the largest degree-awarding body in the UK with over 120,000 students on courses leading to its awards, nearly a third of the total studying for a first degree in the UK (CNAA 1981). Yet the Council has no teaching staff, prescribes no curriculum, conducts no examinations and teaches no students. Instead it validates courses through a hierarchy of committees, subject boards and working parties, detailed visits to colleges and scrutiny of extensive documentation.

The Council has always been controversial: fierce debate surrounded its establishment and there has been continuing pressure from many of its associated colleges for academic independence. Now it has to cope with constrained economic circumstances, one result of which has been the creation of the new National Advisory Body for public sector higher education (NAB). What then is the Council's place in British higher education and what future does it have? In order to answer these questions we have to look both at the purposes that the Council serves and the process or means by which it attemps to fulfil them. (In passing, I note that CNAA is not the only external validating body in higher education: this chapter is restricted to it on grounds of remit, not interest.)

PURPOSES

The Council can be seen, first, as an instrument of national policy for higher education — in fact, as a means to other wider ends. Successive governments have used the Council as an instrument of 'binary' policy though it is worth recalling that this was not the role originally intended for it. When the Council was established in 1964 after the Robbins Committee, it was simply to replace the National Council for Technology Awards (NCTA) which had until then awarded the Diploma of Technology to successful students in the colleges of advanced technology and other leading technical colleges.

Although the guiding principle behind the Robbins Committee's recommendations was that of 'equal academic awards for equal performance', this did not mean that that committee saw the colleges under the CNAA's aegis as equal in all respects with the universities. Indeed the creation of the Council implied that these colleges needed some form of supervision that the univesities did not. The Council in the Robbins system could be seen as part of a kind of tutelage scheme, replacing that of the external degree system of London University, for junior members of the higher education system. This purpose was completely changed as Robbins' view of higher education was replaced by that of the authors of the 'binary policy', who flatly rejected the Robbins 'ladder' concept of higher education and announced the aim of developing two separate but equal sectors — the university or 'autonomous' sector and the public sector of colleges of further or teacher education. In the binary system CNAA had a powerful purpose as the main validating body for a rapidly expanding, independent and distinctive sector of higher education; rather than a tutelage body, it was to be an institutionalized system of peer review by public sector — and other — staff. This was not a function that the Robbins Committee had foreseen for the Council, and Lord Robbins was outspoken in his resentment of what he called this 'perversion' of it. But the policy was confirmed by successive governments in, for example, the 1972 white paper *Education: A Framework for Expansion*, and by additions to the areas of work covered by the Council, including art and design (1974) and more recently management education. The future of the Council obviously depends on future policy for the public sector.

The Council can be seen, second, as having one fundamental purpose. This is as a device for giving national validity to courses of study created and administered by local institutions. In this, the Council is heir to an important tradition in the public sector. This kind of device was first employed in the creation of the National Certificate Scheme in the early 1920s. The National Certificate Scheme was further developed by the NCTA with the DipTech to degree level and the principles of this system substantially taken over by the Council in 1964.

Whether an instrument of tutelage for aspiring universities or a component of a separate sector of self-confident but unchartered institutions, the Council guarantees the standard of individual courses. It does not create the courses, but validates those created in the institutions in response to their perceptions of the demands and needs of students and the local and national economy. It is an attempt therefore to reconcile two basic components of academic life — academic freedom in the institutions, and the maintenance of academic standards.

An important principle underlying this function is the idea of separation of roles. The Council is responsible only for *academic* validation: it has no power to decide if the course is needed, nor if it can be financed. These administrative and financial responsibilities lie elsewhere, with the secretary of state, the local authorities and the institutions. The Council's future depends on the preservation or otherwise of this distinction.

We can identify a third main, though implicit, function of the Council. That is to encourage innovation. The debates of the 1960s emphasized the need for educational change. This was reinforced by the reforms of teacher education and the creation of the DipHE in 1972. The CNAA as the main validating body for public sector colleges would be an agent of innovation in subject matter, course design and process.

Achievements

As an instrument of binary policy, the Council's record is an undoubted success. It has offered the academic base for the unparalleled expansion of degree and postgraduate work in the public sector colleges. In the UK as a whole, over 1,200 first degree courses, 45 DipHE courses and 423 postgraduate courses approved by the Council were running in 1980-81. In addition to the 120,000 students on first degree courses were 6,000 on CNAA DipHE courses, whilst 1,700 were following the Council's certificate of education courses and there were nearly 12,000 on CNAA postgraduate courses.

The Council's courses reflect the public sector's emphasis on vocational and practical education. Nearly 40 per cent of first degree enrolments were in science and technology, with another 10 per cent in business and management studies and 11 per cent in education. Twenty-eight per cent of all enrolments and 49 per cent of science and technology students were on sandwich courses — a remarkable proportion given the difficulties of finding placements and the demands of these courses.

The Council is remarkably successful, too, in serving the aim of innovation. It has become its common practice to validate courses, mainly in technical subjects, which have not yet (or in some cases at all) received recognition in universities as appropriate for degree level study. The 1979 *Annual Report* records for example the validation of courses in scientific and technical graphics at Plymouth Polytechnic and timber technology at the Buckinghamshire College of Higher Education. New postgraduate courses were approved for the first time in earth sciences, pressure vessel design, shipping and maritime studies, and international shipping (CNAA 1980). The history of CNAA validation is, one is tempted at times to think, the history of innovation in higher educaiton in the UK.

PROCESS

Whilst the Council can be regarded as successful as an instrument of policy and of innovation, in terms of its process it has problems. Many of these arise from its own success; it has had to cope with the explosion in its workload as it has facilitated the expansion of degree and postgraduate work in colleges. Similarly, its procedures create their own problems. It would be unfair to detail these problems without first noting some important positive aspects of the Council's processes. The Council has, for example, been remarkably effective as an instrument of validation in giving national standing to courses created and run by local institutions. There is little dispute as to national standards. Indeed there are some, including those who have served on the Council itself, who hold that the standards for some of its courses could not be met by the universities. In part this results from the membership of the Council, its committees, boards and subject panels. On all of these are distinguished members from both public sector and university institutions — an important form of trans-binary co-operation. In addition, when approved, the Council's courses are usually controlled not only by the general responsibility of the institutions to keep the Council informed of developments, but also by the familiar system of external examination, again utilizing university and public sector academics. But structure is not all. A key factor in the maintenance of standards is the process of validation and continuing supervision itself. It is this, as much as anything, which secures standards. The scrutiny of proposals can be detailed — and daunting for those making them. In addition to visitations for each course, there are the quinquennial visits to examine an institution's general suitability for offering the Council's courses.

The process of validation not only secures standards, but has, itself, promoted innovation: it is worth looking briefly at how this happens. It is generally assumed in academic life that good teaching relies upon independence. Robbins considered that it was 'fundamental that an institution should be able to prescribe the requirements of its own courses.... We know of no argument that would justify the imposition of content and method as one of the surest guarantees of efficiency and discovery. All this is also true of the maintenance of standards... an autonomous institution should be free to establish and maintain its own standards of competence without reference to any central authority.' Robbins saw the issue as an opposition of autonomy against central control, and did not therefore accept that a device like the CNAA could be a permanent feature of an established sector of higher education. But, almost paradoxically, such a device can encourage innovation and the maintenance of standards. The reason is that if proposals have to be argued before a body of external people as knowledgeable as the proposers, basic assumptions have to be justified, and proposers and examiners may well be led to question them. The need to defend proposals, often in tedious detail, requires the proposers to establish how their courses cohere and to give serious thought to what they are teaching. Out of this greater understanding, innovation is more likely. It is not clear that courses would be more radical if institutions were entirely free of this academic oversight. And a radical course which has passed the scrutiny of academic conservatives is likely to be very much better than one which has avoided it. Through this method, the Council has been a force for innovation in higher education that the new universities, for example, though they were established at about the same time, and have the academic freedom Robbins advocated, have not been, as Perkin (1970) was obliged to lament: 'Soon the new universities of the 1960s will become older ones and will be committed to existing systems. If they cannot learn any better than previous new universities to remain flexible and to continue to make radical changes and interesting experiments, then the conclusion... must be that... there ought to be once in every generation the founding of a wave of new universities as numerous and experimental as those of the United Kingdom in the 1960s.'

The Council's processes have three further important consequences for institutions. The quinquennial institutional visits have been an influence on the government and structure of institutions, and the CNAA has often helped institutions to argue for resources in order to secure or maintain validation of courses. Secondly, quinquennial visits, for all their failings, have encouraged institutions to embark on serious self-examination and self-evaluation and because of their extent and scope have involved substantial proportions of staff in these processes (see Locke, Pratt and Spencer 1980). Third, in some ways in contradiction to the first, CNAA has offered staff in institutions, particularly junior staff, a means of combating their own academic conservatives. This has occasionally meant that staff have been, in effect, able to appeal to CNAA over the heads of their own superiors and secure validation for courses, or support for aspects of them, despite internal resistance.

The problems of process that the Council faces are of several kinds. First is the bureaucratic nature of the Council's procedures. In order to assess any course, the Council demands information. This can mean that an individual college has to produce a stream of documents, and may be engaged in a substantial and lengthy correspondence. An institutional visit may tie up the time of several hundred members of staff for several days, to say nothing of the preparation. One of the reasons why it has required so much paperwork of institutions is that the Council has attempted to meet its charter obligations to ensure comparibility of standards with university awards by requiring information on as many aspects of courses and institutions as possible. Visits to colleges are thus sometimes concerned with matters of minute detail rather than academic principle; the Council has sought to assure itself on a host of technical as well as more general matters.

A second problem arises from this. It is the difficulty of using this information as a basis for jduging proposals (see Locke, Pratt and Spencer 1980). What often appears to happen, at least to staff in colleges, is that the key decisions are taken on the basis of visits by visiting parties or subject boards. They undoubtedly bring with them views based on the documentation: Do they change these views on the basis of the visits? Are the visits only the basis of their judgements? How are the two kinds of information related? The problem is compounded by the complex structure of the Council. The Council itself is a body representative of interested parties. But the lower bodies in its hierarchy become increasingly composed of experts/academic peers. Occasionally, visiting parties are unable to take decisions on academic grounds because policy has not yet been settled by a subject board.

A third problem is that of the inquisitional nature of Council-college relations. Colleges put forward proposals to be judged. In the end, the Council has the whiphand. It is difficult to be frank about worries with a course if the course could be closed as a consequence. It is difficulties such as these which have contributed to some sense of resentment in colleges about CNAA's existence and to pressures for academic independence. And it was in response to these problems and in recognition of the colleges' growing capacity to create and run satisfactory courses that the Council introduced the idea of 'partnership in validation' (CNAA 1975 and 1979).

Partnership in validation has been described by the Council's chief officer, Dr Edwin Kerr as 'possibly the most fundamental change in the Council's relationships with the institutions which run courses leading to its awards since its foundation....' The new procedures, introduced from the 1979—80 academic year, recognized that many of the institutions offering CNAA courses have developed, in Dr Kerr's words, 'into establishments of very considerable academic strength and experience'. As a result the emphasis of the Council's work has moved steadily away from validating proposals put up by institutions making their first application towards validating additional courses or developments in existing courses at institutions which the Council knows well and with which it has developed' very close and informed relationships'.

The principal innovation was the introduction of approval for an indefinite period of well established courses. To enable the Council to maintain its oversight of course standards, a system of progress review visits was introduced. Instead of being inquisitorial revalidation visits, they were intended to enable the Council and the colleges to discuss the progress and problems of the course, drawing wherever possible on the documents prepared by the college itself in the normal course of its operation. The second main change was greater freedom for colleges to modify approved courses within previously agreed limits. The third feature was the establishment of a major new committee of the Council, the Committee for Institutions. This became responsible for quinquennial visits and now has the aims of ensuring that the review procedures complement the course validation process more closely than in the past and to foster the development of relationships between the Council and its associated institutions.

One way in which this development may take place is through a fourth feature of the new process, which allows colleges to suggest variations in validation procedures to suit particular cases. It is the task of the Committee for Institutions to assess these proposals.

The final feature of the new procedure is a series of improvements in the existing procedures for the validation of new courses, to introduce greater flexibility into the process, involving the college and the Council in discussions at an early stage, drawing on the Council's knowledge of the institution, and allowing greater reliance on the college's own procedures for course development.

Partnership in validation does offer several improvements. It promises a much needed reduction in the time spent and the paperwork produced by colleges and the Council in preparing for validation of new courses, and eliminates the superfluous revalidation of successful existing courses. It promises the opportunity of greater dialogue between colleges and Council in the preparation of courses, leading, one hopes, to better courses and understanding, as well as again less unnecessary documentation. These may be matters of detail, but they are the ones which most affect staff involved in developing and teaching the courses, and the improvement here must not be overlooked. The new system also offers institutions the opportunity of proposing variations in validation procedures. If used imaginatively, this will be a major gain. Colleges putting forward more adventurous courses have often felt themselves shackled, perhaps inadvertantly, by procedures designed for more conventional courses. Much responsibility rests upon the Council, and the colleges, to use this provision to good effect.

But changes in procedural detail, though welcome, do not mean that the Council has been able to break through into genuine partnership with the institutions offering its awards. First, the CNAA system is still unequal. Partnership implies that both partners share both risks and benefits, and operate within broadly the same rules. Yet colleges will continue to do the bulk of the work, produce elaborate documentation, be questioned rather than questioning, and obey rather than make the rules. Second, much of the gain in the new arrangements is undermined by the Council's other regulations. These explicitly limit the kind of course proposals a college may put forward; they attempt to 'delineate' the range of course structures which the Council regard as acceptable and go on to prescribe in extensive detail matters such as examination and assessment procedures, admission requirements, the objects of practical training, and the qualifications of teachers.

In doing this, the Council is relying on false assumptions about comparability of standards. By prescribing requirements such as the conventional university entry requirements of two GCE 'A' levels or equivalent (though being more generous than the universities in allowing exceptional entry), or similar lengths of courses to university degree courses, the Council has assumed that the standard of its graduates is therefore comparable with university graduates. But university awards, as Robbins recognized, do not have national or international standing because they are all the same, or because they are comparable, but because there is confidence in the process by which they are gained. Neither a host of technical detail nor regulations or procedures governing the acceptable pattern of course structures or the philosophy of courses will ensure comparability of standards. These are not fixed components of courses, but they change in differing social, economic or educational climates. The Council can maintain standards only by establishing confidence in its own processes for judging the validity of courses. In other words, the Council needs to examine and regulate itself as much as its courses. The obligation should be on the Council and its committees to ensure that the arrangements in proposed courses are adequate to ensure that the award is comparable in standard with others, but they should not prescribe what these arrangements should be.

The basis for such an approach already exists in the statutes which prescribe the matters to which the Council must have regard in approving courses of study. Let us take the example of examinations and assessment. The Council could regulate that a committee of Council approving a course must satisfy itself that the arrangements for assessment are adequate, fair to the student, command public confidence, be apt for the award for which they are designed, state what body is responsible for the assessment, what its membership is and what its terms of reference are. The arrangements should include the possibility of review by the academic board of the institution and appeal by students. Submissions should distinguish between final and course assessment and should state whether the latter is diagnostic or qualifying. All these matters (and there may be others like them) would be subject to the approval of Council, but Council need not make regulations about what they should consist of.

This issue illustrates that the Council still faces fundamental problems about the process of validation; which become crucial in the light of the new circumstances that the Council and the higher education system face and it is to these that we now turn.

NEW CIRCUMSTANCES

Amongst the major changes of circumstance is financial stringency. The CNAA has been a successful instrument of policy in times of expansion. Can it serve as well in times of stagnation or decline? Similarly, CNAA has been a successful instrument of a policy to develop and sustain a distinctive public sector. Will the future pattern maintain this distinction, and the need for a validating body within it? CNAA has been needed in the past to give national validity to courses created by local institutions. Will the future see such institutions becoming academically independent and able to award their own degrees? A new body has been created in the public sector to allocate the funds for advanced further education. In doing this it intends to employ 'academic judgement'. Does this mean that CNAA no longer has a purpose? And what of the problems the CNAA faces with its own procedures and processes. Does partnership in validation point the way to the ultimate redundancy of the Council?

Higher Education Policy
The key policy issue for the future of the CNAA is the future of the binary policy. A variety of scenarios can be envisaged. If there is to be a continuing binary policy, then there is a second issue as to whether the public sector institutions are to be self-validating or not. If the binary policy is to be continued on much the same basis as in the past, then there is a need for a central validating body for the public sector institutions. If, on the other hand, the distinctions between the sectors are to be reduced or eliminated, the likelihood is that all or some institutions will attain the power to award their own qualifications. CNAA may then become the body that Robbins originally foresaw, perhaps ultimately withering away when all aspirants have reached the promised land. The current signals from the government are conflicting. The consultative document on the management of the public sector (DES 1981) presented as rigid a statement of binary policy imaginable, delineating the tasks of the two sectors more exclusively than any previous statement. But other ministerial indications are that the system, whilst remaining binary, should be less so. NAB to some extent nicely reflects the dilemma. As a central focus for the public sector it emphasizes the binary distinction, yet it seeks to relate provision in the two sectors.

Economic Constraint
Government has made clear that current economic circumstances heighten the need for higher education in general and the public sector in particular to relate to the needs of the economy. The discussion document spoke of the public sector's 'key contribution' lying in 'the provision of courses specifically designed to reflect the opportunities and requirements of the country's employment market.' Even disregarding some of the crass instrumentalism of the document, there is case for a distinctive form of higher education provision in public sector institutions, maintaining the 'service' tradition of response to local and national needs, with a validating body on the CNAA model.

This need is heightened by pressures of economic circumstance. The consultative document emphasized the need for value for money and cost effectiveness. Financial constraint makes it more difficult to respond to needs, in that funds are not available for growth. New needs cannot be met, as they have been in the past, by expansion. Nor is there any indication that the need for change will be less in the future than in the past. Economic recession and the hoped for recovery from it requires innovation in education to meet the new circumstances. And whether or not we emerge from recession, new courses are needed, since the pattern of provision reflects the past not the future. The pressure is on institutions to produce different courses. The premium will be on innovation, and the evidence of the past is that external validation on the CNAA model has been more successful in this than other forms of academic control, though in an expansionary environment. The question arises whether the CNAA can encourage innovation in times of contraction or constraint.

CNAA and the Universities

All these changes, of course, relate to both sides of the binary system. The growth of the instrumentalist view of higher education; the demands for greater accountability in times of economic constraint, and the increasingly difficult choices that have to be made in allocating scarce resources are all faced by the universities too. For them, they raise questions of how long the universities can be self-validating and to that extent self-justifying, and how the UGC can make resource decisions (as in July 1981) without independent advice on the quality of its institutions or parts of them. These questions suggest that a form of external validation like that in the public sector may become necessary for the universities, and more radically that the CNAA's remit might be extended to all institutions of higher education.

CNAA and NAB

The NAB's task of relating the pattern of provision in the public sector to national need and national resources implies, as the consultative document, the work of the Pooling Committee and the NAB itself acknowledge, the need to make educational judgements. Sooner or later, resources to colleges will be allocated on the basis, to some extent or other, of judgements about which courses are preferred. This has raised the question of CNAA's relation to NAB or indeed whether CNAA is any longer needed. Again, a variety of different futures is possible. Lewis (1982) identified several kinds of 'loose' or 'tight' relationships, and argued for different relationships in the shorter and longer terms, with CNAA remaining independent of NAB at first but ultimately merging with it, such a merging resulting from a move from course to institutional validation. Others (SRHE 1981) have argued that this issue calls for a complete restructuring of both NAB and CNAA into a different kind of funding and validating body. In its own response to the consultative document, CNAA (1981b) acknowledged the validity of the argument that 'planning and funding cannot be satisfactorily done without taking matters of academic quality fully into account. Planning and funding inevitably involve making academic judgements....' The response went on to set out the arguments against CNAA's involvement in this process.

The first was that it violated the general constitutional principle of the separation of powers; second was that until now CNAA had been involved in judging whether courses met a certain minimum standard, not in ranking them, and third was that CNAA members were experts in curriculum development rather than planning. But, as the response went on, there are strong arguments why CNAA would be unwise to ignore NAB. There was firstly CNAA's data and experience which would be of value to NAB, secondly the danger of duplication of effort by NAB and CNAA, thirdly the likelihood that CNAA reports would be used by NAB anyway. All of this suggested to the Council that there was no body as well placed as CNAA to give objective academic advice to NAB and that it was willing so to do.

This meant, as the response noted, that CNAA would become an academic arm of the NAB, and it was clear that the Council was not wholly satisfied with this supportive role. The response went on to identify some more radical approaches, centring around around the idea that CNAA should become the national body, an idea which obviously did not find favour with ministers in the short term and is unlikely to be developed in the longer term arrangements (if they ever happen).

Validation and 'Academic Judgement'
The desire to stay close to the centres of power in the public sector, whilst understandable, fails to recognize the strength of the Council's own role and position. The key is the idea of separation of roles, and it is crucial here to distinguish between two apparently similar ideas — validation and 'academic judgement' — for they are not the same. The Council is right to emphasize its task as simply that of validating courses which meet certain minimum standards. This is different from judgements about value for money or whether a course should be provided. It is not the Council's job to decide whether or not a course is needed, or whether some course better meets needs than some other and whether or not to finance it. Those decisions, about the allocation of public resources between competing interests, are political in nature, and should be made by bodies accountable in some way to the public who ultimately fund the activities. In principle, the education system established by the 1944 Act offers such accountability, at least for the public sector, through elected local authorities and the secretary of state. Pooling and the creation of the NAB make accountability, at least for the public sector, through elected local authorities and the secretary of state. Pooling and the creation of the NAB make accountability less direct, but the NAB system could be developed as I have argued elsewhere to more closely resemble the pattern envisaged in the 1944 Education Act than at present (Pratt 1982). In

any case it is not the task of a validating body to determine which course should be run at any institution. Moreover, as Lewis (1982) has argued, there are objections to the concentrations of academic power that such an arrangement involves.

This is not to argue that CNAA has no part at all in this judgemental process. Far from it. But in order to contribute, it will have to reassess its processes as a validating body. It is to this aspect of its functions that we must now return.

Education Value Added

The basis of CNAA's function lies in distinguishing between the functions of a national body, such as NAB, and individual institutions. A central body cannot of its nature prescribe educational solutions. Its job, if there is one at all for it, is to determine the national problems to which the higher education system can put forward educational courses as solutions. I have suggested that it should do this by the creation and publication of some kind of 'national scenario'. Institutions would put forward plans for their future development, which the NAB would judge and then fund. Part of the process of judging which proposals are to be funded via NAB will involve deciding which courses offer the best prospect of solving some aspect of a national problem. This judgement will involve decision about the likely success of the course in doing what it says it will do, and in combination with this, some assessment of the cost, so that it is possible to distinguish between courses doing similar things and those doing different ones, and those doing similar things for different costs, or different things for different costs. The problem at the moment is that no one, CNAA, NAB included, has a way of making these kinds of judgements. So far costs per student have been the only measure of cost benefit. These of course fail to recognize the main purpose of education, which is to achieve change. Students enter courses with one set of skills, knowledge and abilities and, in theory at any rate, leave them with another. What is needed is a way of assessing the educational value added to the student by the course. And this is where CNAA comes in, as this is pre-eminently an academic function. But it will require change in CNAA's approach to its work. The CNAA's approach to comparability has been to validate not the output of courses, but the input. It has concerned itself with the entry qualifications of students, the time taken on the course, the qualifications and experience of staff, the academic environment of the department and the college, the organization and structure of decision-making bodies and so on. Such an approach is not only unhelpful, in some respects it is anti-educational. Determining such inputs as entry requirements and lengths of duration of courses implies a self-fulfilling prophecy. Only those likely to succeed in that time can enter the course. So far the Council has failed to offer a way of assessing the output from its courses. In some ways this is very fundamental criticism, since its charter obligation is to ensure that its awards are comparable with those of universities. But it is also a criticism that can be made of the rest of the education system. It has evolved few, if any, ways of measuring the quality of its products. Most assessment is tautologous in that an examination is set and prepared for and the success of this preparation then judged. There is little which enables comparison to be made of supposedly similar outputs, like degrees; nor are there clear ways of discovering what difference the process has made to the student. If output levels were validated, then the opportunity would be open for students of varying abilities to embark on a course and take whatever time is needed, by whatever methods are appropriate to attain the exit level. The able will get there quicker, as there will be less educational value to add to them.

An approach such as this would oblige educators, in colleges, to begin to identify the characteristics of their student input that they wish to act upon and what sort of characteristics they propose the output should have. Ideally the students might play a part in this. This done, the college is in a position to design a process which will get the student from where he is to where he wishes to be. There will be many processes which might do this. There will be many combinations of inputs (staff, buildings, etc.) which will produce a given output. There will be as many outputs as there are students, and educational value added will vary with them and the changes in enrolments over time.

If all the courses in a college are designed in this way, the college can determine which characteristics of output are common to all its courses and which peculiar to particular courses. It can begin to describe its output in general and particular terms. It will be able to attribute to various outputs the cost of various inputs. It will be able to decide which combination of inputs (ie cost) is most apt for which combination of outputs. In other words, it becomes possible to do the job that the NAB has been established to do.

It is important to note in this what the nature of the process is. It is a judgemental process. The measure available to help in it will be one of qualitative output compared with quantitative inputs. A college will be able to say 'we can produce these kinds of graduates for this cost'. The separate judgement will still have to be made as to whether this kind of graduate is what is wanted and at what cost. It may be possible to produce similar graduates at different costs or different kinds of graduates at similar cost. The decision as to the benefit of the education will still have to be taken, and that, as argued above, is properly the task of elected accountable bodies.

It is also important to note that this approach to CNAA validation is course-based and is incompatible with validation of institutions or broad programmes of work, as advocated by Lewis and increasingly favoured by the CNAA. The basis for arguing for it lies again in the distinction between validation and funding. It is possible — and in my view desirable —

for NAB's institutions to move towards 'programme approval' for funding purposes, and individual course validation. CNAA will help in the process of deciding which courses — or programmes — to fund by offering public information about education value added (thus avoiding the problem of 'confidential' information about institutions' standards reaching NAB). And this information will help NAB to distinguish between apparently identical courses. In the end, even if courses remain apparently identical, the choice of which to fund can be left to the 'market'. Adequate systems — some of us would argue excessive controls — already exist for closing under-subscribed courses.

CONCLUSION

This chapter has argued that, building on its successes as an instrument of policy and innovation, the CNAA has a future in the pattern of higher education emerging as a result of current policy. Although a variety of scenarios can be envisaged for the future, some form of binary distinction seems likely to remain for some time, with a role for CNAA as the main validating body in the public sector. The pressure of financial constraint and the desire of government to relate higher education provision more closely to the needs of the economy suggest that the promotion of innovation will continue to be a major task for the Council. These developments also suggest that the CNAA style of validation might need to be extended to the university sector. The creation of the NAB, although it will be concerned with 'educational judgement', does not mean that CNAA has no future. On the contrary, CNAA's function as a validating body will continue to be needed, and is quite distinct from NAB's function of advising on the allocation and distribution of courses. In this sense the Council stands as an important bulwark against the excessive control by the centre not only of the provision but the content of courses. It can act in this way, and in so doing help the NAB with its tasks, only if it considers afresh how it carries out its basic task of validation. The problems of the past in CNAA's processes need to be resolved. The way forward is for CNAA to help institutions to assess the *educational* changes they bring about for their students. This involves a shift of emphasis in the Council's procedures, from their present concentration on the process to the new and more difficult area, the outputs of education.

The challenge is to maintain an approach to validation that derives from educational rather than economic requirements yet, in the traditions of the public sector, offers ways in which educational standards and economic demands can be accommodated together. It is a challenge which will tax the accumulated experience and expertise of the Council and its institutions, but it has to be met if higher education as a whole, as well as the Council itself, is to have a future.

REFERENCES
Council for National Academic Awards (1975) *Partnership in Validation*
Council for National Academic Awards (1979) *Developments in Partnership in Validation*
Council for National Academic Awards (1980) *Annual Report 1979*
Council for National Academic Awards (1981) *Annual Report 1980*
Council for National Academic Awards (1982b) *Response to the Government's Consultative Document on Higher Education in England outside the Universities: Policy, Funding and Management*
Department of Education and Science (1981) *Higher Education in England outside the Universities: Policy, Funding and Management*
Lane, Michael (1975) *Design for Degrees* MacMillan
Lewis, Richard (1982) *The Relationship between a Funding Body and an Academic Validating Body* Paper for the Leverhulme Programme of Study into the Future of Higher Education
Locke, Michael, Pratt, John and Spencer, Andrew (1980) *The CNAA Quinquennial Visit to North East London Polytechnic: Monitoring the Polytechnic's Performance* NELP
Perkin, Harold (1970) *Innovation in Higher Education: New Universities in the United Kingdom* OECD
Pratt, John (1982) *Resource Allocation in the Public Sector of Higher Education* Paper for the Leverhulme Programme of Study into the Future of Higher Education
Society for Research into Higher Education (1981) *Draft Comment on CNAA Response to DES Consultative Document on Higher Education in England outside the Universities*

DISCUSSION AND COMMENT

Discussion centred more on the changing role of the CNAA than the position of the NAB. What relationships should CNAA have with NAB? Had the creation of NAB made the CNAA redundant? Alternatively had the CNAA a role in relation to the universities?

The CNAA had harboured ambitions to perform the role of the national body and it was evident that the experience built up by its various panels could play an important role in assessing quality amongst public sector institutions. It was represented on NAB's board but it needed to discuss with the institutions it validated how far its academic judgements about institutions arising from its validation role could be transmitted to NAB. The discussion revealed some support for the view that two bodies concerned with academic judgements, one not involved in resource allocation, represented a duplication of effort.

The CNAA had been invited by the secretary of state to consider what constitutional changes might be required to extend its remit beyond the public sector. Many speakers testified to the formative role of the CNAA in the development of public sector institutions and to the importance of the peer review system it had established but the proposition that such a system should be extended to cover the universities commanded only limited support. The likely pressure for some form of quality control over the whole of higher education was, however, recognized. It was noted that the UGC through its subject committees undertook peer group review of research and courses together and took resource allocation decisions based on their findings. The CNAA only reviewed courses, the NAB was responsible for advising on funding. The comparison highlighted the need for continuing discussion of the future role of CNAA.

At the same time wide-ranging criticisms were made not of the CNAA per se but of the elaborate system of course controls in the public sector, of which CNAA validation formed only one part, and which included: LEAs, HMIs, RACs, CNAA, and finally DES. Even the most optimistic scenario, it was suggested, produced a two and a half year approval period for a new course. This made planning almost impossible. Why, it was asked, did DES need to retain course controls? The answer apparently was that it was holding them as long-stop powers while it assessed how effective the NAB could be. It was clear from the discussion that some rationalization of these procedures was an urgent priority.

More direct comment was made on the proposition that CNAA validation had encouraged innovation. The acceptance was quoted of a number of highly specialized degrees (eg in timber technology) as evidence of innovation, but several speakers argued that such specialized qualifications contradicted rather than supported that assertion. A further question was the extent to which the existence of CNAA validation procedures institutionalized academic second class citizenship.

The role of the NAB vis à vis the CNAA has obviously still to be worked out. The NAB plans to be interventionist in regard to academic programmes or portfolios of courses but is still in the early days of establishing its powers. Co-ordination of higher education is in part achieved by monthly meetings of NAB, WAB, and UGC, but the existence of a range of 'primary funders' while good from the point of view of the need for a multiplicity of funding agencies, nevertheless raises co-ordination problems. There is going to be a continuing role for LEAs, both as funding agencies and in the formulation of policy, but the modus operandi and the effectiveness of the NAB both in relation to institutions and to the DES has yet to be established. One speaker suggested that the acid test would be how many university degree courses were closed as a result of UGC/NAB trans-binary discussions. The NAB had already, however, made an important contribution by establishing open and public procedures and this was likely over time to have an impact on the UGC's approach to decision making.

7

REGIONALIZATION IN HIGHER EDUCATION GOVERNANCE THE REGIONAL DIMENSION: SOME CONSIDERATIONS FROM A EUROPEAN PERSPECTIVE

by Guy Neave

For anyone who has been following the development of higher education in Western Europe over the past decade or so, the issue of the 'regional dimension' has been one of growing significance. What this means and why this is so is by no means clear, for as with everything in this world, the motives are mixed and those behind the horrid term 'regionalization' no less so. On the one hand, one of the most powerful pressures towards regionalization is the cultural argument which in the case of the Bretons and Versailles chateau in 1978 was literally explosive. On the other, there are various forms of utilitarian justification, put forward with reference to such matters as regional economic development, industrial efficiency or the need to ensure that higher education corresponds more closely to what are perceived as regional labour market requirements (Levy Garboua and Orival 1982; Neave 1979; Ruin 1977). Very often the two basic justifications are married together: cultural revival requires economic renaissance to underpin it. Or its converse. In both instances, higher education is seen as a catalyst and at the same time as instrument of economic and cultural mobilization. It confers, or is thought to confer, in those areas where no university exists a certain degree of cultural legitimacy which is not surprising for those who remember the importance of central European universities in translating tongues and cultures held to be rustic in status to enjoying a literary and civic standing. One thinks for instance of the Czech universities in the early nineteenth century and the revival of the various Slavonic languages later in that century (Kohn 1960).

But before going into some of the more contemporary trends towards the regionalization of governance in the higher education systems of Europe, it is important to place this in historical perspective.

HISTORICAL BACKGROUND

What I want to suggest is simply that in tackling this topic we are in a curious manner reverting to a very old model of relationship between higher education and its surroundings. Long before higher education systems were either recognized as 'systems' or brought together as national entities, the university was a regional body — founded by local duke or princeling as in the case of Grenoble (1329 under the insistent pleas of duke Humbert II), by the municipality as in the case of Leiden (1575) or

Groningen (1614), or by the local archbishop as in the case of Glasgow (Dreyfus 1976; Cohen 1982). The governance and external control were largely a matter of local importance, though in certain foundations based in capital cities, the church, monarch or his servants might sometimes intervene.

In the Seven Provinces of the Netherlands, for instance, the city fathers kept an unremitting watch on the activities of the foundations, less to ensure good living than to impose Godliness. They controlled and appointed the college of curators, appointed professors in the various faculties, though left the university to find its own funds — a sense of economy that is both modern and righteous! The classic example of the local university is, of course, that which dwelt in the Italian city state, patronized by the local prince and looked upon at all times with a good deal of suspicion by Holy Mother Church. As we all know, their local nature did not preclude their enjoying an international attraction. In this context, the university stood as one of a series of quasi-autonomous corporations — the others being the churches, free cities, guilds and merchant companies — each jealous of its privileges, each engaged in a continuing battle for autonomy and dominance (Eskstein 1979).

If you will forgive the rather summary nature of this sketch, the point I want to make is that the major influence that began the move away from the 'local' or 'regional' university was the emergence of the modern central state, this being understood as that machinery and those institutions which had the power to make laws and which subordinated all other entities within its territory to the directives it issued. It was also capable of enforcing them in a uniform manner on pain of sanction. The modern state emerged as an imposer of 'orderliness', as an arbiter between contending factions or, alternatively, as a superordinate body standing above and beyond the fractional and factional interests of the various quasi-autonomous corporations I have just mentioned.

The emergence of the modern — as opposed to the medieval — university in Western Europe is usually held to be coterminous with the emergence of the modern state. Crucial to this was the establishment of a central and formal bureaucracy, the drawing up of formal rules and regulations for its recruitment, its workings and for determining promotion and advancement within its ranks. This was set down in the form of administrative law. Taken together, such developments were of the highest significance for the regional nature — or, for that matter, the locally based governance structures — of the university. First, because gradually it substituted the state as its prime patron; second, because the development of formal entrance examinations, nationally standardized, for entry to the higher ranks of the central civil service had long-term repercussions on the university curriculum itself. It is not entirely irrelevant in this connection to point out that the standing of the various disciplines — law in Germany, Austria and Italy, engineering in France — derives directly from the paths of high preferment they opened in the administration. Such reforms not only linked the university with the state, but also associated it with a national rather than a local élite (Coleman 1966).

It is usual when examining the links between the university and the state in Western Europe, to cite as evidence the reforms introduced by the Prussian minister of education, Alexander von Humboldt, in 1809, and in France, the establishment under the direct intervention of the Emperor Napoleon of the 'Université Imperiale' in 1811 (Künzel 1982; Archer 1979). In fact, this process was well underway even before those two countries were overwhelmed by the twin disasters of the battle of Jena and the Corsican clan. The principle that universities were state institutions and thus subject to administrative law had been enunciated by Frederick II of Prussia (1712—1786) (de Ferra 1982). This gradual incorporation of previously independent establishments proceeded throughout the eighteenth century. In Sweden, the rise of clear-cut 'curricular pathways' leading to posts in the central bureaucracy took place during the half century from 1720 and 1772 and involved the insertion of specific academic subjects held to be of a vocational nature because they led to direct state employ. A committee, reporting in 1749, suggested the division of academic disciplines into five areas closely corresponding to civil service departments — a move which, curiously, anticipated by some 225 years the reforms recently introduced on a similar realignment of knowledge (Svensson 1982). It was thrown out to the rejoicing of all right-minded academics. Even so, the proposal stands as an important pointer to that broader pehenomenon — namely, the uprooting of the university from its regional context. In Austria, the firm and unequivocal subordination of the university to the requirements of the state bureaucracy were the hallmarks of that version of 'enlightened despotism' pursued by the Empress Maria Theresa (1717—1780) and her son, Joseph II (1714—1790) (Gruber 1982).

Similar developments may be seen in the course of the nineteenth century, particularly in those countries which, whether as a result of the upheaval following the Napoleonic wars or the rise of nationalism, attained the status of fully independent nations. In the case of the Netherlands, the French occupation had marked effects upon the regional nature of governance in higher education. Gone was municipal overlordship, and instead, though lipservice was paid to local sensitivities, the broad lines of higher education policy were determined from 1815 onwards by central government (van Kermenade 1980). Symbolic of this was the change in the role of the curator. No longer the creature of municipal rectitude, his became the task of implementing the ukases from on high, not to mention the delicate job of recommending to king and ministers those suitable for professorial posts. University budgets became the direct concern of central administration, and professors, as in Austria, Germany and France, had the mantle of civil servant thrust upon them (Cohen 1982). Parallel moves could be seen following the unification of Italy under the Kingdom of Piedmont. The removal of princely particularism — or, it could be argued, the formal power of local institutions — over the university was the principal achievement of the Casati Law, passed in 1859. Heavily inspired by French administrative practices (which was hardly surprising since the Piedmontese court was itself French not Italian speaking), it laid down a system of uniform control from the central Ministry of National Instruction in such matters as budget, course structure and curriculum content as well as a de jure control over professorial appointments, which, in essence persists to the present day (Clark 1977).

The Rise of the Jacobin University
There are, of course, notable exceptions to this trend which I shall deal with in a moment. Suffice it to say that one of them was Switzerland and the other Great Britain. It is, nevertheless, clear from these various examples that the rise of one of the major variants of the continental university was closely associated with their direct juridical and administrative accountability to the central state (Nitsch 1965; Gruber 1982). The recognition of 'academic autonomy' did not infringe this. Rather, it stood as a particular and exceptional instance of the state voluntarily and explicitly holding in abeyance its residual rights of intervention in areas of teaching and research. Thus the importance of the principles of *Lehr- und Lernfreiheit* was not because of their recognition — though that indeed was precious enough, but because the state explicitly operated a self-denying ordinance. Academic freedom, as the present day constitution of West Germany points out, has never meant the unconditional surrender of state authority to science and higher learning in its institutional form (*Bundesverfassungsgericht* 1973 quoted in Künzel 1982).

What are the implications of these developments for the broader issue of regionalism and governance in higher education? It is important, I think, to try and understand what the advent of a strong central state meant, not merely for the university, but also for those instrumental in bringing it about. And here I would try to avoid that in-built suspicion of the 'overmighty state' which has long been central to much of British public life. To those brought up in the tradition of the Anglo-Saxon university (to use a Gallicism for a moment) it goes without saying that academic autonomy, self-government by academe and its essential underlying concept of 'collegiality' are conditional either upon the absence of a 'strong' state or on placing as many layers of intervening responsibility as possible between central government and the individual universities. It was, after all, this principle that inspired the establishment of the University Grants Committee in 1919. From the standpoint of either the French, Dutch or German university world, the contrary proposition holds good: namely, that only with the presence of a strong state, acting through formal legal ruling, is it possible to protect academe from the intervention of particularisms and arbitrariness and to lay down relatively clear boundaries within which academic autonomy may flourish (Ringer 1968; Neave 1982). Thus institutions originally the creation of regional interests or local suzerains were gradually welded together as a 'system', the operation and functioning of which was made uniform (and to this extent equal) by the interposition of administrative law operated by the state. Administrative law stipulated the formal entry conditions (ie the holding of the Baccalaureat, the Abitur or the Studenteksamen), regulated the nature of university degrees (a national diploma is still in France held to be superior to that delivered by a particular university without national recognition), set down conditions of service for those with civil servant status (the equivalent of tenure), and, finally, introduced a certain measure of immunity to external local pressures by close budgetary oversight of university expenditure.

All this is, of course, nothing new to those already familiar with some of the major Western European university systems. But, when placed in the context of our present topic, such developments assumed a new significance, namely that they translated the focus and mission of the university from the local to the national setting. Thus, alongside the Jacobin state rose what I have termed elsewhere the Jacobin university (Neave 1979b). The price of this 'protection from local particularism' or 'esprit de clocher' was, however, the disappearance of the university as a quasi-autonomous corporation in the legal sense though not, obviously, in its internal behaviour or in the conducting of its internal affairs.

The rise of the nation state and its concomitant institutions, such as a national bureaucracy and a publicly financed system of education (the latter acting as a cultural underpinning to the concept of national unity) were all part of that drive which, throughout the nineteenth century and well into the present, sought to strengthen the territorial integrity of the nation. And this, by the same token, meant the undermining of regional claims to legitimacy or droit de cité. Thus, in continental Europe, higher education became a direct emanation of the nation in just the same way as did the civil service to which many of its graduates were destined. This long drawn out process, seen from the regional perspective, is perhaps one of the most outstanding examples of that phenomenon later to be known as 'institutional drift'.

Counter-developments
One should not think, however, that the denial of higher education's regional dimension was a universal phenomenon, though one has to look hard to find counter-illustrations. One of these was the development of higher education in Switzerland and the other in Great Britain.

Because of the particular nature of the Swiss confederation, which gives sovereign powers to the twenty-six cantons, university development throughout the nineteenth century — and still today — retains a highly local pattern of administration. There are two exceptions to this. The federal law of 7 February 1854 set up a Federal Higher Education Council to administer and supervise the two federal institutes of technology of Zürich and Lausanne. Otherwise each university (there are seven today) depends for its finance and administration on the department of education of the canton in which it is situated (Crausaz 1979). In effect, the constitutional pattern of Swiss government has served to preserve a very strong regional dimension both in the university's role and also in its governance patterns. The power of the federal state compared to that of the cantons in the field of university policy making is very limited, as witness, for instance, the fate of the federal law on financial support to higher institutes of learning and research. Designed to give the confederation the means of co-ordinating university budgeting across the country, it was approved by parliament in October 1977 only to be rejected at a national referendum the following May (Crausaz 1979). Popular referenda (which in certain instances are mandatory), plus direct and proximate local administration, mean that Swiss universities come under far closer direct public scrutiny than has ever been envisaged, even, for instance, in the discussion over a devolved system of higher education for Scotland at the height of the devolution debate.

Yet the financial power of the confederation is considerable. It provides around half the investment costs and around a sixth of running expenditure (Wyss 1982). This two-tier system of governance is further distinguished at canton level by a considerable difference in the strength of external control by cantonal departments of education. Broadly speaking, the French language cantons confer a considerable degree of freedom on the university's internal management. This tends not to be the case in the German speaking areas, where the role of the cantonal administration is particularly strong. In the latter case, the role of rector is more a representative of academia whereas in the former the rector enjoys real powers to influence internal decisions (Wyss 1982).

It is perhaps significant that, at precisely the time when countries such as Yugoslavia, Norway and, to some extent, France began to reconsider the question of regionalism in higher education — during the mid- and early sixties — Switzerland began to entertain serious doubts about the development of higher education within a cantonal framework. In part, this sprang from serious financial difficulties (pas d'argent, pas de politique universitaire Suisse!) allied to an outmoded financial structure by which cantons with universities had, hitherto, assumed full financial responsibility for their upkeep. From this emerged two developments: first the passing of the Federal University Law of 28 June 1968 to enable federal finance to cantonal universities; second, the setting up of two advisory boards at national level to draw up non-mandatory guidelines within a loose federal structure. The first of these two bodies was the Swiss Board of Science, the second, the Swiss University Conference.

The Swiss Board of Science has a strategic role in policy decisions.

It advises the Federal Council on all national and international aspects of education policy, draws up recommendations on the development and co-ordination of higher education, and assists with advice and guidelines those universities involved in structural or academic innovation. The role of the Swiss University Conference is that of the main discussion forum, where both universities and cantonal administration get together to reach agreement in such matters as admissions policy to individual establishments and the distribution of the number of places in medical schools (Wyss 1982). This may be seen as a tactical role but is no less important since it involves a delicate balance between cantonal autonomy on the one hand and closer collaboration at national level between institutes of higher education on the other (Crausaz 1979). Such agreements are, however, voluntary, though some commentators have pointed out that the growing complexity of both the administrative and financial systems of control makes for even greater difficulty in reaching bilateral agreements between cantons.

The third exception, I would suggest, is to be found in Britain. In England, though to a lesser extent in Scotland, the ancient universities tended to conserve far longer than in Europe the characteristic of 'an autonomous property owning corporation' (Eustace 1982). Such a pattern, at least in Austria, Germany and Italy, tended to predominate prior to the translation of regional universities into a nation-state system by legal and legislative incorporation.

Yet the minimalist interpretation of the role of the state, the hallmark of nineteenth-century British economic Liberalism, has allowed areas of initiative the importance of which are only today being recognized in Europe. Local initiative and enterprise, independent of the state, founded the great municipal universities. And, whereas in Europe many national university systems were busily engaged in eradicating regional cultures — another dimension to the Jacobin state (in France see for instance de Certeau, Julia and Revel 1975) — the federal University of Wales was founded, largely to give recognition to that old and particular nation. The discovery of 'lay representation' on decision-making bodies which represents one of the most important aspects of the Swedish U68 reform of the university (Ruin 1977) has long been a practice in Britain, though whether it is effective in bringing the voice of the community to the groves of academe is a different matter.

From a European point of view, British universities constitute a loose federation in which the exact relationship between itself and the state is largely unspecified except in terms of practice and on the basis of what might equally be termed 'private understanding'. Unlike Germany where theories of the state and higher education have long been the object of inquiry from Kant onward, there is an absence of any equivalent constitutional theory for the simple reason that the British constitution, as every schoolboy knows, is unwritten. This means, in effect, that whilst you have a far greater latitude to reaffirm a specific regional commitment, you have little in the way of protection, other than the initiative of a few key individuals, against the short-term arbitrariness of political parties, or even against that of your fellow representatives. You are, in short, faced with the collapse of all those procedures that in times past guaranteed a high and admired self-governance among universities, whether this be the quinquennial grant system or the University Grants Committee. It is then very strange that, having suffered from the gradual erosion of the buffers placed between universities and central government, universities should seek refuge from the latter by having recourse to the regional dimension. But perhaps, like Sir Richard Grenville, it is felt to be:

'Better to fall into the hands of God
Than the arms of the King of Spain.'

Trends towards Regional Governance in Western Europe

The first examples of higher education institutes with a specifically regional remit in Western Europe can be traced to the mid- to later sixties. In Britain, Mr Crosland's Woolwich speech suggested that closer public control over the newly created polytechnics should aim at ensuring their continued responsiveness to the social and economic demands of the locality (Pratt and Burgess 1974). In other words local or regional governance was a specific instrument for ensuring that such establishments developed in keeping with perceived regional needs, be they qualified manpower, research facilities, assistance to industry or to local government services. This initiative followed very closely that carried out in France by the Comité des 18 which, sitting in 1966, drew up the guidelines for the future university institutes of technology (IUTs). In Norway a similar remit was given to the experimental District Colleges which, from 1976, have been fully incorporated into the Norwegian system of higher education (Kyvik and Skoie 1982; Kyvik 1981; Domency and Gilly 1977).

In the case of the French IUTs, the French government did not assume — though they did later — that regional responsiveness of necessity involved regional governance. Rather they separated the two issues, conferring a regional mission upon those institutes but controlling it by traditional means of governance — that is to say, they adhered to a reinforced and even closer form of Jacobin centralism than was ever the case for the universities (Neave 1979). This was exercised not only by close control over budget and expenditure (rumour had it that the court of audit was even more savage with the IUTs than ever it was with the universities) but also by the appointment rather than the election of IUT directors. The regional element, in theory at least, was to be provided by the presence of 'prominent personalities' of an industrial and commercial provenance on the Administrative Council and by the use of part-time lecturers who themselves worked in the local economy. In short, tight formal direction from above was to be linked in with a staff recruitment policy at the base. Governance was not seen as a crucial element in redirecting the thrust of these new institutions towards the regional dimension so much as a central government interpretation of what were considered to be regional requirements.

The Norwegian District Colleges grew out of a series of reports, five in all, presented by the Ottosen committee between 1966 and 1970. The committee sat at a particular time when doubts emerged, first, about the desirability of continuing the traditional pattern of central administration in Norway and, second, about regional policy. The proposal to establish several regional colleges correspond to both these considerations. Their task, it was suggested, would be to provide an organizational superstructure of all short-term higher education in a particular region (Kyvik 1981) both as an alternative to universities and, at the same time, as a focus for all non-university education in each of the twelve regions designated. Amongst the various goals attributed to them were the training of new manpower in the light of technological innovation and the introduction of fields of study held relevant to the local context. It was expected, then, that the colleges would stimulate social, cultural and economic activity and thus act as a counterweight to the licentious attractions of the great urban centres. Equally important, the regions were expected to influence the development of the various courses presented.

Unlike the French IUTs, however, underpinning the regional remit did involve major structural changes in the patterns of governance. Agreed the Ministry of Church and Education retained its traditional control over the budget and over the validation and regulation of examinations. But, in 1976, the Norwegian parliament interposed a new board, operating at county level. The membership, of nine in all, is appointed by central government. Five are nominated by the county assembly for a period of four years, two more are drawn from the staff of participating institutions and two are students. Its remit and responsibility is to ensure that the planning, establishment and development of all higher education in a region be considered as a whole, though this does not include the universities. It may prepare budgets for post-secondary education within its particular area though subject to centrally prescribed financial limitations and subject to those rules and regulations determined by central administration. It is also responsible for examining the need for post-secondary education within the region and may propose the allocation of training facilities amongst various fields of study. In addition, each regional board has responsibility for promoting contact between individual institutions, central authorities and the various regional economic interests (Kyvik 1981).

Though these powers seem, at first sight, considerable, there are a number of factors intervening that detract from them. The first is that despite this move towards co-ordinating responsibility for post-secondary education at regional level, most of the other types of non-university education (teachers colleges, colleges for training social workers, etc.) still tend to operate within other lines of management. These are both financial and administrative. Kyvik, examining the regional colleges from the standpoint of implementation theory, has argued that, so far, the intention to carry through integration has not met with much success. Second, the regional boards do not appear to have effective power, with the result that the higher education system is 'almost as fragmented as before the launching of the reform proposals' (ibid. p.65) Third, there is the inevitable question of legitimacy. Most non-university institutions, it has been pointed out, tend to look upon the wretched regional boards as superfluous and bureaucratic bodies, interposing themselves incontinently between institution and central ministry (Kyvik and Skoie 1982). And, as if to add insult to injury, they have been accused of leading to yet further centralization inasmuch as they infringe some of their powers, particularly in the area of determining, through the financial allocation priorities, the type of studies that will find grace and those that will not. Thus, an exercise which is still wantonly and persistently regarded by ministry officials as leading to decentralizing and opening up greater public participation in educational decision making, seen from the base, has totally different overtones. What is one man's centralization is another's participation.

The common feature of both the IUTs and the regional colleges is that their 'regional commitment' did not extend to other sectors of higher education. In neither case were universities involved and certainly not the French grandes écoles, the true élite sector of French higher education. If anything, the emphasis on 'regionalism' in one area served to increase the determination of the remainder to assert their 'national status'. This was not the case in Sweden. The reform of higher education, recommended by the U68 Commission and implemented in July 1977, involved a root and branch reform of both institutional and governance structures and also the undergraduate curriculum (Premfors 1979). If the outcome of these reforms was the establishment of six regional boards with effective oversight for all post-secondary education in their territorial area, the motives behind this development were profoundly different from the Norwegian exercise. In the first place, the principle of integrating administrative oversight for higher education was not limited to the non-university sector alone. The U68 reforms, on the contrary, brought together both university and non-university institutes under one organizational umbrella in a species of 'comprehensive university'. In the second place the main consideration turned less around regional policy than the need to decentralize decision making, to give students greater representation in university decision making, to bring in 'outsiders' to boards of governance in individual institutions and, finally, to make higher education more amenable to changes in the labour market (Premfors 1982).

The regional boards, then, serve many purposes. By bringing in outside representatives — students, representatives of white and blue collar unions — they may be seen as extending into academic governance the industrial principle of 'co-determination' (Ruin 1977). Though they cannot directly influence traditional full-time undergraduate courses they can have considerable impact over what are termed 'single' or local 'study lines'. These do not lead to the award of a degree, but tend to be specialized. Regional boards have financial responsibility for these and for distance learning courses. They may allocate money to different institutions to support such courses. This means that through the intermediary of these bodies, the region has the power to exert pressure or persuasion to ensure that particular needs of a regional nature will be reflected both in the type of courses offered and, it is hoped, by the research undertaken (OECD 1981).

However, their discretion in awarding subsidies to 'single' courses is not total. Allocation to a particular institution is affected by its range of 'general' courses and these are decided centrally at a general level by parliament and in detail as well as for their budgetary implications by the National Board of Universities and Colleges. This dichotomy of control over the curriculum and resource allocation has direct implications for the de facto influence of the regional boards. It has been pointed out, for instance, that those institutes created out of non-university establishments are more likely to have 'single' course elements in them than their fellows which emerged from long-standing and highly reputed university foundations. This implies that the regional boards possess greater effectiveness in influencing the former than the latter, which still look towards central administration for guidance and direction.

There have, not unnaturally, been numerous objections to reinforcing the powers of regional administration. First was the argument that an over-involvement of local interests in the life of the university would prove detrimental to effective research. Research criteria, it was argued, were international where not national in scope. To subordinate the type of research undertaken to purely local interests would be tantamount to withdrawing Swedish academe from the Republic of Letters and instead, make it little more than a serf of the regional glebe (Ruin 1977). Second was the protest voiced by students anxious lest too much local involvement would detract from the national value of their diplomas. And, third, that the licentious proliferation of regional boards would not merely lead to an equally licentious proliferation of bureaucrats, but that the decision-making structure itself would become increasingly atomized between central government, regional boards and local boards of higher education, the latter being concerned with economic administration and planning and personnel matters (OECD 1981). And, last but not least, it was feared that, as a result of political participation at regional level, the distribution of resources within a region would obey geographic or party political considerations rather than those of academia.

If these three countries — France, Norway and Sweden — are amongst the more outstanding examples of the way in which the twin issues of regionalism and governance are receiving increasing attention in Western Europe, there is a further model which merits consideration. This is the Yugoslavian one.

Yugoslavia is a federation of six republics and two autonomous provinces dedicated to the principle of 'socialist self-management' (Tanovic 1982). This involves a fundamental transfer of power away from the central state and its investment in the regional and local communities and, at the same time, the incorporation of industrial workers and farmers into industrial and agricultural management. At the federal level there is no body responsible for regulating higher education either in the federal parliament or in the government. If the legal framework is provided by a Higher Education Act, its application, interpretation and administration is the work of the Committees of Education, Science and Culture, located in every republic and autonomous province. In addition to validating the statutes of the university as a whole, such bodies also have responsibility of making sure that the curriculum and the type of manpower to which it leads are in keeping with the constitution and the law. This does not mean, however, that, as in Sweden, either curriculum or staff appointments are made at central government level. This is carried out at the level of individual establishments by means of an Academic Council of which one third are teaching staff, one third students and the remaining third representatives of outside political or community interests (Tanovic 1982).

In a curious manner, it would appear that through its particular interpretation of socialism and its legislative enactments, Yugoslavia's model of higher education has resurrected many of those structures which characterized governance in the medieval universities of Bologna and Paris. The legal basis for both the Communal Council and the Academic Council is enshrined in the Law of Associated Labour. This states that every university, college or academy is an independent association in which teachers, scholars, non-teaching staff and students manage the property of the establishment on an equal basis and participate in its affairs. It is from this act that both the Academic Council and the Communal Council, which is also involved in appointments and promotion, derive their powers.

If higher education governance has been pushed to well below the regional level, so too has funding, both for recurrent, capital and equipment expenditure and for research allocations. The former lies in the hands of Communities of Interest for Higher Education the latter under the ambit of Communities of Interest for Research. The first of these bodies acts as an autonomous assembly responsible to parliament in financing higher education. Their revenue is raised from that proportion of his income which every employed individual pays to higher education. It has been argued that this direct form of tax levy and its local disbursal is more democratic than the previous system of state grants. The Communities of Interest for Research seem to have been less successful. For, though they finance research applications on a competitive basis, this system of local control appears to have driven research out of the university and into industry. Eighty per cent of research funds, it has been pointed out, go to research centres outside higher education, primarily in industry (Tanovic 1982).

The Yugoslav model of self-management can be seen as an interesting extension of that model of autonomy usually identified with higher education in the pre-modern era in Western Europe, but applied to social organization as a whole rather than to higher education alone. This, one might argue, derives less from considerations of a regional nature than from the imperative of a particular ideological reconstruction of society in general.

THE MODERN CONTEXT

There is sufficient evidence from the various national examples I have presented to suggest that the regional dimension in governance is an issue of major importance at the present time in Western Europe. Nor has the discussion ceased, even today. In Spain the passing of the Organic Law on Higher Education in the course of 1980 placed financing of universities in the hands of the so-called Autonomous Communities — effectively Catalonia and the Basque country though there are calls for a similar statute to be promulgated for Galicia as well (Neave 1980). Whilst in France, recent proposals put forward by the Fréville Commission, reporting in March 1981, suggested that a greater degree of financial autonomy was desirable for the university sector and that French universities should look increasingly towards their immediate regions for research and teaching contracts with local economic interests. Others have argued that greater regional control would make for more response to regional and local labour markets rather than have graduates perpetually looking towards the traditional, national labour market (Levy Garboua and Orival 1982).

There are, of course, many ways in which one may look upon the 'regional aspect' — as an exercise in greater participation by the outside community, as an instance of 'democratic control', as an example of recognizing the legitimacy of sub-national cultures — all of which are value judgements; alternatively, it can be viewed as part of a technocratic imperative — more efficient decision making through devolution, a recognition that perhaps the fundamental assumption of the nineteenth-century legislator that 'uniformity of legal stipulation equals equality of conditions' is perhaps less well founded. Or, finally, that the present-day administration of government is so complex that centralized decision making down to the last detail is counterproductive and in the end makes for greater arbitrariness than would be the case if central government merely contented itself with laying the overall framework and left the executive details to be elaborated the nearer they come to the point of operation.

Either way, within the context of the classic Western European systems, what we are witnessing is a swing of the pendulum of history, away from what some French writers have called the 'University of Napoleon' (Girod de l'Ain 1979) and which I have termed the Jacobin University. But this is only in one dimension, namely that of governance. In some countries, often precisely those that see, formally speaking, a greater devolution towards the base, also see a tightening up of financial control from the centre. France would be a good example of this. And here it is very likely that that which one gains on the swings of a revised form of governance one loses on the budgetary roundabouts.

If regional governance is *necessary* to refocus the mission of higher education upon its immediate surroundings, it is not *sufficient*. For it is a remarkable feature of those institutions founded with a regional remit, be they regional colleges, university institutes of technology or the non-university sector of Yugoslavian higher education, that they very quickly to try and shed this regional overtone. It does not automatically follow that *because* there are public and regional forms of governance then sensitivity to the social, cultural or economic hopes of that region *shall* be taken into account in a manner that endures. Indeed, studies undertaken into these three systems of higher education suggest that the two propositions are largely non sequiturs. What is determinant in the development of these institutions and the relationship with their region is an outcome of the dynamics of the academic profession itself. Irrespective of which side of the binary line, the values of that profession have a universal quality and are perceived by its members as capable of accommodation only with considerable difficulty to what might be presented — perhaps incorrectly — as the short-term concerns of regional executives and their municipal masters. I have already noted, though in passing, the strength of feeling amongst certain sections of Swedish and Norwegian academics against a proximate rather than a distant bureaucracy. Similar feelings are now being expressed in Switzerland (Rivier 1978).

Given the historic centralization of most university systems in Western Europe, it would be erroneous to see in their new emphasis upon the regional 'mission' any real parallel with the characteristic British model of independent but mutually isolated institutions with separate charters. The nearest European example resembling it is , to my mind, that of Yugoslavia. Nevertheless, the salient feature of most of the examples analysed here is the thickening of the administrative layers interposed between central government and the individual university establishment. In short what one is seeing in Europe is the strengthening — though variously motivated — of the buffer between higher education and the ministry through the presence of additional intermediary monitoring and governance agencies. In this connexion, it is worthwhile noting the recent proposals of the French Freville Commission which tended directly and explicitly in this direction.

The Freville Commission recommended that an intermediary organ, similar to, if not directly inspired by, the University Grants Committee, be set up to negotiate on behalf of the French universities with the Ministries of National Education and of Finance. It is a curious irony that just at the moment when the UGC retains a mere shadow of its former self, so France — the Jacobin state par excellence — is contemplating an arrangement which resembles the UGC in its earlier and better days.

CONCLUSION
Viewed historically, Britain is seeing a move by central government to unify and control its system of higher education — a development which in continental Europe emerged far earlier either as part of the 'enlightened despotism' of the Germanic world or the construction of the nation state during and in the aftermath of the Napoleonic wars.

However, in any attempt to compare the new buffers being set up between university and central administration in Europe, and the apparent attempts to break down their counterpart in Britain, it is important to remember that the respective end-products may not be so dissimilar. Relations between state and university in Europe will continue to be defined by formal rules, regulations and procedures (rather as in Britain, formal regulations define the relations between a university and its constituent colleges). These rules are backed with hallowed procedures for implementation and challenge. The strength of the centrally imposed legal framework — even in the more dispersed systems such as Yugoslavia and Switzerland — will remain considerable. An important area of latitude still exists for experimentation within these legal frameworks as well as through the formal negotiating processes whereby regulations are tested and modified.

The main mechanism for imposing regional commitment in some European systems is not exhortation and resource starvation as in the case of the UK. Nor yet the broadly local control exercised in the polytechnics. Rather the region's needs tend to be promoted through a central government directorate which uses financial means to control key specific university matters. These include, in addition to the overall budget, the balance of posts in the different specialisms within higher education and between higher education sectors, ratification of staff appointments according to strict criteria of qualifications, national validation and standardization of degrees and diplomas, and indicators for research priorities.

Comparative evaluation suggests that, given present circumstances in Britain, the essential problem is less the location of the governance of higher education, whether institutional, local or regional. Rather the problem relates to the clarity and openness of the constitutional, administrative and financial framework which regulates and controls higher education as a whole, and the need to stipulate its foundation formally and legislatively. Once that has been done, *then* and only then, does the regional issue become of importance, but not, I think, before.

REFERENCES

Archer, Margaret S. (1979) *The Social Origins of Education Systems* London: Sage

Becher, Tony, Embling, Jack and Kogan, Maurice (1977) *Systems of Higher Education* New York: International Council for Educational Development

Clarke, Burton (1977) *Academic Power in Italy: Bureaucracy and Oligarchy in a National University System* Chicago: University Press

Cohen, Adolph (1982) The state and higher education in the Netherlands *European Journal of Education* 17 (3)

Coleman, James A. (1966) *Education and Political Development* Princeton: University Press

Crausaz, Roselyne (1979) Higher education in Switzerland *European Journal of Education* 14 (1)

de Certeau, Michel, Julia, Dominique and Revel, Jacques (1975) *Une Politique de la Langue: la Révolution Française et les Patois* Paris: Gallimard

Domenc, Michel and Gilly, Jean-Pierre (1977) *Les IUTs: Ouverture et Idéologie* Paris: Editions du Cerf

Dreyfus, Paul (1976) La ville et la région de Grenoble *Paedagogica Europaea* xxi (2)

Eckstein, Harry (1979) On the 'science' of the state *Daedalus* 108 (4) Fall

Eustace, Rowland (1982) The state and higher education in Britain *European Journal of Education* 17 (3)

de Ferra, Giampaolo (1982) Italie: la nouvelle donne *CRE Information* 58, 2 ème trimestre

Girod de l'Ain, Bertrand (1979) Le retour à l'université de Napoléon *Le Monde* 17 August 1979

Gruber, Karl-Heinz (1982) The state and higher education in Austria *European Journal of Education* 17 (3)

Kohn, Hans (1960) *Le Panslavisme* Paris: Payot

Kyvik, Svein (1981) *The Norwegian Regional Colleges: a study of the establishment and implementation of a reform in higher education* Oslo: Institute for Research and Studies in higher education

Kyvik, Svein and Skoie, Hans (1982) Recent trends in Norwegian higher education *European Journal of Education* 17 (2)

Levy Garboua, Louis and Orival, François (1982) Recent developments in French higher education: an economic perspective *European Journal of Education* 17 (2)

Neave, Guy (1978) *Nouveaux Modèles d'Enseignement Supérieur et Egalité des Chances: prospectives internationales* Bruxelles: Commission des Communautés Européennes

Neave, Guy (1979a) Education and regional development: an overview on a growing controversy *European Journal of Education* 14 (3)

Neave, Guy (1979b) Regional development and higher education *Higher Education Review* (3) Summer

Neave, Guy (1979c) Academic drift: some views from Europe *Studies in Higher Education* 4 (2)

Neave, Guy (1980) Accountability and control *European Journal of Education* 15 (1)

Neave, Guy (1982) La notion de limite: modèle des liens existant entre l'université et l'Etat *CRE Information* 58 2 éme trimestre

Nitsch, Wolfgang (1965) *Hochschule in der Demokratie* Neuweid: Luchterhand

OECD (1981) *Reviews of National Policies for Education: educational reforms in Sweden* Paris: Organisation for Economic Cooperation and Development

Pratt, John and Burgess, Tyrrell (1974) *The Polytechnics: a report* London: Pitmans

Premfors, Rune I.T. (1979) The politics of higher education in Sweden: recent developments 1976—1978 *European Journal of Education* 14 (1)

Premfors, Rune I.T. (1982) *Values and Higher Education Policy* Stockholm: Department of Political Science (mimeo)

Ringer, Fritz (1968) *The Decline of the German Mandarins: the German academic profession 1809—1934* Harvard: University Press

Rivier, Dominique (1978) La gestion de l'université contemporaine: planification et décentralisation *CRE Information* 44 4 ème trimestre

Ruin, Olof (1977) *External Control and Internal Participation: Trends and Policies of Swedish Higher Education*, Stockholm: Department of Political Science (mimeo)

Tanovic, Arif (1982) Yugoslavia: an autonomous model *CRE Information* 58 2 ème trimestre

Svensson, Lennart G. (1982) State, class and knowledge: a history of Swedish universities *European Journal of Education* 17 (3)

van Kermenade, Jos (1980) *Onderwijsbeleid en-bestel* Groningen: Wolters Noordhof

Wyss, Franz (1982) La Suisse: pouvoir éclaté *CRE Information* 58 2 ème trimestre

8

REGIONALIZATION IN HIGHER EDUCATION GOVERNANCE
A REGIONAL DIMENSION IN THE UNITED KINGDOM

by David Morrell

THE CONTEXT OF REGIONALIZATION

The United Kingdom as a whole does not have any clear or balanced basis for division into regions. Some areas have a long history of discontent with central government often based upon historical, geographical or even emotional sentiments. However, with the publication of the Kilbrandon Report[1] in 1973 it was possible to set aside less reliable motivations and consider the rational factors relevant to the possible regionalization of the United Kingdom. The report and its important memorandum of dissent[2] formed the background to the white paper (1975) and subsequent bill for devolution to Scotland and Wales[3], which in their turn provoked much thought and debate, particularly in the areas concerned, on the subject of decentralization.

Traditional and emotional mists were dispelled to reveal real problems of psychological remoteness, centrality of conception, and sense of powerlessness resulting in apathy. Devolution became clearly distinguished from delegation and geographical identification was distinguished from functional identification. The concept of regionalism could be seen as a method of increased democratization and participation relevant throughout the Kingdom and not just to the restless periphery[4].

All the Kilbrandon commissioners agreed that centralization of government had already gone too far and that the need to increase or restore opportunities to participate was real enough to warrant the establishment of new representative institutions at regional level for Scotland and Wales and for up to eight regions in England. Interestingly the majority would have conferred the special privilege of legislative devolution upon Scotland and Wales giving only indirectly elected regional councils in England, whereas the minority preferred uniformity of political rights as a more equitable solution.

Some would consider it unfortunate that the commissioners did not give consideration to the possibility of evolving an appropriate version of the structure now operating in most large democratic countries, namely federation. However, they were not prepared to question the doctrine of the undivided sovereignty of the Westminster parliament which was so dear to Dicey[5] and so fatal to Westminster-Irish relations[6]. This chapter will not be so inhibited.

The sequence of the Kilbrandon Report and the important reports on local government reform in England[7] and in Scotland[8] was unfortunate. Two-tier local government was accepted before the fertile debate on the decentralization of functions from central government ran its course. To many people yet another tier of government was unthinkable.

However, the desire for community participation in social policy and for accountability continues to increase. This participation can take the form of more central government intervention but there is clear evidence that limits to the acceptability of distant and less well-informed central control have been reached. The alternative is more participation at local government level but there appear to be a number of functions which it may not be desirable to devolve to that level. There is a wide gap between the government of two and a half million people and the government of fifty million. The unit of two to ten million people is near to the scale of many states in federations and would cover the smaller nations of Europe. Five out of the six political parties represented in the House of Commons in recent years are committed to some form of decentralization and even the sixth has made certain gestures in that direction. The issue is therefore still very much alive and it is important that those who are concerned about the future of higher education should debate the matter and formulate opinions and not be caught unprepared as many were in Scotland in the seventies.

A leader of Britain's newest political party has described the tendency of governments to centralize, bureaucratize, and stifle the roots of democracy[9]. He has warned that centralized policy will inevitably lead to confrontation[10] and that ordinary people are reacting against impersonal and distant organizations, public or private, which seem to interfere increasingly with their lives[11]. He deplores the submersion by press and media of all cultural distinctions under London[12] and quotes opinion based on polls indicating that most people believe that local and regional control is now at an irreducible minimum[13]. A director of CBI Scotland has referred to the vortex effect of the south-east of England, which increasingly concentrates the power and the decisions around London[14].

Many, perhaps most, of Britain's universities have deep local roots and a genuine concern for the economic, social and cultural life of their neighbourhood, and therefore will feel the need to respond to regional consciousness. But universities are funded by central government in London on the advice of a national committee which would find it very difficult to be aware of all regional pressures and distinctions and which has no special remit to consider regional factors. This central mechanism is now the subject of a sharp tightening of control by central government, which has taken over decisions not only on finance but also on student numbers. Centralization of control is leading to confrontation, just as Dr Owen forecasts, and is already reducing the power of institutions to take into account regional factors in making their own decisions.

Universities are under pressure to collaborate with each other and to rationalize the provision of higher education with the public sector. The efforts of the University Grants Committee (UGC) to promote such activity on a national scale merely draw attention to the structural vacuum at regional level. Universities have a well recognized need to reconvince the population of the critical nature of their function and mission. Universities must not only be aware but also demonstrate their awareness of regional needs such as those of industry and commerce in both technical training and in the development of personal qualities[15].

Decentralization is therefore a live issue. It can be seen as an effective way of responding positively to certain of the pressures of our time. Its revelance to higher education is evident. Self-identification and scale appear to be important factors with profound implications for morale and motivation. Regionalization is one possible form of decentralization and in spite of the lack of obvious regional areas and of our centralist constitutional traditions it is an option which must be explored.

SCOTLAND: A REGIONAL DIMENSION IN THE UNITED KINGDOM

Scotland is being examined in more detail, not because it is in any way a typical region of Britain, but because it is one region in which the debate upon the merits of regionalization of higher education has already been rehearsed.

When the British parliament came into being in 1707 Scotland retained a distinctive school system and educational tradition. Although the early continental influences upon the Scottish universities were clearly modified by English influences in the nineteenth and twentieth centuries they are still known for their emphasis upon opportunity of access, breadth of study, and something more difficult to describe which is encapsulated in the concept of 'the democratic intellect'. The administrative devolution represented by the Scottish Education Department has protected the school system from anglicization but the universities, financed through the UGC since 1919, have become conscious in recent years, as accountability and control have increased, that they are being subjected to criteria which can take only marginal account of long-established Scottish traditions.

Political devolution has been an issue in Scotland for a long time. The Balfour Commission (1957)[16] recognized a Scottish dimension and, although the Wheatley Report (1969)[17] rejected devolution, by 1970 the Douglas-Home Report[18] was recommending a 'Scottish Convention' without a Scottish university grants committee but voicing some doubts about the London UGC's access to information on Scottish universities. (It was two academic members of the Douglas-Home Committee who dissented from the convention proposal.)[19]

The 1975 white paper provoked sudden and intense debate. The SNP predictably demanded a peculiar form of Scottish UGC[20]. This was opposed by the Committee of Vice-Chancellors and Principals (CVCP) and National Union of Students (NUS) (Scotland)[21] (although for different reasons). The

Association of University Teachers (AUT) (Strathclyde) proposed a Scottish Higher Education Grants Committee but the AUT (Glasgow) rejected university devolution. Informed press reports of the time deplored the immaturity and confusion of the debate and emphasized the importance of thorough discussion and a soundly based conclusion[22]. In 1976 the Scottish Education Department and the universities were compelled by the apparent imminence of devolution to begin formal consideration. The secretary of state produced a green paper proposing a Council for Higher Education which was considered by an inter-senate working party which the eight universities had already set up. A collective decision to support a consultative council covering all degree and equivalent work was arrived at by the eight universities. However, as the secretary of state eventually decided to establish a tertiary education council covering all non-university post-school education the universities were deemed to have excluded themselves. This impression was confirmed when the annual conference of University Courts resolved in considering the latest white paper on 28 May 1976 to publish their agreement with its conclusion that responsibility for the universities should not be devolved.

The main arguments against devolution were its association with provincialism (rather than internationalization), the danger of isolation from national sources of research funding, and threats seen to academic freedom and institutional autonomy. In an interesting pamphlet[23], Nigel Grant and Alex Main, both well-known educationists, set out their refutation of these arguments and emphasized the need for the integration of the Scottish education system, the defence of the tradition of democratic intellect (contrasted with the élitist English tradition), and the defence of the broad curriculum (avoiding specialism). They argued that anglicization was the inevitable result of an increasing London influence and that without university devolution there would be a widening gulf between the schools and the universities and also between the universities and certain professions (law, teaching, and the Church).

The universities were strongly criticized by the press and by other voices in the educational system for being conservative, complacent, fearful and unimaginative[24]. The current climate of opinion is more difficult to define, but one of the most perceptive reporters of the Scottish university scene has sensed 'a remarkable change of emphasis' since the Scottish universities rejected devolution and pointed out that in the recent crisis they were co-operating in their reaction to UGC and were not split by 'the Oxbridge versus the rest mentality prevalent in England'.[25]

The Council for Tertiary Education which was set up in 1978[26] has recently (1982)[27] produced a report which recommends the separation of public sector tertiary education into advanced education under a body analogous to the UGC and other tertiary education under local authorities. The establishment of a public sector grants committee in Scotland would undoubtedly raise again the question of a Scottish UGC. The Council is very conscious of the need to co-ordinate tertiary and university education and the universities are also aware that the simpler pattern and scale in Scotland provides 'a potential framework for complementary development'.[28] Regular meetings now take place between the universities, as a group, the Scottish Education Department, and representatives of colleges, to discuss course planning. The Council's identification of early tasks illustrates regional problems, eg the employment/qualification match and the interface with secondary education.

In 1981 the all-party Campaign for a Scottish Assembly[29] published a report which recommended that 'an Assembly should have full control over primary and secondary education. It must also have responsibility for Scottish universities'. It reflects the earlier realization that were an assembly to be set up which would assume political oversight of the Scottish Education Department the Scottish universities would be in an anomalous and isolated position if they remained under the auspices of the 'English' Department of Education and Science.[30]

The Scottish universities guard their autonomy as fiercely as any others but nonetheless they have found it convenient to establish many collective bodies for specific purposes.[31]   Student awards are handled by the Scottish Education Department, not by local authorities, and this arrangement, by the consistency of its operation combined with the reasonableness of its scale, made a favourable impression upon the Rayner inquiry into aspects of civil service operation. However, administrative advantages do not continue into the policy sphere because Scottish civil servants are inevitably outranked by those in London and civil service links are stronger than political ones: 'the principal value of the Scottish Office lies not in the independent ability to make policy but in translating policy into action on the ground'.[32] For political contact it has been possible for the eight universities to act collectively to receive a visit from the under secretary of state and subsequently the eight principals met the Secretary of State for Education and Science. The possibilities of collective action have been foreseen for some time but the dire pressures of 1981 have helped to close the ranks.[33]

After the UGC letters of 1981 *The Scotsman*[34] argued for a Scottish UGC on the basis (1) that eight universities would be more reasonable to deal with than forty-five, (2) that collective independence would promote diversity and mobility, and (3) that the separation of the universities from other areas of education was harmful. The Scottish universities are united in their broad curriculum, desire to be accessible to all classes, four-year courses, and strong lay governing bodies (Courts) which are composed of distinguished local citizens who are aware of regional traditions and to whom the universities are genuinely and effectively accountable. It was an English-born principal who said 'we will not readily see the Scottish University system mortally wounded.' Recent government and UGC decisions have had a critical impact, whose effects in a particular region may be at best random and at worst damaging in the inevitably slight regard for regional considerations. The exercise of increased central authority has drawn attention to this problem and may have created a centrifugal force which could swing opinion in favour of a rationally planned course towards devolution.

PROVINCIAL STRUCTURE IN CANADA

Canada is a country which is still concerned to establish its national identity, and yet it is said 'that Canadians who love their country have chosen to gamble on the feasibility of maintaining a political community by embracing rather than by suppressing diversity'.[35] The provinces differ in their cultural patterns, social needs, and prospective demographic situation and each province has its own structure of educational institutions at the post-secondary level.

The federal principle has been defined as the method of dividing power so that the general and regional governments are each, within a sphere, co-ordinate and independent.[36] Under the British North America Act[37] responsibility for education was divided but in practice the financing of universities, apart from certain research support, is now a provincial matter. In 1967 by transfer of tax points from Ottawa to the provinces the federal government implemented its policy to permit diversity among the provinces. They retained some leverage through nominal control of cash transfers in certain areas,[38] such as national loans to students (but with the provinces acting as agents)[39] , and research funding. The universities protested that they wished to deal directly with federal sources and although the Council of Ministers of Education in 1974 expressed concern that the provinces should preserve their autonomy in an area as crucial as research and higher education, the system which resulted was a partnership involving both levels of government.[40] The provinces wanted a say in defining national policies[41] and federal officials were tempted to use the research councils as instruments of federal policy[42] , but eventually the Candian Committee on Financing University Research was established as a consultative body. However, the prospects for arriving at and implementing a jointly formulated federal/provincial policy for Canadian university research are still regarded as too slight to propose any single design, and on the whole this competition to influence research direction seems not disadvantageous to the universities.

The degree of provincial diversity which is nurtured under this system is of particular interest to us. Provincial participation rates vary from —38% to +32% of the average among the provinces.[43] The systems differ to reflect culture, population size and distribution, financial resources, electoral motivations, judgements and priorities in each province[44]and result from a mixture of design, preference and 'happenstance'. Vocational instruction is geared to the support of industries which bulk large in the provincial economy (eg forestry in New Brunswick) and discretionary grants[45] (as distinct from formula grants) are used to encourage diversity and to promote excellence. The provinces are seen as institutionalizing diversity and education is seen as of key importance in creating a set of institutions which express, preserve and promote the development of a culture.

The impact of proximity of provincial government upon institutional autonomy is clearly worth looking at but the result is surprising. It is accepted that the innovative and critical functions performed by universities are better served by setting these institutions at some distance from the state apparatus[46] and as long as a way could be found to limit total spending there seemed to be no reason to interfere with the way in which universities spent their revenues[47]. It is well understood that external control of universities is the enemy of excellence in teaching and research, that 'collegial government' down to the department level is required, that administrative decentralization and an element of academic anarchy are important[48]. Almost every province has an effective buffer body between universities and state which normally operates on a public basis without the secrecy of the British UGC.

The effects of public funding derived from two levels of government are seen to be favourable as the greater the diversity in sources and types of funding the greater the autonomy of the university[49]. There is nevertheless some worry that provincial governments might attempt to design and manage university systems too precisely. Recent developments have equipped them with expertise and tools which could be used in this way. A centrally directed provincial system might risk becoming self-contained and inward-looking[50]. Stultification and mediocrity might be the result if universities are not allowed to take fundamental decisions about their own development and to have latitude to determine how to fulfil their responsibilities to society[51].

In case the existing degree of autonomy seems to imply irrationality and waste it is necessary to take into account the planning processes. For example, Manitoba considers that each university should have some specific role and Ontario has several universities which are distinctly local in that they draw most of their students from the immediately surrounding area. Differentiation of institutional purpose is conscious policy expressly supported by the Ontario Council on University Affairs (their enhanced and public UGC) which believes that differentiation would assist in the effective utilization of public funds through elimination of areas of unnecessary duplication. There is also a peer review of graduate courses. Regional development priorities have some impact upon academic development and pressure upon institutions to collaborate with one another is more easily exercised in a regional context.

Expansion made regionalization easy but contraction will make it imperative and there may be very strong pressures upon provincial governments to assume direct responsibility for financially insolvent universities[52]. Provincial operating grants make up between fifty-eight and eighty-five per cent of university income[53] but as always it is income at the margin which promotes diversity within the system and conduces to excellence[54]. Formula financing has been tried by seven provinces, but four have now abandoned or suspended it, and even the main enthusiasts, Ontario, have modified their system considerably.

The Canadian experience shows that it is possible to combine three different factors, namely national policy, regional policy and university autonomy. All three are regarded as important and all three have their impact. This is achieved within a well-established political federation by a process of constant negotiation which appears to provide an acceptable balance of interests. There are elements of public accountability at both national and regional levels which appear more convincing than those offered by UK universities at present and yet there is clear evidence of respect for the importance of autonomy and academic freedom in the pursuit of excellence. This example may be from a different context but it seems to indicate that a regional dimension can be of positive value.[55]

A POLICY ON REGIONALIZATION?

The general view of universities is that they have always been reluctant and slow to respond to economic and social needs. Some even propagate this view or actively resist the accommodation of a 'community resource purpose' as a threat to 'the integrity of the academy'.[56] This general view has been quite untrue for some time but until there is public realization of the responsiveness of many universities and there is increased responsiveness in the others, pressure for greater public accountability will grow. Such accountability, in purely democratic terms, can only be to national or local government.

It has long been argued that the academic community should retain its autonomy and integrity by finding more ways of making more positive reactions to political and other pressures.[57] Individual institutions can find ways of doing this in detail, but the universities in general have failed to develop a collective policy which would obtain the initiative which they should justify. The initiative for change remains therefore with political masters who are reluctant, who have only indirect influence, who are not well qualified to assess academic needs, and who constitute one of the most highly centralized national governments in the free world.

The UGC is qualified in academic judgement, but is not well qualified to argue social and economic priorities with government. The UGC is now well aware that the resources they are given are inadequate for their purpose. The UGC, too, is remote, centralized, and not as well informed on such matters as regional variations in the need for qualified manpower. Government and UGC have now moved from allocating finances to dictating total student numbers, and to advising on what appears to them to be a rational distribution of student places by institution and by discipline. Recognizing that the volume of public money involved and the resulting need for accountability has made such moves inevitable it is now becoming evident that the machinery whereby these decisions are being made is inadequate. The national scale of operation means rough justice and the frustration or enfeeblement of responsiveness and accountability at regional and local level.

Scotland is a natural region but the other part of the United Kingdom is both too large to form one region of reasonable scale and, Wales apart, difficult to divide into natural regions. England has only developed an adequate higher education provision within this century, much of it in the last thirty years. Before that university education was highly concentrated socially and regionally. Nevertheless the English system remains dominated by a small number of institutions in one region, which play a significant part in the education of the majority of university staff throughout the country. The fact that these institutions are peculiar and untypical, and that a large number of politicians and the majority of senior civil servants pass through their gates, has a very strong influence on the system as a whole, which is counter to the close identification of institutions with their regions. The cult of attending a university far from home originates in the same collegiate tradition and is nowhere so strong as in England. The attempt to cultivate this pattern in the new universities led to serious problems of alienation which were not experienced where most students remained involved with the non-academic community. Regionalization of higher education in England might be seen by some as the final disintegration of a long-established academic, social, and political establishment, and would make them feel insecure. However, others would welcome a new era of freedom and self-expression in which the rich character and talent of each region might flourish in a new way.

Would regional consciousness in England be strong enough? Tentativeness is evident in the proposals which David Owen describes as 'dependent upon the extent to which a regional identity developed'.[58] It is not easy to see what regional division of England would be most relevant to higher education. Local government units are too small for this purpose, concerned as they are with populations of two million to three million (excluding London). It is possible to group these units into nine regions with populations of two and a half million to five million, but even that would mean only three or four universities per region, hardly enough to justify a regional university policy. The inclusion of other institutions of higher education could provide a regional pattern of higher education, including two to five universities. The Scottish group of eight universities, which is a natural region in many ways, might become rather large when looked at as a group of twenty-six higher education institutions. Quantities are probably much less important than questions of purpose and function of grouping and regional consciousness, and until, or unless, there is an upsurge of regional involvement and pride in institutions of higher education the regionalization of higher education in England may remain a fairly remote prospect.

The relationship between universities and public sector is obviously a very important aspect of any regional dimension. It would be wrong to ignore the trends and pressures for rationalization of post-school education as a whole. Suggestions for bodies composed of groups of local authorities[59] and for action by existing group organizations[60] seems to suggest a need for some decision making in larger groupings, but such proposals tend, naturally enough, to favour united action by local authorities rather than the introduction of a new level of democratic decision making. There must be dangers in any proposals in which the democratic accountability would be distinctly indirect.

In a stimulating paper dated 17 March 1980, Dr G.S. Brosan[61] proposed regional consortia for further and higher education, 'publicly accountable bodies responsible for ... all post school education'. His proposal implies groupings, which would 'consult in detail with industry, commerce, professional organizations, trade unions, employer associations, and so on'. To achieve democratic accountability he insists 'LEAs (local education authorities) should have the dominant voice'. Indeed the chairman of Rochdale LEA believes so strongly in local government wisdom that he wishes the whole of higher education to be run by them![62] The concept is attractive in its simplicity but again draws attention to the wide gap between national and local priorities and to the need to temper purely political influences.

National and local governments are clearly finding it difficult to reallocate responsibility for post-school education between them in any rational way. The concept of level is confused with the concept of locality and the results are educationally harmful. Could there be an answer in a new level of locality?

There are a number of distinctive and valid educational traditions represented in our higher education provision today. Increasingly detailed central decisions on university policy and funding are interfering with such traditions and favour standardization. There are many who sense that increased centralized authority is inevitably imposing a minority view which is alien not only to diverse regional traditions, but what is much more important, insufficiently sensitive to regional needs. What is insensitive to regional needs must eventually be, in sum, insensitive to national needs.

The prominence increasingly being given to national priorities, as perceived by national government and Whitehall, derives from a natural desire that post-secondary education provision should be rational and accountable. The assumption that the process is best conducted through central government arises from the lack of other credible agencies. We should consider whether a new approach, for which there are many precedents in other countries, might be preferable. Canadian federalism is not only a form of government but it also represents 'a principle of social organization which insists upon the diversity and complexity of social life and believes that the development of the human person normally requires a plurality of autonomous communities, having their own rights, their own freedoms, and their own authorities'. The state is only one of the vast network of associations within society and is expected to obtain for such associations what they are unable to obtain for themselves. This is the principle of state subsidiarity which calls for a pluralist and decentralized organization even in the political sphere[63]. In Canada this concept is possible because of the existence of provincial government. Each province has its own structure of institutions at post-secondary level recognizing the difference in cultural patterns, social needs and demographic structure. Britain is not a federal state, but it is argued that the study of federal methods does disperse the fears which inhibit us in considering the possible benefits of deliberate and controlled decentralization. It has been said by Mrs S. Williams that 'the institutions of higher education in Britain do not see themselves as research centres for their own cities or countries in the way American universities do ... there need be no tension between this role and the role of being internationally recognized centres of academic excellence'.[64] There are examples of this dual fulfilment in Scotland where regional consciousness is significant.

During the period when the establishment of a Scottish Assembly seemed a real probability the concept of university devolution was not merely contemplated but hotly debated. It can be argued that had the Assembly been established, university devolution with suitable safeguards for autonomy would have come. The Education Committee of the General Assembly of the Church of Scotland recently expressed 'regrets that the reductions are not based on a co-ordinated plan for tertiary education which would ensure that monies would be best spent in accordance with a total educational policy', and 'worry at the apparent narrowing of the broad basis of education, so much part of the traditional education scene in Scotland'.

Evident accountability is a clear necessity as long as higher education consumes significant public finance. But accountability should be a mechanism of reassurance rather than control. Increased accountability to national government inevitably means stultification of initiative. Accountability for funding in three roughly equal parts, national, regional and local, would encourage institutions to respond to national patterns, regional needs and local factors in a responsible and fruitfully diverse way. The local dimension is best represented by a governing body of informed and interested local people, including representatives of local government, controlling the expenditure at institutional level of a budget which derives significant income from student fee income which reflects both prestige and market forces. A UGC which was less academic and more open would enhance the credibility of national accountability. An equivalent body for national funding of the 'public' sector should on the other hand have adequate academic participation to achieve credibility in the educational community and avoid widening the gap between the sectors. Thereafter the existence of regional differences based upon history, local circumstances, and institutional choice 'within a common framework of cost norms and public accountability is a strength of systems of higher education'.[65]

University responsiveness to national needs is generally underrated. Much rigidity in the system derives from government methods of funding, and government attempts at planning have been responsible for mistakes which have been all the more damaging because they are on a national scale. Dispersal of accountability to a new and additional level of democracy would modify the scale of such errors and increase the chances of arriving at a better policy. As the resources available for education contract the decisions become more difficult. There never was a better time for devolution of decision making to levels as near as possible to where the sacrifices are being made.[66]

The 'friendly neighbourhood university' (with an international reputation) is a source of pride and concern to a community which feels a genuine involvement with its purpose and function. National recovery will come from grass roots enthusiasm and effort rather than from national policy. Major failures in regional policies for industry are now very evident, as is the need for intensive industry/education liaison practicable only at regional level. The assumption that there can be permanent national centres of excellence is ridiculous in that it presupposes a fixed continuity of excellence, but it is also divisive in that it inhibits the development of a diversity of regional and specialist centres of excellence.

The vertical lines which tie the institutions of higher education to London could reasonably be weakened, but the horizontal lines which relate them to one another and to their regions must be strengthened. Course planning and student support are two areas in which Scotland has some coherent regional action under way. Schools and employer liaison are also co-ordinated in different ways on regional bases. Even the government, in recent months, has met the Scottish universities collectively to discuss policy without disrespect to UGC. Perhaps Scotland will see itself as the area for an experiment in regional devolution of higher education.

NOTES

1   Royal Commission on the Constitution 1969-1973 (1973) *Vol. I Report* Cmnd 5460
2   Royal Commission on the Constitution 1969-1973 (1973) *Vol. II* Memorandum of Dissent by Lord Crowther-Hunt and Professor A.T. Peacock. Cmnd 5460 — I
3   *Our Changing Democracy, Devolution to Scotland and Wales 1975* Cmnd 6345, 6585 and 6890

4   Calvert, H. (Editor) (1975) *Devolution* London: Professional Books Limited
5   Dicey, A.V. (1887) *England's Case against Home Rule* 3rd edition, p.168. London: John Murray
6   Kier, Sir David L. (1950) *The Constitutional History of Modern Britain* p.441. London: Adam and Charles Black
7   *Royal Commission on Local Government in England* (1969) Cmnd 4040
8   *Royal Commission on Local Government in Scotland* (1969) Cmnd 4150
9   Owen, D. (1981) *Facing the Future* p.18. OUP
10 Op. cit. p.214
11 Op. cit. p.XIV
12 Op. cit. p.188
13 Lispey, D. (1980) Councils of Despair *New Society* 31 July
14 Checkland, S.G. (1981) *The Upas Tree* p.113. UGP
15 Checkland, S.G. (1981) *The Upas Tree* p.118. UGP
16 Cmnd 9212 (1954, 1957) p.12
17 Cmnd 4150 (1969)
18 *Scotland's Government, Report of the Scottish Constitutional Committee 1970* p.45. Edinburgh
19 Sir Charles Wilson (Glasgow) and Professor J.D.B. Mitchell (Edinburgh)
20 *Organization of Scotland's Institutions of Higher Education under a Scottish Assembly* (1975) SNP 1975
21 *Times Higher Education Supplement* 21 February 1975 NUS (Scotland) Conference
22 *Times Educational Supplement* (Scotland) 21 February 1975
23 Grant, N. and Main, A. (1976) *Scottish Universities: The Case for Devolution* Edinburgh: EUSPB
24 *Times Higher Education Supplement* 18 June 1976. *Scotsman* 17 June 1976
25 Wojtas, Olga in *Times Higher Education Supplement* 4 December 1981
26 *Hansard* 3 August 1978, 500—503
27 *Review of Structure and Management* CTE(S) Report. 29 September 1981
28 Principal Burnett, in *Scotsman* 9 November 1981
29 *Blueprint for Scotland 1981* Campaign for a Scottish Assembly
30 Drever, Grant and Morrison *Scottish Universities and Devolution* (1977) Department of Education, University of Stirling
31 Examples: Scottish Universities Council on Entrance, UCNS (Scotland), Regional Computing Organization, O and M Unit, Meeting of Faculties, of Principals and of Registrars, Regional Training Organizations, etc.
32 Keating and Midwinter (1981) *Policy Analysis* Centre for Public Policy, University of Strathclyde
33 Morrell, D.W.J. (1977) *Future of Higher Education* Proceedings of the Conference of University Administrators
34 *Scotsman* 12 October 1981

35 Leslie, P.M. (1980) *Canadian Universities 1980 and Beyond* Ottawa p.367. AUCC
36 Wheare, K.C. (1963) *Federal Government* pp.364—5. London: OUP
37 Leslie, P.M. (1980) *Canadian Universities 1980 and Beyond* Ottawa p.363. AUCC
38 Op. cit. p.157
39 Op. cit. p.368
40 Op. cit. p.209
41 Op. cit. p.207
42 Op. cit. p.206
43 Op. cit. p.22
44 Op. cit. p.73
45 Op. cit. p.235
46 Op. cit. p.234
47 Op. cit. p.237
48 Op. cit. p.359
49 Op. cit. p.132
50 Op. cit. p.361
51 Op. cit. p.361
52 Op. cit. p.129
53 Op. cit. p.5
54 Op. cit. p.133
55 Other sources:
   Morrell, D.W.J. (1978) *Report of ACU Travelling Fellow (unpublished): Further argument*
   Conseil des Universités de Québec *Annual Reports* Québec: Conseil des Universités
   Council of Ministers of Education of Canada *Annual Reports* Toronto: Council of Ministers of Education of Canada
   Maritime Provinces Higher Education Commission *Annual Reports* Maritime Provinces Higher Education Commission
   Ontario Council on University Affaris *Annual Reports* Toronto: Ontario Council on University Affairs
   Hurtubrise Rowat Report (1970) Commission on Relations between Universities and Governments
   New Structure New Environment: Review 1972—75 (1976) Toronto: Council of Ontario Universities
   Pressures and Priorities (1979) Twelfth Congress. London: Association of Commonwealth Universities
   Trotter and Carrothers (1974) *Planning for Planning* Ottawa: Association of Universities and Colleges of Canada
56 Jacka, Cox and Marks (1975) *Rape of Reason* p.19. Churchill Press
57 Morrell, D.W.J. (1977) *Possible Structural and Constitutional Evolution of Higher Education in the U.K.* p.39. Proceedings of the Conference of University Administrators

58 Owen, D. *Face the Future* p.177. Op. cit. p.xiv
59 See Redcliff Maud Report
60 *A Time to Listen — a Time to Speak Out* (1982) Convention of Scottish Local Authorities
61 Brosan, G.S. (1980) *Evidence to Select Committee on Education and Science*
62 *Times Higher Education Supplement* 12 February 1982
63 Leslie, P.M. (1980) *Canadian Universities 1980 and Beyond* p.378. AUCC
64 Williams, S. (1981) *Politics is for People* Penguin
65 Lockwood, G. (1981) *International Journal of Institutional Management in Higher Education* 5 (3) 183—185
66 Morrell, D.W.J. (1981) *Management of Resources in Higher Education in Scotland* Conference paper given at Queen's College, Glasgow; June 1981

DISCUSSION AND COMMENT

Arguments for a greater regional involvement in the governance of higher education have been growing in strength but the discussion suggested that some of the issues were extremely controversial. The evidence from continental Europe gave little support for regionalization. In Sweden the decentralization of higher education and the establishment of regional boards highlighted the danger that institutional powers might be subsumed in regional control mechanisms. In Germany, it was argued, decentralization to the Länder had brought no greater community participation or local involvement and the Federal Government had tried to re-unify the system in the interests of better co-ordination.

A carefully worked out scheme outlined in Lord Crowther-Hunt's paper, for granting powers for primary legislation to regions and for making them responsible for the administration of higher education, with NAB and UGC having advisory powers only, received little support. It was argued that the creation of a third layer between the central authorities and the institutions would increase bureaucracy and costs without any compensating inprovement in public participation. Graduates and research output were a national rather than a regional commodity. In addition the present distribution of institutions would immediately raise a requirement for increased expenditure to rectify inequities. Most people favoured the regional arrangements established by the NAB and thought that except in Scotland that was probably as far as it was desirable to go. Indeed there was some evidence that the present exercise of local powers gives rise to a number of problems such as inequity of treatment over discretionary grants, entry to schools, and so forth, and that there was a need for a greater commonality of practice between LEAs.

There was agreement that localism was more important than regionalism. The role of the Regional Advisory Councils was considered and while there was no serious disposition to follow the Select Committee's recommendation that they be abolished, there was a concensus that the highest priority should be given to an improvement in local links. It was agreed that local co-operation was particularly important for continuing and part-time education. Such co-operation was more likely to be achieved between institutions if it was voluntary than if compelled by some external authority. At the same time institutions needed to take more trouble to relate to their local community. The benefits to be gained could be seen in the support obtained by Salford after the cuts letter of July 1981.

In Scotland it was agreed that different factors applied. The present administrative structure tended to emphasize and strengthen a sense of identity. Whether or not governmental devolution in some form took place there was a case for recognizing the regional dimension in Scotland and in some way building it into the structure of higher education there.

9

HAS THE BINARY POLICY FAILED?

by Peter Scott

So far as we have in Britain any policy for higher education it is the binary policy. For the division of higher education into a university and a polytechnic and college sector not only establishes the political, administrative, and financial context in which detailed decisions about both educational and resource priorities are made, but also serves as an influential metaphor about the future shape and direction of the system. The binary policy is the nearest thing we have to an authoritative statement about the purposes of higher education. In this important sense it is both a primary and a qualitative policy; other policies that have been developed by the DES or within the system since 1965 have been essentially secondary, because they are concerned with administrative adjustment within the accepted context of the binary structure, or quantitative, because they are concerned with reconciling the resource needs of higher education with the public expenditure available for this purpose. This dual nature of the binary policy, as structural status quo and normative metaphor, has often led to confusion and ambiguity. So it has at times become difficult to continue a serious and constructive debate about the advantages and disadvantages of the binary policy without paying very close attention indeed to the terms of reference of the debate: is the binary policy being regarded as an administrative arrangement or as a semi-political statement? This ambiguity causes particular difficulty when the question that must be addressed is the title of this chapter — has the binary policy failed? It is, for instance, perfectly acceptable to argue both that the polytechnics and colleges have been successful as institutions and even that the present binary structure of higher education provides an essentially sound administrative framework, *and* that the binary policy has failed as normative metaphor or political statement about the future direction of the system. Conversely it is possible to accept entirely the aspirations for a more accessible and more relevant system which were embodied in the original decision to go (or rather stay) binary, *and* to argue that the present administrative and financial division of the system into two distinct sectors was always or has become an obstacle to realizing these aspirations. So there is no natural congruence between the two aspects of the binary policy. It may have succeeded administratively only to fail normatively or — and this is the view that will be supported with qualifications here — it may have failed or be failing administratively while succeeding normatively.

Although this duality of the binary policy as status quo and as metaphor is the most significant complication that must be taken account of in any discussion of its success or failure, there are others. First, it must be emphasized that the binary policy was not created in the mid-1960s by Anthony Crosland aided and abetted by Sir Toby Weaver. Mr Crosland began his second binary policy speech, at Lancaster University in January 1967, by underlining this point: 'I must begin by mentioning a severely practical reason for this policy and the system of higher education that goes with it. That is that the system already existed. I did not invent it; it had been developing steadily since the turn of the century or earlier....This was the plural or binary system — whatever you choose to call it — which we inherited. Were we to convert it into a unitary system entirely under university control? ... The plain fact is that we did not start off *tabula rasa;* we started off with a given historical situation. A plural system already existed.'[1] There is a substantial and highly significant truth in the statement that the binary policy has always existed and probably always will exist. The effective question has always been not whether a binary line should be drawn but where it should be drawn. Indeed one of the most important motives for drawing the line where it was drawn between autonomous universities and maintained polytechnics and colleges was precisely to prevent its being drawn in a place that might have made better administrative sense but would have caused greater normative offence, between higher education of all kinds and 'non-advanced' further education and adult education. The only way in which the need can be avoided to draw a binary line somewhere is by abolishing entirely the present distinctions between higher, further, and adult education. Indeed, with the present turmoil in upper secondary and lower further education as a result of the development of the Manpower Services Commission and the growing attraction of tertiary colleges that straddle both sectors, even that might not be sufficient. What this means is that under present and foreseeable future conditions there will always be a binary policy. In this sense the question, has the binary policy failed, is inherently implausible. The only realistic question therefore can be: would a different binary policy have worked better?

A second complication arises from a widespread confusion about the nature of the binary policy that was adopted in the mid-1960s and has remained the administrative framework for British higher education. This policy is over-interpreted in two critical respects. First, it has sometimes been defined in terms that go far beyond the, at any rate publicly stated, aims of the policy. Some, most notably and most eloquently Eric Robinson in his book *The New Polytechnics*[2], have argued that the binary policy should have become the basis of a radical policy for higher education which would cast the polytechnics in the role of 'people's universities'. Others have argued that the binary policy was an unnatural attempt to restrain the legitimate ambitions of the polytechnics and colleges, a device to preserve the traditional élitism of the universities from the consequences of the rather thoughtlessly expansionist mentality which the Robbins Report had perhaps unwittingly encouraged the universities to adopt in the early 1960s. Both are interesting and stimulating points of view which help to illuminate important and difficult choices facing British higher education. But neither is an approximately accurate description of the binary policy, the first being very much a plea for the binary policy-that-might-have-been and the second only sustainable in terms of psychohistory. In fact the aims of the binary policy were clearly laid out in Mr Crosland's speeches at Woolwich and at Lancaster, in the subsequent white paper *A Plan for Polytechnics and Other Colleges*[3], and in the various modifications to the original policy that have emerged in the last ten or twelve years. It is possible to take these publicly stated aims and to examine to what extent they have been achieved by the polytechnics and colleges since 1965. Such a task may be less exciting than politicized speculation but it is more useful in terms of both improved policy analysis and the feasibility of reforming the present binary structure. This does not mean, of course, that the binary policy should be judged entirely as an administrative framework without normative content. What it does mean is that the validity of the binary policy as a normative metaphor must be tested not by indisciplined speculation but by careful analysis of whether it has encouraged or protected those types, aspects, and styles of higher education which were regarded as especially significant in the promotion of those values which the binary policy aimed to reflect.

Secondly, the binary policy has been misinterpreted by those who confuse the primary principles of the policy with the secondary means of implementation that were chosen to give it effect. The binary policy is not the same thing as the polytechnic policy. The first is ends; the second means. This distinction is important because the binary policy is about both more and less than is commonly imagined. It is about more in the crucial sense that it is a policy for *all* higher education. After all, the binary policy first and foremost was a decision not to establish any more new universities. As a result it embodies a particular view of the correct balance of types of institution and of the styles of higher education which they represent within the total system. In both these respects, the negative and the system-wide, the binary policy is as much a policy for the universities as for the local authority (and voluntary college) sector. But it is about less than many people suppose because it did not require to be implemented in the way in which it has been implemented, broadly through the concentration of advanced courses in a small number of large comprehensive institutions called polytechnics. It has been argued that this process of concentration was mistaken because it tended to create within further education a more systematic split between higher education and the rest, an outcome which the binary policy itself on a wider stage had been designed to prevent. This argument may lack weight because it ignores the difficulty in terms of both the most efficient use of resources and the desire to achieve parity of esteem with the universities of an anti-polytechnic policy which would have made no attempt to concentrate advanced courses. But it does perhaps demonstrate that the detailed implementation of the binary policy was not predetermined. Again this is an important qualification if the question is Has the binary policy, as opposed to the polytechnic policy, failed?

The third complication is that 'binary' has come to be used not only as the description of a policy but as the characterization of a system. We talk as much of the binary system as of the binary policy. This is a misleading habit. It implies a system neatly and symmetrically divided into two homogeneous sectors, which was not an accurate description in 1965 and is even less accurate in 1982. The non-university sector in particular is a heterogeneous collection of institutions which have little in common with each other except the fact that none is a university in the rather precise constitutional sense which we have adopted in Britain. Not only must a distinction in legal, administrative, and financial terms be made between maintained local authority colleges and voluntary colleges with their denominational histories, but in terms of educational balance and style it is possible to distinguish four main institutional types within the non-university sector; the 30 polytechnics which act as the flagships of this sector; the 14 Scottish central institutions, centrally funded by the Scottish Education Department as their name implies, but in other ways more diverse than the English and Welsh polytechnics, with some like Robert Gordon's in Aberdeen and Paisley effectively polytechnics but others specialist monotechnics (the Scottish structure is still further complicated by the presence of polytechnic-style colleges like Glasgow College of Technology which are not central institutions but are maintained by regional authorities); the 64 colleges and institutes of higher education formed from the debris of the contraction of teacher education in the mid-1970s, which again can be sub divided into four types   proto polytechnics like Ealing, Hull, or Derby Lonsdale, liberal arts colleges like Bulmershe, colleges of education still almost exclusively involved in teacher training like North Riding, Matlock, or Bishop Grosseteste, and embryonic community colleges on a semi-American pattern like Bradford; and the more than 300 colleges of further education which continue to provide some advanced (ie higher education) courses. This last group is sometimes regarded as a residual anomaly. This point of view can be questioned, partly because the contribution of ordinary further education colleges to higher education is still substantial, particularly in the important areas of part-time and higher technician courses, and partly because in many of the best colleges excellence and specialism are defined in terms of areas rather than levels of work.

Alongside the diversity of the non-university sector the 45 universities may appear a homogeneous group of institutions. But again it would be a mistake to place too much emphasis on this quality. The technological universities, the former colleges of advanced technology, have always stood a little apart from other universities, protective of their peculiar histories and highly, even hyper-conscious of their distinctive mission. Their presence within the university sector has often acted as an irritant to the conventional and convenient symmetry of the binary system (although not necessarily of the binary policy). Within the rest of the university system the ebb and flow of subject preference among students and the not always harmonious ebb and flow of 'knowledge formation' within disciplines have both encouraged an institutional volatility which is not sufficiently recognized. Most recently the selectivity practised by the University Grants Committee in July 1981 in its distribution of a much reduced grant to universities has intensified this accelerating process of differentiation and even stratification between univerisities. The less visible and so more acceptable selectivity that is practised by the research councils has had a similar effect. The result is that even among the universities the appearance of homogeneity tends to dissolve the more closely it is examined. When this growing differentiation among the universities is set against the historical diversity of the non-university sector, the tidy symmetry of the binary system so often relied on by macro-policy-makers disappears almost completely. This conclusion, of course, says nothing about the success or failure of the binary policy. Indeed it is possible to argue that the diversity of British higher education in 1982 is an outcome of that policy or more modestly that this diversity would have been much less had the recommendations of the Robbins Committee been put into effect. But this conclusion does mean that to talk of a binary system of higher education is a nonsense. Mr Crosland, it should be remembered, preferred the adjective 'plural' even in the mid-1960s. 'Plural' is an even more appropriate adjective today. The most accurate formula therefore is to talk of a binary policy within a plural system. With these four complications/reservations in mind, the rest of this chapter is divided into five main sections: i) a description of the objectives of the binary policy as expressed in the speeches of ministers at the DES, in white papers and other statements, and in the developing policy of the department; ii) an analysis of the extent to which the binary policy, or its institutional instruments the polytechnics and colleges, have achieved these objectives; iii) an examination of the inherent flaws in the binary policy as it has been implemented; and iv) a discussion of the broad principles which should inform any revision of the binary policy.

OBJECTIVES OF THE BINARY POLICY

The first objective of the binary policy was to prevent the total domination of the higher education system by the universities. The Robbins committee, it must be remembered, had recommended that, in addition to the transfer of the colleges of advanced technology to the universities and the establishment of the new universities which had already been planned, a further six universities should be founded and the colleges of education should be brought under the wing of the universities. If the Robbins pattern of expansion had been followed, of the 558,000 full-time students expected in 1980/81 346,000 would have been studying in the universities and a further 146,000 in the 'client' colleges, leaving only 66,000 in further education. The government decided that this balance would be quite wrong and announced that no more new universities would be created and that the colleges of education would remain either local authority or voluntary institutions. These two decisions made up the initial and the essential binary policy. In this first form the policy was both radical and conservative. It was radical in the sense that once the government had concluded that the universities could not be allowed to become the semi-monopoly instruments of the expansion of higher education which everyone desired in the first half of the 1960s it was obliged to go on to conclude that the university was not the only conceivable model for a fully mature institution of higher education. In 1963 this was an unfamiliar idea. Although it was recognized that non-university institutions made an important contribution to higher education, such institutions, particularly those in further education, were regarded as either peripheral or half-formed. The binary policy was conservative in the sense that it represented an attempt to hold the balance that existed in the early 1960s between universities, colleges of education, and further education within the total system of higher education, a balance which the Robbins recommendations, if accepted, threatened to upset. In this perspective the binary policy can be seen as a successful attempt to preserve the status quo in the face of the university imperialism fomented by Robbins. Even in its first stages, therefore, the policy exhibited the duality between administrative status quo and normative metaphor. What Robbins was proposing was conservative in normative terms, because it could envisage no other model for a fully mature institution of higher education than the university, but radical in administrative terms, because this myopia led inexorably to the conclusion that a much expanded system of higher education would naturally be a system even more entirely dominated by the universities. In contradiction the binary policy was conservative in an administrative sense, because it sought to preserve the existing balance between university and non-university components of higher education, but radical in normative terms, because this affection for the administrative status quo led equally inexorably to the need to 'invent' new types of institution.

The second objective of the binary policy was to encourage the development of vocational or 'relevant' courses within higher education, a task which it was felt the universities were not well equipped to undertake or alternatively with which they should not be expected to bother. This point of view was expressed with least equivocation by Mr Crosland in his first binary speech at Woolwich Polytechnic in April 1965[4]. He later admitted that he regretted parts of his Woolwich speech and the first of these two passages must surely have been among those he regretted. In an interview in 1970 he admitted that he had accepted the advice of his civil servants to make a major speech on higher education at a time when he had only a superficial knowledge of the subject, and that 'every change I made in the draft of the speech made it worse'[5]. But he added that the more he had thought about it the more he had become convinced that the binary policy was right, and that he had set out the real arguments for it in his second binary speech at Lancaster. This is an interesting and revealing comment because it makes it possible to compare the two speeches and see which bits were missed out of the second speech. The most obvious omission in fact is this second objective of the binary policy, the need to have an alternative sector which will offer a distinctively vocational and 'relevant' form of higher education. Clearly, on reflection Mr Crosland felt that the contrast between university-style and polytechnic-style higher education in this respect was less than he had at first supposed. Yet it is not clear whether his greater reticence at Lancaster reflected a significant decline in his, and the DES', belief that the non-university sector could provide more relevant and more vocational courses than the universities, or simply a recognition that this idea had been crudely and antagonistically expressed at Woolwich.

Certainly the idea that in some important sense the polytechnics offer a more relevant form of higher education has not gone away. The 1966 white paper *A Plan for Polytechnics and Other Colleges* naturally enough followed the emphasis of the Lancaster speech because it was almost a contemporary document. It justified the binary policy and the creation of the polytechnics in more administrative and less ideological terms. But the objective of greater 'relevance' in the non-university sector surfaced again in the 1972 white paper *Education: A Framework for Expansion*[6]. Mr Crosland's first formulation of this objective for the binary policy in his Woolwich speech may have been crude. Certainly it begged many questions. His comparison with the grandes écoles and the technischen hochschulen in particular was dubious support for his argument that a new, non-university sector needed to be created: the Robbins committee no doubt would have pointed out that their proposal to establish SISTERS (Special Institutions for Scientific and Technological Education and Research) would probably make a serious contribution to the fostering of really high-level technological education in Britain and moreover would have been a more logical extension of the policy laid down in the 1956 white paper on technical education which had led to the creation of the colleges of advanced technology. After all in France the grandes écoles enjoy resources and esteem far superior to those enjoyed by the universities, and there was no suggestion in the original binary policy that so radical an inversion of priorities was ever contemplated by Mr Crosland or Sir Toby Weaver in their wildest moments.

An unfortunate result of Mr Crosland's second thoughts after Woolwich was that this second objective of the binary policy, to foster a more relevant form of higher education through the polytechnics and other non-university colleges, was never properly developed. It was raised at Woolwich and then dropped from sight, never to be properly debated or even articulated. But nevertheless it remained immensely influential in the popular interpretation of the binary policy. For example, it is possible to imagine that a most interesting debate could have been developed about the appropriate educational level for the most effective intervention to remedy Britain's apparent technological inadequacy: Robbins, and previous government policy, suggested that such intervention should be at the highest level through colleges of advanced technology (CATs) and SISTERs; Crosland and Weaver seemed to be suggesting rather clumsily that intervention should take place at a lower level (ordinary degrees? technician diplomas and certificates?) International comparisons would suggest that they were right and Robbins was wrong. The same kind of issue is at the heart of the present inchoate debate between 'Cambridge' engineering and 'Salford' engineering within the university sector. But sadly this debate has never taken place within the all-important context of the binary policy. Instead the argument about 'relevance' in higher education has often taken place on what might be called the socio-sentimental plane rather than in terms of a coherent policy of scientific and technological manpower. At times even it has drifted perilously close to the shoals of personal fulfilment far from the deep channels of economic need. No doubt the growing presence of the social sciences within the non-university sector and the gradual assimilation of colleges of education to the maintained sector mainstream have contributed to this drift. But an important reason was the failure in the mid-1960s to address the issue of relevance with sufficient rigour and directness.

The only other context in which the differences between university-style and polytechnic-style higher education can be discussed is that of philosophical abstraction, as higher education for knowledge generation on the part of the universities and higher education for practical problem solving on the polytechnic and college side. Or finally it may be seen in the context of a Manichean struggle between Lord Robbins, strongly committed to the extension of liberal forms of higher education, and Sir Toby Weaver, equally strongly committed to higher education for capability. None of these perspectives is at all useful to the policy maker. To see the binary policy in terms of Newman v. Popper may be the basis for an interesting conversation but it is not only unprofitable in the context of practical policy but also a misleading over-interpretation of that policy. This second objective of the binary policy, athough immensely influential, has remained ill-defined and undebated. Yet it cannot for that reason be ignored. Leaving aside treacherous concepts such as 'applying knowledge to the solution of problems, rather than pursuing learning for its sake' [7], it is possible to identify certain characteristics of higher education courses that might be regarded as more 'relevant' than those traditionally offered by universities. First, it should be possible to study less traditional subjects at degree level (this was frequently not the case in 1965). Secondly, such courses might be more likely to be sandwich courses. Thirdly, such courses might have a more flexible structure than that of conventional degrees. All three characteristics were mentioned by Mr Crosland in his Woolwich and Lancaster speeches. They, and other characteristics which he did not mention, such as the nature of the student intake, student perceptions of the differences between university-style and polytechnic-style courses, and any differences in the pattern of the employment of their respective graduates, may help to provide a framework in which the success or failure of this second binary objective can be tested.

The third objective of the binary policy was more clearly defined and is much more straightforward. At both Woolwich and Lancaster Mr Crosland placed particular emphasis on the need to sustain both full-time sub-degree courses, and part-time advanced courses of all descriptions. At Woolwich sub-degree and part-time students were placed after full-time degree students in importance; at Lancaster the order was reversed with the presence of full-time degree students in the non-university sector being largely justified because it was essential to sustain sub-degree and part-time courses. This emphasis on these latter two groups of students was continued in both 1966 and 1972 white papers and became a common even stale ingredient in all subsequent ministerial statements on the binary policy. The 1966 white paper, for instance, stated: 'The Government believe it to be of the utmost significance that the leading colleges concerned with higher education should be comprehensive in the sense that they plan their provision of courses to meet the needs of students in all three categories (ie full-time degree, full-time sub-degree, and all part-time advanced).'[8] However, an important qualification must be made. It was not intended that all non-university institutions should be equally committed to all three categories of students. The white paper made it clear that the government would like to see the concentration of full-time courses in the polytechnics so far as practicable. Although it specifically stated that full-time courses should continue to be offered in non-polytechnic colleges when there was adequate student support, it also stated that colleges not already engaged in full-time higher education should not embark on it except in the most exceptional circumstances. But the white paper also made it clear that a much wider distribution of part-time courses was both inevitable and proper, although this liberalism was qualified by the subsequent statement that 'proposals for part-time courses will not be entertained from colleges which have no full-time higher education courses unless the course is to be conducted in close association with a polytechnic or other college that is offering degree courses in the same field.' So two areas of ambiguity remained. Did the government expect full-time sub-degree courses to be concentrated to the same extent as full-time degree courses in polytechnics and other major colleges? And did the government believe that part-time courses should be more widely dispersed than full-time courses, or did it believe that a tight association between the two was necessary for both educational and efficiency reasons? Neither was clear in the mid-1960s and rather than gradually being answered by the pressure of events they have tended during the 1970s to become more obscure. Yet in broad terms this third objective of the binary policy seems fairly straightforward: the polytechnics and colleges were intended to be comprehensive institutions offering not only full-time degree courses but also (and perhaps more so) full-time sub-degree and part-time degree and sub-degree courses.

The fourth objective of the binary policy was to keep a substantial part of higher education 'under social control and directly responsive to social needs' to borrow the phrase used by Mr Crosland at Woolwich. In his Lancaster speech he elaborated on this objective by emphasizing that he had not intended to suggest that the universities were not socially responsive but that 'given the high degree of autonomy which they enjoy, there is a sense in which the other colleges can be said to be under more direct social control.' What precisely did Mr Crosland mean by social control? It is clear both from his Lancaster speech, in which he gave as two examples the (then) recent 20 per cent productivity exercise in colleges of education and the control over courses and class sizes in further education, and from his 1970 interview with Maurice Kogan that what he intended was the whole panoply of administrative controls exercised by regional advisory councils for further education, regional staff inspectors, and the Department of Education and Science itself. One of the objectives of the binary policy was therefore an essentially negative one, the fear that with the drift to university status that would have taken place under the Robbins scheme for the future a series of important control levers would have been lost by the government. An important advantage of the non-university sector in the eyes of the Government was that it would remain subject to detailed administrative control. In this sense 'social control' was a rather limited and even negative concept. The course approval system after all is basically a mechanism for assessing the proposals put forward by colleges in the light of national or local need, likely student demand, and so on. It is not a mechanism for generating proposals in the first place. So 'social control' should not be confused with democratic control. The need in the middle 1960s did not appear to be to stimulate new proposals from institutions for courses, many of them 'directly responsive to social needs', but to regulate and direct these proposals so that specific national needs could be satisfied and that in general a well-balanced higher education system would be produced. The danger at that time appeared to be that the very rapid expansion of higher education which nearly everyone supported or believed was inevitable would be disorganized and even anarchic. Hence the need for firm administrative control.

It is certainly important to distinguish between 'social control' in this sense and the closely related objective of the binary policy which was to retain a substantial local authority stake in higher education. It is clear from both the Woolwich and the Lancaster speeches that Mr Crosland saw them as distinct objectives. Apart from the general principle of democratic accountability, three other reasons were advanced for maintaining this local authority stake. First, it was argued that at a time of rapid expansion and changing ideas it was better to have a variety of institutions under different control rather than a monopoly (Mr Crosland said at Lancaster that 'a unitary system would surely imply an omniscience which we do not possess'). This argument for pluralism was particularly applied to the colleges of education, which in the mid-1960s were in the middle of a particularly rapid expansion and which it was felt would suffer from 'a change of horses' in midstream. Secondly, it was argued that both local authorities and voluntary bodies were willing to allow liberal changes in the government of colleges to reflect their new status. Thirdly, the need for close links with the schools was emphasized (although interestingly the same emphasis was not placed on the organic links between non-advanced and advanced further education). But there is nothing to suggest that the government intended to encourage a more active involvement of local authorities in setting institutional priorities. The notes of guidance on the government and academic organization of polytechnics issued in 1967 made it clear that local authorities were expected to adopt a 'hands-off' policy towards their polytechnics and colleges[10]. The role of local authorities in the non-university sector seemed to be envisaged as ensuring good financial housekeeping by the institutions and as guarantors of pluralism, variously and confusingly defined as maintaining the status quo and encouraging the development of a more diverse system to meet more diverse needs. It was the Regional Advisory Councils (RACs), the Regional Staff Inspectors (RSIs), and the DES which were to exercise the 'social control' recommended by Mr Crosland.

The fifth objective of the binary was only half an objective. It was not mentioned at all in the Woolwich speech and mentioned only obliquely in the Lancaster speech. This was the potential capacity of polytechnics and other non-university colleges to attract students from a less restricted social constituency than the universities. This capacity had two aspects. First, the polytechnics and colleges, because of the more populist tradition of further education, would act as an alternative route into higher education for those potential students who would be dismayed by the university route. At Lancaster Mr Crosland placed particular emphasis on this aspect. It is sometimes assumed that the polytechnics and colleges were intended to be a 'working-class' form of higher education to complement or compete with the 'middle-class' form provided by the universities. In fact there is little in the official formulations of the binary policy to support such an assumption. The Lancaster speech contains perhaps the strongest, official, statement of the 'egalitarian' objectives of the binary policy. Yet with the exception of the reference to first-generation aspirants to higher education there is little in it which could be called a specific reference to social class. However it does provide a more modest check list of the kinds of students which the non-university sector designed to help: i) under-achievers at school who have not demonstrated that they are of university calibre; ii) those who do not come to higher education straight from school because they left school at 16 (and then spent some time gaining qualifications in non-advanced further education?); iii) mature students; iv) first-generation students who probably for social reasons did not want to apply to a university. It may of course be that there is a correlation between such groups of students and social class. But this was not made explicit in any formulation of the binary policy however common it may have become subsequently in populist interpretations of this policy. The second aspect of the capacity of the polytechnics and colleges to meet the needs of new types of students was more structural. It was the belief that if universities were given a virtual monopoly of degree-level work by creaming off either the relevant courses in further education or the further education institutions themselves, this would create a socially and educationally damaging 18 plus divide. In Mr Crosland's words, 'it would be truly "binary" with a vengeance, converting the technical colleges into upper-level secondary modern schools and dividing the 18-year-olds into a privileged university class of full-time degree students with the remainder in FE. I can imagine nothing more socially or educationally divisive'. This belief that an 18 plus of this nature would be undesirable was clearly closely linked with the subordinate beliefs in the need to maintain diversity in higher education, and to maintain the non-university colleges as comprehensive institutions offering a wide range of courses, full-time, part-time, and sub-degree.

The binary policy was clearly a complex set of practices and attitudes, prejudices and aspirations, which add up to more than the formal objectives of the policy as enunciated in the middle and later 1960s and which are equally distinct from the specific development of the polytechnics and other colleges during the 1970s. Yet to test these objectives against outcomes is an essential precondition to bringing some order and coherence to what it is admitted must be a wider and more ideological debate.

OUTCOMES OF THE BINARY POLICY

The first outcome of the binary policy neatly fits the first objective of the policy. However radical in a normative sense, this first objective was conservative in administrative terms; it was to maintain the existing, 1962/3, balance between university and non-university components within the expanding system of higher educaiton. This objective has been achieved with considerable accuracy. In 1962/63 130,000 of the 216,000 full-time students were in universities, or 60 per cent. In 1980/81 297,200 of the 516,300 full-time students in higher education were in universities, or 58 per cent[11]. Although in 1962/63 there were five students in colleges of education for every three in advanced further education and nineteen years later there were almost five times as many students in advanced further education as there were in the much shrunk colleges of education, the proportion of all students in higher education studying in the non-university sector had remained almost the same, creeping up from 40 to 42 per cent. So in these global terms the binary policy succeeded in freezing the balance between university and non-university components of higher education. This is a more considerable and a less conservative achievement than it appears. If the recommendations of the Robbins committee had been followed the number of students in higher education would have been divided as follows: 346,000 in universities (63 per cent), 146,000 in colleges of education which would by then have had a much closer relationship with the university sector (26 per cent), and only 66,000 in advanced further education (12 per cent), making a total of 558,000 full-time students in higher education[12]. If this Robbins projection is adjusted in the light of the unforeseen contraction of teacher education during the 1970s and the actual total of 41,000 is substituted for the 146,000 assumed by Robbins, the drive towards a system dominated by the universities in the Robbins proposals is even starker. This revised Robbins projection would be: 350,000 in universities (77 per cent), 41,000 in colleges of education (or successor institutions) (10 per cent), and 66,000 in advanced further education (13 per cent), making a new total of 453,000. So if the Robbins projection, with this adjustment, had been followed, the binary split would have been 77:23 in favour of the universities. In fact as a result of the rejection of Robbins and the substitution of the binary policy the split is 58:42. Or to put it another way the non-university sector has enrolled more than 100,000 'extra' full-time students than it might have been expected to have enrolled under existing policies, half of their gain being represented by the universities' 50,000-student 'shortfall' compared to the Robbins projection and half by the 50,000 extra students the higher education system has enrolled above the adjusted Robbins total. To what extent this latter gain was achieved by substituting full-time for part-time students will be discussed later.

The success of the binary policy's second objective, the promotion of courses in subjects that are more vocational and 'relevant' than those offered in universities, is almost impossible to assess. Is vocational relevance to be measured in relation to the input, the intentions of the student when he/she starts a course; to the process, the content of the course which presumably reflects the intentions of those who designed it; or to the outcome, the use of which the qualification eventually gained is put in the labour market? Depending on the answer rather different interpretations of vocational relevance will be preferred. Nor is it possible to express simply the contrast between the university and non-university sectors in terms of vocational relevance by pointing to those clearly vocational subjects which are only offered in the latter and those equally clearly academic or liberal subjects that are only offered in the former. For the spectra of subjects offered in the two sectors largely coincide. The difficulty still experienced in the early 1960s whereby certain subjects could not be studied to degree level because of the conservatism of the universities, then the only degree awarding bodies, has dwindled away to insignificance as a result of the success of the Council for National Academic Awards (CNAA). So the need for a non-university sector to be strengthened because in important areas of study of considerable vocational relevance the award of a degree was impossible has disappeared. Indeed the criticism is sometimes the other way round: that universities have been more liberal/sloppy in their approach to validating courses in other institutions than the CNAA.

However, although no simple or satisfactory evidence is available to settle this question of whether the polytechnics and other non-university colleges offer more 'relevant' courses, it is possible to apply some suggestive tests as to whether such a claim is true or not. The first is the input to the non-university sector, in broad terms the characteristics and perceptions of their students. The characteristics of polytechnic and college students will be discussed later in this paper in the context of the binary policy's record on part-time and sub-degree students and on allowing greater social mobility. However, there is evidence that polytechnic and college students do regard their institutions as more 'relevant' than universities. Surveys conducted among students at the (then) Enfield College of Technology (now part of Middlesex Polytechnic) in 1970[13], at the Polytechnic of Central London in 1972[14], and in a later national survey found that the majority of polytechnic students saw their education as 'more relevant to the needs of society', although, paradoxically but perhaps realistically, they expected university students to find it easier to get jobs.

The second test is of the process itself: do the polytechnics and colleges offer a distinctively vocational balance of subjects, modes of study, and methods of teaching to such a degree that it could be claimed that this second objective of the binary policy had been fulfilled? The evidence is not decisive. One test is simply to take a static snapshot of the subject balance in the two sectors. If all subjects are allowed rather arbitrarily to three clusters, 'science', 'social studies', and 'arts', the picture in 1978 was that proportionately more university students were studying science and technology subjects than polytechnic and college students, and conversely that proportionately more advanced further education students were studying in the 'social studies' cluster[15]. Such comparisons prove much less than they suggest. The measures are inevitably crude because they take no account of the great differences in vocational relevance between courses which bear the same name. It would also be misleading to equate vocational relevance with science and technology or vocational irrelevance with the arts. In the case of advanced further education this latter category includes art and design. On both sides of the binary line the 'social studies' group includes a hotch potch of subjects, some highly specific in their vocational application, others highly irrelevant. What this analysis does perhaps show is first, that although the charge popular in some universities that the polytechnics have become 'polyartnics' cannot be sustained, their most rapid growth has taken place in subjects which are not those in which further education has traditionally been considered to be strong, and secondly, that the ebb and flow of subjects seems to be a common phenomenon across the whole of higher education that does not respect the binary line.

If the mode of study is taken into account a sharper contrast emerges between the two sectors. It is, of course, hazardous to rely too much on measures of interdisciplinarity, and there are in any case few courses that spread across the boundaries of broad subject groups. However, the impression is that polytechnics and colleges have been more adventurous in experiments with a traditional structure of the Honours degree. The idea of modular degrees which allow students real although guided choice is more common in the non-university sector, although a survey of polytechnic staff attitudes has shown that it is not always easily accepted[16]. Many of these degrees, however, are in the broad area of social and professional studies which have been hit by the resurgence of engineering. What impact this has had on the movement towards interdisciplinarity in the polytechnics has not been examined. But there is one measure of the difference between universities and polytechnics which is fairly unambiguous; that is the relative fortunes of sandwich courses. Sandwich courses were seen in the mid-1960s when the binary policy was first forcefully articulated as an important element in the distinctiveness of the non-university sector. This is supported by what has happened since. In the university sector the sandwich course has remained imprisoned within the ghetto of the technological universities and has not commended itself to the traditional universities. The result has been that between 1973 and 1978 the number of students in sandwich courses in universities rose only gradually from 12,923 to 14,741, while in advanced further education they rose from 33,574 in 1973 to 55,999 in 1978. In 1973 there were less than two sandwich students in the non-university sector for every one in the universities; today it is almost four to one. As the cuts in universities have been particularly directed towards the technological universities the relative advantage of the polytechnics and colleges in this respect is certain to increase.

The third test of 'relevance' is the output of the two sectors: do non-university students seem to go into more obviously vocational jobs? On the face of it there is little difference in their pattern of employment. In 1979 51.1 per cent of university graduates went into permanent employment in the United Kingdom compared with 54.5 per cent of polytechnic graduates[17] . More university graduates went into further academic study and teacher training (20.7 per cent compared with 13.5 per cent), while polytechnic graduates were marginally more likely to be unemployed (7.3 per cent compared with 4.9 per cent). However, on closer examination differences emerge. In biological sciences, for example, 40.9 per cent of polytechnic graduates went into permanent UK employment, compared with 35.4 per cent of university graduates. A substantial proportion of the latter continued in further academic study, 26.6 per cent compared with only 15.2 per cent from polytechnics. If the kind of jobs which the two sets of biology graduates obtained is then examined another difference emerges: the most common area of employment among university graduates was research and development, while among polytechnic graduates it was quality control and analysis. A similarly revealing contrast can be seen in the patterns of employment among management and business studies graduates. For university graduates the most common area was financial work while among polytechnic graduates it was marketing and selling. In mechanical engineering a much higher proportion of polytechnic graduates ended up in jobs in production, 34.6 per cent compared with only 21 per cent of university graduates. Since 1979, because of the recession, a smaller proportion of polytechnic graduates has gone into permanent employment; there has been a precipitate fall in the number going into further academic study; and a significant rise in those undertaking further vocational training. The general impression created by these figures is of a greater willingness (if not always success) among polytechnic graduates to enter permanent employment and for that employment to be at the 'sharp' end of industry and commerce, in production rather than R and D, in marketing rather than in financial control.

The success of the third objective of the binary policy, the encouragement of sub degree and part time courses, is much more easy to assess. It is also perhaps a crucial test of the success of the policy. Critics of the polytechnic pattern of development have concentrated in particular on this aspect of the binary policy. In fact the record is rather more ambiguous. The policy for polytechnics can only be condemned if it can be properly demonstrated that the pattern of courses in the polytechnics has radically diverged from the pattern in further education as a whole. The polytechnics, after all, can hardly be expected to buck the wider trends that are affecting all further education. Yet taking all course enrolments in further education, non-advanced as well as advanced, it is clear that there has been a rapid increase in the number of full-time and sandwich courses and virtual stagnation in the number of part-time students whether studying during the day or in the evening. It is against this background that the performance of the polytechnics and other non-university colleges must be judged. Clearly, all further education was subject to broad secular trends, the bias towards full-time study embodied in the mandatory grant system, the growing unwillingness of employers to release their employees, the entrenchment of degree on professional qualification, and so on, which affected advanced courses as much as or more than non-advanced courses. It is within this generally hostile environment for sub-degree and part-time courses that the record of the non-university sector must be assessed. First, sub-degree courses. Between 1968 and 1978 the number of student enrolments on Higher National Diplomas and Certificates, Technician and Business Education Council higher awards, and the Diploma of Higher Education rose from 58,504 to 68,297, an increase in the number of students enrolled on full-time degrees in advanced further education from 25,540 to 85,911. However, it is probably best to be cautious in any interpretation of this disparity. First, the number of students on full-time sub-degree courses rose by 63 per cent. The overall percentage rise was dragged down by only a 7 per cent increase in the number of students on part-time day sub-degree courses and by a 40 per cent decline in evening only sub-degree courses. Secondly, during the first decade of the polytechnics there was naturally a substantial process of up-grading the level at which less orthodox subjects could be studied. So the role of the CNAA cannot be overlooked as a powerful agent in expanding the scale and the scope of degree level work in the non-university sector. Nor can this process sensibly be condemned. It is therefore reasonable to regard the explosive growth of degree students in polytechnics and colleges as an exceptional phenomenon. Perhaps a fairer comparison is between the growth rates of university degree students and sub-degree students in polytechnics and colleges. Sub-degree courses come well out of such a comparison, growing at almost twice the rate (63 per cent compared with 36 per cent).

The second part of this third objective, the encouragement of part-time students both at degree and sub-degree levels, is also easier to assess than to interpret. In 1968 76 per cent of all student enrolments for degrees were on full-time or sandwich courses, and ten years later the proportion had risen to 83 per cent. This is perhaps less of a shift in favour of full-time degrees than one would expect from some of the more categorical criticisms made of the polytechnics' and colleges' record in sustaining part-time work. If all advanced courses, except teacher training, are included, the shift becomes even more moderate. In 1973 the polytechnics had 71,586 student enrolments on full-time and sandwich courses and 44,910 on part-time courses, producing a ratio in favour of full-time work of 62:38. Five years later they had 113,935 and 62,681 respectively, producing a split of 64:36. These figures hardly support the charge that the non-university has abandoned part-time courses wholesale.

The fourth objective of the binary policy was first, to keep a substantial part of the expanding higher education system subject to greater 'social control' than the universities, and secondly, to maintain a substantial local authority stake in higher education. The first of these has been sustained almost without qualificaton. Polytechnics and other higher education colleges have remained subject to the prevailing system of course approvals, although in the years of expansion that system was applied with considerable liberalism. In the case of teacher training the DES has used its regulatory powers to fix not only the output but also the balance of the output of student teachers and to determine their institutional origins. Independent colleges of education have been closed, amalgamated with further education colleges to form diversified colleges of higher education, or swallowed up as the education faculties of polytechnics. Whether this detailed and continuous exercise of administrative powers actually produced the well-balanced and efficient system which was its object can of course be disputed. The system of course approvals has remained a reactive rather than a stimulatory mechanism. It disposes but does not propose, a weakness that assumed greater importance when, because of the cuts in public expenditure from 1979 onwards, development in higher education could no longer be simply additive. This weakness has been compounded by the crude and inflexible inputs into this system of control, most particularly the attempt to regulate courses by means of minimum student numbers. It has become clear that these essentially administrative tools of control are no longer able to regulate in any acceptable way a system in the process of enforced contraction, however they may have coped with the gentler challenges of expansion, and that they must be supplemented by more sophisticated political and academic tools. The newly established National Advisory Body for local authority higher education (NAB) seems to be about to move away from a system of course-by-course approval as a means of steering the system and towards approval on the basis of whole programmes of work or even ultimately whole institutions. The NAB is also in the process of bringing financial and course planning together at a national level for the first time.

The second part of this objective, the maintenance of a strong local authority stake in higher education, has to some extent been a prisoner of these developments in the course regime and in the financial mechanism of the pool. In fact there has been remarkably little serious and sustained debate about the role of local authorities in non-university higher education. Links with the local community, local schools, and between advanced and non-advanced courses have been used as secondary arguments in a primary debate about financial and course planning. The value of democratic accountability in a substantial part of higher education has received even less consideration. Yet throughout the 1970s and into the 1980s many local authorities have been generous supports of the polytechnics and other maintained colleges both through the advanced further education pool and directly from their rate income. Certainly the maintained colleges appear to have been better resourced than the voluntary colleges, even after allowances have been made for their different subject mixes. As a result of the investment made by both local authorities and central government since the adoption of the explicit binary policy in the mid-1960s unit costs

184 THE STRUCTURE AND GOVERNANCE OF HIGHER EDUCATION

in universities and in the non-university sector have tended to converge. The extent to which local authorities have continued to cherish their polytechnics and colleges can also be valued precisely by the extra money they spend on these institutions over and above those sums allocated through the pool, which represents the assessment of their needs by central government. In any case, whatever view is taken of the need for a local authority stake in higher education, there is no doubt that the present government, and any likely future government, intend to maintain it. In January 1981 civil servants in the DES proposed, and ministers half-heartedly approved, a proposal to remove the polytechnics and other major colleges entirely from the control of local authorities and to establish a quango on the approximate pattern of the UGC. This plan met with widespread oppositon and was abandoned. Later in the summer a consultative paper was issued which offered two contrasting models — model A which would have reproduced in broad terms the January proposal for a UDI, and model B which amounted to continued local authority control although with significant modifications[26]. Although this paper is still formally on the table, the government effectively preempted the outcome of such consultation when it established the NAB, a result which was much closer to model A than to model B. However, it is important to keep the question of local authority control in proper perspective, although it sometimes grabs more than its fair share of attention. The issue of the local authorities' stake in higher education was as much a sideshow in 1981 as it had been in 1965 when the binary policy was first articulated. The primary issue was and is 'social control' in the form of administrative regulation: it was freedom from such regulation which Mr Crosland was unwilling to grant the non-university colleges in the 1960s. Today the issue has broadened out into the larger question of the proper co-ordination of financial and academic planning, in the context inevitably of dwindling public expenditure on polytechnics and colleges. The true significance of the NAB lies in its role as the effective possessor of the powers that formally belong to RACs, RSIs, and the DES itself, rather than a potential supplanter of local authority control.

There is one final dimension of this fourth objective of the binary policy that remains to be discussed; that is the development of the internal government of the polytechnics and colleges. As a quid pro quo for acquiescing in continued local authority control, the non-university institutions were promised a more liberal regime. The DES insisted that they should be allowed much greater autonomy than had previously been the tradition in further education. The actual outcome has been mixed. It is probably fair to say that on academic questions there has been little inclination on the part of local authorities to interfere. Indeed there have been complaints that local authorities provide too little purely educational input into the institutions they maintain, and that as a result the arguments for the close association of advanced and non-advanced further education and for intimate links with the schools have been considerably weakened. On the other hand, because polytechnics and colleges have no corporate autonomy and do not employ their own staff, it has been impossible to disentangle the financial affairs of institution and of maintaining local authority. How to reconcile the demands of good housekeeping with the rights of institutions to reasonable autonomy has proved in practice to be difficult.

There are two other issues. The first is the real as opposed to the constitutional balance of power that the confused and even contradictory arrangements for internal government have produced within polytechnics and colleges. On the whole it is the management of such institutions that has won, and the local authority and the academic staff that have lost. Local authorities may be able to make the director account for the consumption of alcohol in the hotel and catering department, but it is the director who in practice has the largest say in determining the overall direction of the institution. Indeed it can be plausibly argued that the confusion of college government has encouraged the development of a strong managerial interest in non-university institutions. The second issue is closely related. If the Robbins Report had been followed, all fully mature institutions of higher education would have enjoyed university-style government: vice-chancellors who were chairmen of senate rather than managers of their institutions, minimalist central administrators, and powerful oligarchical organs of academic self-government. Although without particular emphasis, the binary policy suggested that an institution could be regarded as fully mature without necessarily enjoying such a form of internal self-government. So it can be argued that from the start the intention was to foster strong management within the polytechnics and colleges. Certainly there is a case for saying that strong management is necessary in institutions which are asked to undertake as wide a variety of tasks as the polytechnics. In a traditional university it was safe to assume that the overwhelming majority of those within the institution shared common intellectual values which were expressed in a broad consensus about the objectives and balance of the institution and about the teaching and research priorities necessary to achieve these objectives and to maintain this balance. Whether this assumption can be as safely made today in the universities, of course, can be doubted. But perhaps polytechnics were necessarily more fissiparous institutions, embracing within a common administrative and resource framework a very wide variety of objectives which could not be traced back to common intellectual values.

The fifth objective of the binary policy was to open paths into higher education to 'new students' who could not or would not aspire to enrol in a university. As has been pointed out, it is doubtful whether this should really be counted among the original objectives of the policy. Partly it was simply a natural consequence of the second (more relevant courses) and the third (more sub-degree and part-time students) objectives; partly it was an objective attributed to the policy by enthusiasts afterwards. Nevertheless it is worth trying to assess the extent to which this fifth objective has been achieved. First, in most subjects in which there is a common student market across the binary line degree students in polytechnics and colleges have less impressive scores in terms of grades at 'A' level than those in universities. Yet the standard of CNAA degrees is carefully monitored to ensure comparability with university standards and the proportion of students in each degree classification is broadly similar. This would tend to support the claim that polytechnics are efficient teaching institutions which produce the same output standards although the standard of students at input is often inferior. However, this must be seen in the context of the widespread evidence that 'A' level scores are a bad predictor of degree success and of the suggestion that in the non-university sector students are sometimes over-taught. Secondly, more degree students in polytechnics and colleges enter with qualifications other than traditional 'A' levels. At the beginning of the 1970s only 2.1 per cent of university students had 'other qualifications' for entry, while the percentage for polytechnic and college degree students was 26 per cent. Again, this is not especially surprising. One would expect the polytechnics, growing as they have from further education, to have more students with FE-type entry qualifications while the pressure for places in universities has given them little, too little, incentive to deviate far from the traditional 'A' level route. Thirdly, many more polytechnic and college students come to higher education after a gap from school. In 1978 56,350 of the 175,574 advanced course students in polytechnics were aged 25 and over, or 32 per cent. Among part-time advanced students it was 53 per cent, but even among full-time and sandwich students the proportion was 20.5 per cent. In universities in the same year only 16,150, or 7 per cent, of the 245,933 undergraduate students were aged 25 or over. Fourthly and finally, there is evidence that polytechnics and colleges draw their students from a wider social constituency than universities. In the first half of the 1970s 27 per cent of undergraduates in universities came from working-class families while the proportion of working-class students studying for degrees in the polytechnics was 36 per cent[19]. It also appears that there is a class gradient, with the working-class student better represented on other full-time courses. This fits in with other recent findings that there are remarkably few differences of rates of access between social classes to part-time further education and that 'educational opportunity would be much more unequal if it did not exist'[20].

FLAWS IN THE BINARY STRUCTURE
Although the success of the binary policy should be acknowledged, so too should the force of the criticisms that are made of it. Perhaps a useful distinction can be drawn between the binary *policy,* the objectives laid down in the 1960s which were described in the second section of this

chapter, and the binary *structure* which provides the administrative framework for higher education at the beginning of the 1980s. It is also important to keep in mind the duality of the binary policy as both a description of the status quo and as a normative metaphor. If both these qualifications are kept in mind, the conclusion may be reached that the present binary *structure* no longer provides the most hopeful administrative and financial environment in which to continue to pursue the original goals of the binary *policy*. In this fourth section five flaws, or blockages, in the present operation of the binary policy will be described which tend to support this view.

The first is that although the binary policy could be said to be as much about the universities as about the non-university institutions, all the emphasis and all the attention have been placed on the latter. For a long time we had only half a higher education policy. Despite tentative suggestions for reform like Mrs Shirley Williams' '13 points' in 1969, the universities were left alone until recently. They were, of course, subject to macro-expenditure policies like all services dependent on public support and they were also regulated in the broadest sense by the government's shifting decisions on how the total number of students in higher education should be split between the two sectors. Apart from these two blunt instruments of policy successive governments have had little practical ability to steer the university system in desired directions (teacher education and medical schools are partial exceptions to this). What dirigisme there was was provided by the UGC, formally at any rate quite independently from the DES. In a sense this was why a binary policy was needed in the first place, to maintain a substantial sector of higher education subject to more detailed 'social control'. Also, until the mid-1970s the impermeability of the university system did not seem to matter very much. The expectation was still for substantial expansion, although the projection for more than 800,000 students in 1981 contained in the DES' Planning Paper Number 2 [21] had been scaled down to 750,00 in the 1972 white paper. Moreover the, rather less explicit, expectation was that much of this expansion should take place in the polytechnics and the colleges. As a broad generalization the 1960s were the decade of university expansion, the 1970s and presumably 1980s were expected to be the decades of polytechnic and college expansion. Between 1958 and 1968 the number of full-time students in universities increased by more than 110 per cent; between 1968 and 1978 by only 35 per cent [22]; with the non-university sector the pattern was reversed, although the rise and fall of the colleges of education had tended to obscure the picture. In the middle 1970s it had almost become unofficial DES policy that the universities should represent a static or slow-growth sector of higher education, with the polytechnics and colleges acting as the main instrument of sustained growth. Seen in this context, it did not appear to matter that the universities were left alone. Today, of course, it matters a great deal. Not only is there no real prospect of further significant growth, at any rate of the conventional variety, which means that at the end of the century the universities will still be the largest sector of higher education; but also a central policy for universities has emerged. The fact that this policy is an uneasy combination of the random effects of the overall cut of 15 per cent in the universities' grant by the government and of the selectivity strategy adopted by the UGC to meet this emergency is less important than the simple fact that for the first time it is sensible to talk in terms of a policy for universities. These two developments have produced a double anomaly. First, the ostensibly 'élite' sector of the British higher education will continue for the foreseeable future also to be the majority sector, while the presumably more populist sector under much more detailed 'social control' will only enrol a minority of students (of course, a simple head count would show that the polytechnics and colleges had almost twice as many students as universities but many are part-timers, so the balance of the commitment of public resources to higher eudcation will continue to reflect the universities' majority status). This position is inherently unstable. Secondly, instead of having only half a higher education policy, the Hamlet without the prince position of the years from 1968 to 1978, we now have two separate halves of a higher education policy which are not co-ordinated in any satisfactory way except at the macro-expenditure (and so student-split) level and which as a result do not add up to a coherent whole. Although this unfortunate result is not an intended consequence of the binary policy, the present binary structure does make it difficult to resolve. The first flaw therefore is this missing university dimension.

The second flaw is closely linked with the first. It is the way in which the binary policy let the universities off the reform hook in the mid-1960s. For the existence of 'alternative' institutions cast university development in an entirely new, and possibly more conservative, light. To some degree it took the further democratization of the universities off the political agenda by reducing the educational demands that could be made of them. Universities were no longer the only mature institutions of higher education so they were no longer expected to do everything. Other institutions were available to meet some of the newer, and more destablizing, demands generated by and within a rapidly expanding system of higher education[23]. This was apparent at a rhetorical level. In the early 1960s there seemed to be in the universities a crescendo of interest in reform, of which both the establishment of the new universities and the Robbins Report itself were important ingredients. There was grandiose talk of redrawing the map of learning in exciting and radical ways. In the mid-1960s such talk died away. Instead the new universities settled for what has been called 'the pedagogy of cultivation'[24], while the technological universities have remained incompletely absorbed into a university system with still traditional aspirations. Perhaps this retrenchment would have happened in any case. But it is possible to argue that if the Robbins pattern had been followed, the very pace and scale of expansion would have overridden the cautious instincts of the universities and a significant breakthrough to a mass system of higher education would have taken place on a broad front. Instead the cautious conservatism of the universities was indirectly encouraged by the binary policy and the creation of the polytechnics. Now that the end of expansion has left the universities as the majority sector of higher education, these habits of academic and social conservatism have been entrenched as the hegemonic values of the whole system. Even if this exaggerated interpretation is rejected and the soundness of the original binary decision reaffirmed, an important issue is left. If the objectives of the binary policy, diversity, comprehensiveness, relevance, social control/ accountability, and social justice/mobility, remain valid, perhaps it will no longer be sufficient in the 1980s to confine the attempt to achieve these objectives to the polytechnic and college sector. Perhaps some or all of the universities should also be expected to make a more serious contribution to achieving these 'binary' objectives than they have made since 1965. In short, perhaps the reform of the universities needs to be put back on the policy agenda.

The third flaw of the binary structure is that the original policy was implemented by trying to concentrate advanced courses in a limited number of large and comprehensive institutions, the new polytechnics. Some critics have suggested that this amounted to a pseudo-university solution to a problem which had been defined as the danger of university domination of the entire higher education system. They argue that the binary policy logically tended to abolition, or at any rate blurring, of the sharp distinction between higher and further education by insisting that the values and practices of further education should have more status (and resources?) within the post-secondary system as a whole; but that the means by which it was implemented made it likely that all that would be achieved would be a mild extension and diversification of higher education at the expense of further education. This debate can become an almost metaphysical one in which faith is pitched against faith but it is not irrelevant to the continued validity of the binary policy as a normative metaphor. The binary policy has to continue not only to work well as an administrative and financial framework but also to send out the right kind of message about the future direction of the system. Perhaps such fundamentalist critics have something to say on this second aspect of the policy. However, in a more limited and down-to-earth sense the concentration of advanced courses in the polytechnics has created difficulty, especially over part-time courses. The obscurity of the 1966 white paper on the proper relationship between full-time and part-time courses has not been much reduced by the practice of the polytechnics and colleges. On the one hand it is argued that part-time courses must necessarily be distributed more widely than full-time courses because part-time students are not portable; on the other that part-time courses need the academic and resource support that only full-time courses can provide. This issue has not only remained unresolved, but is likely to create more difficulty in the future as the demand for short courses and other forms of continuing education increases. How can accessibility to such courses be reconciled with their credibility? The 1966 white paper seemed to suggest that some arrangement whereby colleges could offer part-time courses under the aegis of or with the support of polytechnics could provide the basis for a solution. Although a system of consortia with their 'cores' made up of polytechnics or other large colleges and smaller college 'satellites' makes good sense in broad theory, both the details and the politics of such schemes would present considerable difficulty. The growth of a strong and sometimes exclusivist polytechnic interest within the non-university sector has not made much desirable co-operation easy to achieve. One disadvantage of the binary structure certainly is that it attracts all attention to the distinction between (and the interdependence of) university and polytechnic forms of higher education; it distracts attention from the equally important relationships between large and small higher education institutions within the non-university sector and between higher and further education. Yet in terms of the objectives of the binary policy, such relationships are of great importance to the future of non-degree (whether sub-degree or continuing education) and part-time courses.

The fourth flaw in the binary structure is the other side of the coin to the policy of concentrating advanced courses in large polytechnics. It is that, largely because of the vicissitudes of teacher education, this policy of concentration has not been successful. Of the 342,503 advanced course enrolments in the non-university sector in 1978 only 52 per cent (176,716) were in polytechnics[25]. If only full-time and sandwich courses are taken into account the proportion only rises to 58 per cent (114,035 out of 194,034). Substantial numbers of students remain in other maintained major establishments (OMEs) (54,108), and in direct-grant, mainly voluntary, colleges (25,891). It is not possible to regard these two latter totals as a residual element which in the fullness of time will vanish. The non-university sector far from becoming more homogeneous is becoming more heterogeneous. The forced diversification of the colleges of higher education has created not simply an important 'third sector' in higher education, but also a highly diverse sector; some of the colleges of higher education tend towards a liberal arts college model, some towards a proto-polytechnic model, some towards a community college model. Nor by any means do all these institutions place the same value on the traditions and practices of 'relevance' which the polytechnics inherited from technical education. Many are happier with the idea of general liberal higher education along the lines proposed in the Robbins Report. The solidarity of the non-university sector is beginning to break up, to such an extent in fact that it is becoming difficult to accept that a simple binary structure is any longer appropriate. Again there may be a growing tension between the objectives of the binary policy and the rigidity of the binary structure.

Just as it may be necessary to extend these 'binary' objectives to the university sector, so it may be necessary for the binary structure itself to be reformed to reflect the developing diversity within the non-university sector. 'Academic' universities contrasted with 'relevant' polytechnics was never an accurate description of the balance of higher education; today it is damagingly misleading.

The fifth flaw in the binary structure is that it has remained unclear whether its centrifugal administrative intention has been powerful enough to overcome the centripetal forces generated by disciplines. Do teachers in polytechnics and colleges see their role in different terms to university teachers? Or do they see themselves essentially as university teachers do, primarily as members of the 'invisible college' of their discipline or profession and only secondarily as members of the 'visible college' of their institutions? The evidence is ambiguous. Polytechnic and college teachers do appear to have different backgrounds from university teachers. Only 18.9 per cent of polytechnic teachers have first class degrees compared with 42.9 per cent of university teachers and this disparity has not been reduced among recent recruits. University teachers spend 40 per cent of their time on research and 37 per cent on teaching, while polytechnc teachers spend only 18 per cent of their time on research and 43 per cent on teaching. Polytechnic lecturers teach for longer hours (16.7 hours a week on average compared with 15.3 hours in universities). Nor do polytechnic teachers want to do research as much as university teachers: ideally they would like to spend 29 per cent of their time on research, while university teachers would like to spend 50 per cent of their time. Fifty per cent of polytechnic lecturers have never published an article and only 2 per cent have published more than 20. Among university teachers the equivalent proportions are 12 and 26 per cent. On the other hand almost a quarter of polytechnic lecturers said that their interests lay 'very heavily with teaching', while only 6 per cent of university teachers agreed. However, when both sets of teachers were asked which post they would regard as the highest achievement in their profession, the ranking of posts was very similar. Top jobs for both university and polytechnic teachers was a university chair, followed in the case of university teachers by an Oxbridge chair and for polytechnic teachers by head of department in a polytechnic[26]. Such information is necessarily limited. It does not, for instance, tell us whether the greater involvement of polytechnic teachers in teaching rather than research is a reflection of the fact that they do not aspire to research in the same way as university teachers or of an active rejection of the research-oriented values of universities. Nevertheless, rather against the run of anecdotal and 'common-sense' evidence, the empirical evidence does suggest that significant differences remain between polytechnic and university. However, it is not clear what conclusion this evidence tends to support about the success or failure of the binary structure. One interpretation is that 'the reality of the binary system is a blurred division of quality and not a horizontal division of educational function'[27]. But other interpretations less dismissive of the claims of the polytechnics and colleges are possible.

ORGANIZING PRINCIPLES OF A POST-BINARY STRUCTURE

A post-binary structure for higher education must be able to fulfill three conditions. First, it must make it easier to pursue the five basic objectives of the original binary policy. Secondly, it must be designed to eliminate at least some of the five flaws in the present binary structure which were identified in the last section. Thirdly, it must serve as a moralizing metaphor which will help to set a direction and a goal for higher education as successfully as the original binary policy has done. And it must do these three things against a background of no or at the best slow expansion and of declining or at the best static public expenditure on higher education. For there is almost no prospect of a renewal of Robbins, or Crosland-style, expansion in the 1980s and 1990s, partly because of the inevitable shortage of resources and partly because the quality of any new development is likely to be very different from the replication of existing forms of higher education which accounted for so much of the expansion of the 1960s and 1970s. Declining resources, uncertain student demand, the growing demand for more entrepreneurial conduct, will all place the present structure of higher education and the practices and values of its institutions under considerable strain. For this reason it is important to try to identify those organizing principles for a post-binary structure around which higher education can retrench and regroup.

The first and most important of these principles is diversity. This, of course, is common ground. Even Robbins believed that diversity among universities was essential. One of the reasons for the Committee's rejection of the proposal for other-than-university institutions was precisely their belief that such institutions would be too static, trapped in a particular role with no room to manoeuvre and develop. On the other side Crosland argued that diversity was essential because to create a unitary system would imply an omniscience we did not possess. Yet they were not talking about the same thing. The Robbins Committee was supporting the right of individual institutions to make their destiny without artificial restriction; in this way they hoped to create a measure of pluralism within the broad framework of the university as an institution. Mr Crosland, on the other hand, insisted that diversity must be maintained across the system by allocating different roles to different sets of institutions, precisely because he feared that diversity in the Robbins sense would lead to a gravitation, or even regression, towards the traditional university pattern. So it is important to be clear which version of 'diversity' it is intended to encourage. In fact there can be little room for doubt that it must be the latter, system-wide, diversity rather than the autonomous, institution-based variety. Although 'academic drift' has not been as baleful or clear-cut as some binary jeremiahs have alleged, there is still little in the experience of the polytechnics and colleges which suggests that the cordon sanitaire of the binary policy has not helped them to keep to the path of virtue. As the diversity of the needs that higher education must meet and the demands that will be placed upon it are bound to increase still further during the 1980s and 1990s, the need for a more diverse system will also increase to match this heterogeneity. It is unrealistic to expect that from an undifferentiated mass of higher education institutions each one can hope to match its own ambitions to external needs in a way which makes sense across the system. So the need for planned diversity seems clear. However, it is only possible to plan to create the conditions for diversity not diversity itself. National higher education policy should confine itself to constructing broad sectoral boundaries as the minimum preconditions of system-wide diversity, but within them it should pursue policies of course control and resource allocation which stimulate rather than stifle the initiative of individual institutions. The task in the 1980s will be to bring together Robbins-style and Crosland-style diversity. No simple binary, or even tri-partite, division of higher education can hope to match the diversity of higher education that will actually be required. Such crude system-wide diversity will need to be supplemented by much finer diversity between and even within institutions. Any post-binary structure must not only be able to accommodate and to encourage this growing diversity and to establish barriers to creeping conformism, but also send out a clear message that higher education in the last decades of the twentieth century can encompass much more than simply the higher education that developed out of the Robbins expansion, with Crosland amendment, in the 1960s. The second principle must be efficiency. In the future higher education will not only be more diverse but also much leaner. This is not simply an unfortunate and hopefully temporary side-effect of the present reductions in public expenditure, but perhaps a necessary condition for adapting to a new and wider role. Ideas about the organic relationship between undergraduate teaching and research may be much less valid if more and more of the teaching in higher education is of vocationally-directed post-experience courses (or even of much more general first degrees). The belief in the domesticity of the college as an important element, which has been very much eroded during the past twenty years but still remains an important ingredient of the subterranean value-system of much of British higher education, and in the intense and inter-dependent quality of degree study, which has survived in much better shape, will increasingly be questioned in a system with more part-time, 'distance', or other 'casual' students by today's still austere standards. The integrity of the institution itself as something more than a clearing house for client exchanges or a holding company for the resources to be independently exploited by academic experts in specialized branches of knowledge may also come under challenge. All of these will have a fundamental effect on higher education's present view of appropriate staff/student ratios, the balance between teaching and research, and the relationships of departments and other units with the institution. They will have a radical impact on the present configuration of resources which is designed to reflect these older preoccupations. In the long run such developments may have a more significant effect on the economy of higher education than the present cuts.

A third organizing principle must be accountability. Occasionally this issue is discussed in unreal terms as if there were a choice between being unaccountable and accountable when the effective choice is really between different degrees and levels of accountability. So long as higher education receives the bulk of its income from public expenditure in direct and indirect forms, it cannot escape being accountable. The present cuts which the system is trying to absorb are clear proof of that. It can, of course, be argued that for many years after the creation of the UGC in 1919 the universities were barely accountable. Regular grants from the state saved them from their earlier chronic dependence on fees and on support from industry and local government, but so long as the total of such grants remained small in terms of public expenditure and so long as the conventions of respect for the independence of the UGC were upheld, this earlier accountability to students, industry, and town hall was not replaced by an equally rigorous accountability to the state. This allowed a period of what A.H. Halsey has called 'donnish dominion' in which higher education was very much directed by the preoccupations of the academic profession. This period has come to an effective end, partly because of the expansion of the system, partly because of the more recent restriction on the growth of the social state. Yet while the process of accountability has become much more cruel — because there is not enough money to go round — the constitution of accountability in British higher education remains confused. Accountable to whom and for what are questions that the system itself, its paymasters, and its clients, have not been able to answer in a satisfactory way. As a result the age of donnish domination has drawn to a close to be replaced by a confused interregnum. Three main forms of accountability will perhaps eventually emerge — professional accountability, sometimes slipping into a syndicalist mode, which will be the heir to the old donnish dominion; democratic accountability, no longer perhaps simply in terms of resources but also of the quality of higher education itself; and 'market' accountability to students, employers, government and industry (for research and development). In the 1980s and 1990s a whole range of questions concerning accountability — the role of local democracy, the strengthening of democratic accountability at a national level, the opening up of private bodies like the UGC, the rights of the student-consumers, the influence of customers for skilled manpower or research knowledge, even the mass consumption of intellectual culture — will have to be faced. Although the answers to few of these questions are at all clear, it is probably fair to conclude that the theme of accountability will have growing importance in the future organization of higher education. A post-binary structure must somehow find a proper balance of interests to fill the vacuum left by the decline of donnish dominion.

The fourth principle is one that may well get forgotten in the rush to promote diversity, efficiency, and accountability. It is the need to maintain our present traditions of academic and pedagogical freedom. This may at times become difficult. There is a danger that in the enthusiasm for the new utilitarianism the conditions of free inquiry and of free teaching will be undermined. As the customer-contractor principle spreads from research into teaching, it may be difficult to insist upon reasonable autonomy for the individual teacher, department or institution. Yet it will remain important to do so, not simply for the traditional reasons associated with academic freedom such as the right of critical investigation and the duty of balanced teaching, but because if higher education is forced into too subservient a relationship with its diverse clients it will become less efficient as a source of effective teaching and important research. It is not simply that the fiduciary role of higher education must be protected but that higher education must be guaranteed the conditions for academic pluralism as it makes up much of the most important part of the intellectual system. However, it will probably be important to disentangle these conditions for free teaching and research from the decaying fragments of donnish dominion. If this does not happen the intellectual integrity of the higher education system may be compromised by a rear-guard action to defend the institutional autonomy of the old order.

NOTES

1   Speech by Mr Anthony Crosland, Secretary of State for Education and Science, at Lancaster University, 20 January 1967
2   Robinson, Eric E. (1968) *The New Polytechnics. A Radical Policy for Higher Education* Cornmarket
3   White Paper (1966) *A Plan for Polytechnics and Other Colleges* HMSO
4   Speech by Mr Anthony Crosland at Woolwich Polytechnic, 27 April 1965
5   Kogan, M. (1971) *The Politics of Education* pp.193—4. Penguin pp.193—4
6   White Paper (1972) *Education: A Framework for Expansion* pp.30—31. HMSO pp.30—31
7   Woolwich speech, 27 April 1965
8   White Paper (1966) *Op. cit.*
9   Kogan (1971) *Op. cit* p.194
10 *Government and Academic Organisation of Polytechnics, Notes for Guidance* Appendix A in DES Administrative Memorandum 8/67
11 For 1962/63 total, Robbins Report p.160; for 1980/81 total, *Universities Statistics 1980 Volume 1* (1982) Universities Statistical Record
12 Robbins Report (1963) Table 44, p.160. HMSO

13 Donaldson, Lex (1975) *Policy and the Polytechnics* Table 4.1, p.55. Saxon House
14 Donaldson (1975) *Op. cit.* Table 4.6, p.63
15 Calculated from *Statistics of Education 1978. Volume 3 (Further Education)* and *Volume 6 (Universities)* (1981) HMSO
16 Cox, C., Mealing, M., Robinson, S. and Whitburn, J. (1975) *Report on the Polytechnic Survey* Polytechnic of North London (mimeo)
17 *What do Graduates do?* (1981 Edition) Careers and Occupational Information Centre/Association of Graduate Careers Advisory Services
18 *Higher Education in England outside the Universities: Policy, Funding and Management* A consultative document issued by the Department of Education and Science, July 1981
19 Neave, Guy (1976) *Patterns of Equality* Table 7.5, p.85. NFER Publishing Company
20 Halsey, A.H., Heath, A.F. and Ridge, J.M. (1980) *Origins and Destinations: Family, Class, and Education in Modern Britain* p.192. Clarendon Press
21 Department of Education and Science (1970) *Planning Paper Number 2. Student Numbers in Higher Education in England and Wales* HMSO
22 British Universities 1968—78 *Paedagogica Europaea* 1978—2, p.32
23 Ibid. p.31
24 A.H. Halsey quoted in ibid. p.41
25 *Statistics of Education 1978 Volume 3 (Further Education)* Table 14, p.22
26 Survey of university and polytechnic teachers 1976 by A.H. Halsey
27 *The Times Higher Education Supplement* 16 November 1979, pp.10—11

DISCUSSION AND COMMENT

The discussion suggested that whether or not in the past the binary line had served a useful purpose it now represented a hindrance to progress. Speakers from both sides of the line emphasized the commonality of issues that faced higher education and the fact that the binary line served to distract attention from the diversity amongst institutions on either side of the line. Unfortunately no concensus emerged as to what shape a post-binary structure could form. On the public sector side traditional arguments were put forward for the 'seamless robe' but there was a recognition that, for practical reasons, a line had to be drawn somewhere between institutions, although no one was prepared to volunteer a recommendation as to where the line should be drawn. On the university side the spectre of local authority control in a post-binary structure was a deterrent to positive proposals.

The main objectives of the binary line had been to create a balance between the university and the public sector, to protect the pluralistic tradition of AFE, and to produce courses more relevant to societal needs. To some extent these objectives had been met but the line had also fed an acute sense of injustice on the public sector side. This sense of injustice was clearly evident in the discussion. It was generally agreed that the major distinguishing feature between institutions was the quality and quantity of research. For undergraduate teaching there was a good case for funding all institutions on the same basis (with weightings for different subjects), the institutions which were strongly research orientated would need the funding of the research element to be added on. But there were other distinguishing features between universities and public sector institutions, most notably the legal status of institutional autonomy, LEA control, funding arrangements, programme approval and validation arrangements, and the universities' centralized undergraduate admissions systems through UCCA. It was unclear how far these differences constituted a serious obstacle to unifying the two sectors. Obviously the government having established NAB was not going to dissolve it overnight and that and the resource question might delay the implementation of any policy towards unification. Discussion suggested that most people at the seminar were in favour of removing the binary line but were unable to generate positive ideas for a new structure.

10

CONCLUSIONS AND RECOMMENDATIONS

by Michael Shattock

The structure and governance of higher education are never likely to be discussed in Britain in terms of abstract principles. Historically there has always been a strong tendency to see higher education in terms of a hierarchy of institutions and to allot status to types of institutions without defining whether that status derives from academic quality, funding or social prestige. Function was always subsidiary to status. Before Robbins there was a large divide in public esteem between Oxbridge, the 'old' civics and the newer civics. Post-Robbins the creation of the 'new' universities and the transfer of colleges of advanced technology (CATs) to university status led to further layers being introduced into the hierarchy. The establishment of the polytechnics and the enunciation of the principle of the binary line in Mr Crosland's Woolwich and Lancaster speeches produced a yet further division in the British higher education system. By institutionalizing this new divide in funding and control mechanisms quite different from the universities', Mr Crosland ensured that discussions about the structure and governance of higher education would always tend to be overlaid by different and competitive perceptions of status within the higher education system. Concerns about status are reinforced by competition between the two sectors for funding and the allocation of student numbers.

These divisions were at once one of the main themes of the SRHE Leverhulme seminar on structure and governance and the main area of contention between participants. The hostility evident between some local authority education officers and the university sector suggested that for some the 'seamless robe' argument, however strongly advocated, did not extend across the binary line. On the public sector side, there were strong elements of rivalry or jealousy in some contributions about the universities; on the university side, some comments reflected a feeling of being under threat and a sense of virtue unrewarded. Within the public sector there was evidence of internal rivalries between polytechnics and other institutions; within the universities, divisions of view were apparent between those who were and those who were not hard hit in the 1981 allocations of the University Grants Committee (UGC). Relations between civil servants and politicians fared no better and discussions about policy formulation were characterized by bursts of recrimination between the various participants in the process. The resolution of some of these conflicts in a more unified, less stratified higher education system must be a major objective for the 1980s.

A second major theme in the discussion was the extent to which the state had a role in the direction of higher education and how its legitimate interests could be balanced against the need for higher education to retain its character as a self-governing community. The historical model of the UGC was for the first time under serious threat. From the university community itself the UGC's apparent acquiescence to the cuts and the assumptions lying behind its policy of selectivity have led to predictable calls for the Committee to be more representative in its membership, and to perhaps less predictable criticisms of its managerial efficiency. Within the government and parliament doubts have emerged about the extent to which a body largely made up of academics can effectively reflect the nation's priorities in their judgements about the development of higher education and resource allocation to institutions. The new body for the public sector, the National Advisory Body for local authority higher education (NAB), has been created out of a different political culture and is constructed in a very different manner, with direct ministerial and local authority involvement. To what extent should these two bodies be responsible jointly for the governance of higher education or should co-ordination be the function of the DES, or a new ministry of higher education, or should some overarching body be created to supervise UGC and NAB?

Another major theme which organizationally is difficult to separate from governance questions was the balance of powers between central and regional bodies. Historically the universities have been managed centrally and the public sector locally, but the pressures of budget and policy had brought the public sector under greater central control. Both from a political and social point of view, however, doubts were being cast on the centrist model. In Scotland the growing economic and political powers of the Scottish Office, together with an appreciation of the importance of a separate educational identity from the rest of the UK have raised the question as to where the balance of advantage lies for the Scottish universities: remaining under the UGC or integrating themselves fully into the decision-making process of a Tertiary Education Council for Scotland. Elsewhere the extent to which regional or local structures should moderate the role of the centre or even take over control altogether are live arguments on the political scene extending far beyond purely educational matters.

Finally the seminar was concerned to consider the whole area of policy making. Criticisms of the structure of the British governmental system from both the right and the left concentrate on the role of the civil service. Nowhere is this more the case than in education, and particularly higher education. Political parties seem only occasionally to have taken up positions on higher education when out of office and ministers have largely been left to react to demographic or budgetary issues rather than to fundamental questions about the purpose and practice of higher education. Within the DES, officials have tended to react to external pressures rather than be active in the consideration of policy. The incursions of the Central Policy Review Staff (CPRS) into higher education have again reflected concerns about demography and budget rather than educational issues. Policy analysis as a field of interest within government circles has never made much headway, and the lack of such a contribution to policy formulation in higher education and higher education's relationship to economic and social concerns generally has been partly responsible for the dearth of educational policy initiatives in the last decade which itself has led to the loss of a sense of purpose in higher education and a loss of public belief in the system.

The character of the seminar's discussions emphasized even more than rational argument the need for a re-alignment of higher education and a reassessment of the structure and governance of the system as it has developed since Robbins. The fact that the seminar was able to reach agreement on a series of recommendations represents a tribute to the participants' enduring belief in an underlying unity in higher education although on many issues the actual route towards that unity may be hotly contested. The recommendations were reached over extended discussion and represent views widely held at the seminar rather than the views of chairman or convenor individually.

INSTITUTIONAL AUTONOMY

It is important for the future of higher education that the concept of a hierarchy of institutions and divisions based essentially on administrative arrangements should be replaced by a more egalitarian system where institutions are distinguished by function rather than by social prestige or abstract perceptions of status. To achieve this there must be much greater emphasis on institutional autonomy and encouragement for institutional initiative. We need to stimulate greater diversity amongst institutions and create conditions where liberal arts colleges or technological institutions can be good of their kind whether they are universities, polytechnics or colleges of higher education. Partly this can be achieved by the establishment of institutional 'mission statements' which, reviewed at say five-yearly intervals, would lay down objectives for each institution and define in broad terms the kind of programme envisaged. These mission statements would, of course, need to be arrived at through a dialogue between the institution and the funding agency. Funding would be linked to the mission statement. Equally necessary, however, is the preservation of plurality in the sources of funds to encourage institutions to compete in a more open market for funding. Within this plurality responsiveness to societal needs, sometimes called the pressures of the market, needs to be rewarded in order to make institutions more outward looking, and less inclined to sit back comfortably cushioned by a recurrent grant which carries no incentive for innovation.

In such a situation, the binary line, which at the moment is so often seen as reinforcing inequality in funding and public esteem, will tend to wither away. If funding is linked to mission statements there will be no necessary advantage in being in one sector or the other. Some universities may see better opportunities on the public sector side, some public sector institutions may justify transfer to the university sector where base research funding will be more common.

Recommendation 1
That the DES and the UGC and NAB recognize that the protection and encouragement of institutional self-governance and initiative through the operation of multiple sources of funding, responsiveness to external societal demands and strong local/community involvement offers the best prospect for maintaining academic innovation and creativity.

Recommendation 2
That greater emphasis should be given to institutional autonomy. Autonomy, however, should be regulated by agreed institutional 'mission statements' and considerations of national need and the patterns of demand. Funding should be in accordance with institutions' mission statements which should be the subject of a periodic review.

VALIDATION AND COURSE CONTROLS
Public sector institutions suffer from an overload of regulation and validation. This must be progressively removed in order that they can develop an institutional autonomy more comparable to that enjoyed in the university sector. The delays in initiating new courses imposed by the various layers of approval systems puts them at a disadvantage to the universities in reacting quickly to changes in student choice. The DES course control system is currently held in reserve while the NAB sets up its planning mechanisms and it must be hoped that the course control system will soon be dismantled. The more direct controls at local education authority (LEA) and regional advisory council (RAC) level need also to be adapted as the NAB takes over resource allocation and planning for the public sector, so as to encourage much greater flexibility.

The question of validation brings into focus the future role of the Council for National Academic Awards (CNAA). Although CNAA is not the only validating agency it has by far the widest remit over degree courses in the public sector. Over the years it has played a formative part in the development of public sector institutions but the creation of the NAB which will be taking academic judgements on academic programmes and institutions for resource allocation purposes will require a reconsideration of its future role. Opinion at the seminar was divided as to what this role should be. Some urged an extension of CNAA to cover the university sector, others argued that overlap of function with NAB meant that CNAA needed to retrench. It was accepted that the extension of CNAA's role as an accreditation agency over some university courses might be beneficial and need not conflict with university autonomy. On the other hand CNAA's position vis à vis NAB needs to be examined carefully to see where duplication can be avoided.

Recommendation 3
That priority be given to adopting systems of course control which encourage academic initiative and speedy responses to changing student interests.

Recommendation 4
That the role of validating bodies in the future structure of higher education needs review as their role changes in respect to the increasingly autonomous institutions in the public sector.

REGIONAL AND LOCAL CO-ORDINATION

The seminar decisively rejected suggestions that the co-ordination of higher education should be decentralized and specific regional controls built in to the governance of higher education. There was no enthusiasm for regional government or for the argument that the decentralization of government would relieve an overload on the central authorities. On the contrary most members of the seminar felt it would add significantly to the machinery of government, increase bureaucracy and not improve public participation in decision making.

Nevertheless, there was considerable support for adding a regional and a local dimension to the governance of higher education. Even the most research-based, nationally and internationally-oriented institution had regional links and represented an important element in a regional economy. The majority of universities had been founded as a result of local or regional promotion and it was important that they should place a greater emphasis on their regional role than they currently do. One reason for the decline in public support for higher education was a sense that higher education institutions had turned away from their local community. The NAB had rightly placed great emphasis on the need for regional advice in the development of the public sector and it is possible that this framework could be extended to provide a co-ordinating function across the binary line to complement the closer relationships between NAB and UGC at the national level.

In general, however, the seminar placed much greater priority on the local rather than the regional scene, on the development of institutional roles within the locality, and on the growth of collaborative activities between nearby institutions. The first step was to establish local co-ordinating committees to stimulate the development of adult, continuing and post-experience provision. The second was to create a better framework for other forms of institutional co-operation. It was agreed that voluntary association and collaboration was more effective than machinery imposed from above and that such activity would undoubtedly be increased if the UGC and NAB could provide some financial incentives in the way of earmarked grants for particular examples of institutional cooperation. Recommendation 5 below has special implications for Scotland where the public sector is under the responsibility of the Scottish Education Department. The Council for Tertiary Education in Scotland and the Scottish universities should consider the implications of changes in England and Wales for their own situation.

Institutions need to demonstrate a much more sensitive relationship with their local communities and to seek explicit support from them. One necessary step is to establish closer links with local schools and further education colleges, both to break down barriers between higher education and the schools and create personal and professional relationships which will make the 'seamless robe' argument a reality.

Recommendation 5
That representative local committees be set up to co-ordinate and stimulate the provision of adult, continuing and post-experience education, combining the interests of institutions, LEAs and other local providers.

Recommendation 6
That machinery for co-operation at regional level amongst institutions of higher education should be set up by the institutions themselves to complement the closer working relationships between UGC and NAB recommended below (Recommendation 12).

Recommendation 7
That UGC and NAB should take steps to stimulate better inter-institutional collaboration by the provision of funds to support particular schemes involving co-operation between institutions.

THE UGC AND NAB
The UGC has come under inevitable criticism since July 1981. It remains, however, a unique and necessary piece of machinery and its national standing is of vital interest to the universities. The NAB was created partly as a response to criticism that in a contracting situation co-ordination was essential in the public sector, and in particular that co-ordination was necessary with the UGC so that the future of whole areas of study could be considered jointly across the binary line. Close co-operation between the two bodies will be required at every level if priority subjects are to be preserved.

Already the NAB has established a mode of working which emphasizes the importance of ensuring that its decisions are taken openly, and its advice to ministers is made public. The UGC on the other hand has been much criticized for the lack of published criteria for decision making and the extent to which decisions are taken in confidence and without public explanation. In this the NAB's practice is much more in keeping with the mood of the times and needs of the situation and the UGC must accustom itself to a change of practice in these matters.

Comparison with US co-ordinating agencies points up the need for both UGC and NAB to have high calibre staff who are knowledgeable in the field of higher education. The UGC's much depleted staff are drawn solely from the DES, while the NAB's come mostly from the LEAs. Both bodies need an infusion of staff brought in on secondment from the institutions of higher education. In the UGC's case this would remedy some of the present deficiencies in staff work and take some of the burden off its committee members. In some of the submissions to the seminar it was argued that the membership of the UGC needed to be representative of the universities and of the relevant trades unions. There was no support, however, for such proposals, put forward by, among others, the Association of University Teachers (AUT) and it was agreed that UGC members ought to continue to serve as individuals not as representatives. On the other hand the present system of appointment by the secretary of state was open to criticism unless the secretary of state consulted more widely than at present before making his appointments and exposed to public view some of the factors that determined them.

A major public concern over the July 1981 UGC allocation exercise was the extent to which the Committee was aware of the requirements of government as a whole as distinct from any views transmitted by the DES. There was evidence of some concern amongst other departments that the DES was not in a position to reflect accurately to the Committee the specialist requirements of a range of industries and professions. The Department of Industry's memorandum to the seminar suggested that the DoI has separate and distinct interests in qualified manpower and industrial innovation. It seems that adequate machinery does not exist to bring together the views of various departments although the UGC and NAB are required to take account of national needs in their planning. For the long-term future of higher education it is essential to ensure that higher education institutions have an effective interface with government departments other than the DES and that the government as a whole recognizes the contribution which higher education can and does make to the economy at large.

Recommendation 8
The UGC and NAB should place a high priority on the need for co-operation at Committee/Board, subject committee and officer levels.

Recommendation 9
UGC and NAB advice to government should be published as should the criteria they use to make judgements between institutions.

Recommendation 10
The staffing of the two bodies should be adequate to their respective remits and should be appointed independently of the DES, a majority being drawn from higher education itself.

Recommendation 11
The secretary of state should continue to appoint members of the UGC, but should publish the criteria governing the selection in advance and should take the necessary decision only after consultation with the various constituencies involved, including the consumers of higher education.

Recommendation 12
Ways should be found of relating the legitimate interests of government departments other than the DES with the work of UGC/NAB, either by the appointment of assessors on the Committee/Board or at the subject committee level, and with the institutions of higher education, in order to ensure that institutions' research and training responsibilities take proper account of national needs.

HIGHER EDUCATION GOVERNANCE IN THE LATE 1980s

In the short term it is clear that the most urgent need is for the newly established NAB to co-operate across the binary line with the UGC to achieve better co-ordination within higher education. This will not be an easy exercise and the three-year life so far allocated to the NAB will be insufficient to give it time to carry out the important tasks of planning and co-ordination that are needed in the public sector in the light of cuts and contraction required by the government. The period should therefore be extended to five years when a review of both NAB and UGC structures should be undertaken. If Recommendations 1—11 (above) are accepted and acted upon we may expect by then that the binary line may have begun slowly to melt away under the pressure of greater institutional autonomy, better local and regional co-operation and closer co-ordination at the national level. The question then arises as to what governance system would be best suited in the British context. From amongst a number of ideas floated at the seminar two broadly distinct approaches could be identified. The first, a minority view, was that the natural development was for an eventual merger of UGC and NAB into one co-ordinating body. The arguments in favour of this approach were:

   a   That a merger of the two bodies would represent the natural and logical result of a five-year period of close collaboration in an era of contraction in student numbers.

b That a merger of two well established bodies would provide greater strength and continuity than the creation of a new body.

c That a merger would finally remove the binary line and create a more equal and more unified system of higher education.

The arguments against (other than the arguments positively supporting the alternative approach) were:

a That if there was to be a genuine review after five years it would be inappropriate to foreclose such a review at the beginning of the period.

b That if the UGC could be legitimately criticized for its inability to manage forty-five universities effectively now, how effective would a single body covering the whole of higher education be?

c That the present structure offered a protection to the smaller or weaker institutions which might be absent in the larger body.

The second approach was to be less precise about the future but to recommend that UGC and NAB should plan from the beginning for a closer working relationship without defining the end result. At the same time a recommendation should be made for the establishment of a new, overarching, body initially with powers limited to advice only to the secretary of state on the general development of the higher education system and on the division of funding between the two sectors. Such a body might in certain circumstances grow into a full Tertiary Education Commission leaving the UGC and NAB as the bodies which controlled the two main sectors of higher education. The arguments for this approach were:

a That already there was a need for co-ordination of UGC and NAB and this would be better carried out by an overarching body advising the DES than by the DES acting alone.

b That a Tertiary Education Commission would provide a more detached and comprehensive planning structure than a merger of the two bodies.

c That this structure would recognize a likely continuance of different objectives between the two sectors of higher education.

The arguments against (other than those positively for the first approach) were:

a That a second tier body would increase bureaucracy and slow down the process of decision making.

b That the creation of an overarching body would serve as one more layer separating institutions from direct access to the political process.

c   That the secretary of state would also wish to have a more direct relationship with the running of higher education than would be available through a Tertiary Education Commission unless UGC and NAB powers were much reduced.

Under either scenario the seminar was agreed that any governance system must cover all institutions of higher education and must not seek to remove the LEAs from a continuing role in the management of the system. The seminar voted decisively but not unanimously for the less prescriptive approach and for the creation of an overarching body as described in Recommendation 15 below.

Recommendation 13
That, after a five-year review period, the longer-term prospect should be for an even closer working relationship between UGC and NAB and that the two bodies and the DES should accept this as their long-term objective.

Recommendation 14
That UGC and NAB should include within their remit the entire higher education provision including direct grant and voluntary institutions.

Recommendation 15
That in any future arrangements there should be a recognition and reflection of a continuing place for LEAs in tertiary education provision.

Recommendation 16
That an overarching advisory body should be established to offer strategic advice to the secretary of state on matters relating to higher education including the division of funding. The new body should not interfere with the established powers and functions of the UGC and NAB.

THE DEVELOPMENT OF POLICY IN HIGHER EDUCATION
The seminar reviewed the record of successive governments and was agreed that over the last fifteen years neither political party whether in or out of office had developed coherent policies towards higher education except, in the past, for a passive adherence to the Robbins principle, or, in the present, for the reduction of expenditure on higher education as part of a general policy of reducing government expenditure. There is an urgent need, stretching far beyond the limits of the SRHE Leverhulme seminar, for a continuous exploration of policies and policy options for higher education which, on past record, is beyond the capacity either of government itself or of bodies such as UGC or NAB. These policies need to take account of

the important developments in post-compulsory (ie post-16) education. It was agreed that steps needed to be taken to set up a policy studies centre which would undertake research and present reports on policy issues in higher education. The centre would have no formal powers but would derive its influence from the quality of its reports and the extent to which its work affected the day-to-day decisions that have to be taken in the DES, in UGC and NAB and within the institutions of higher education.

Recommendation 17
That priority be given to the establishment of a higher education policy studies centre to serve as an independent source of advice for the DES and other government departments as well as UGC, NAB and the institutions of higher education themselves.

APPENDIX
INTEREST GROUPS IN HIGHER EDUCATION

Policy formulation in higher education depends, inevitably, not just on the inclinations of the government of the day but on the acceptability of policies proposed to the various interest groups or pressure groups involved in the consultation process. More positively in education perhaps than in some other fields policies are generated within interest groups which subsequently the interest groups persuade government to accept. Organizations and known interest groups were, therefore, invited by the SRHE Leverhulme programme to make submissions to the seminar on structure and governance in higher education and papers from the following bodies were circulated for discussion:

AUT	'The AUT and the future of the UGC. A proposed Universities Council'
APT	'Management and governance in polytechnics'
NATFHE	Letter dated 29 June 1982 and a commentary on the DES paper *The Management of Public Sector Higher Education in England*
NUS	'The structure and governance of post-school education' and 'The future of the universities'
TUC	'Public sector higher education' and 'Cuts in higher education'
CBI	'Submission to the Leverhulme Seminar on structure and governance'
CNAA	'Response to Government's consultative document on higher education in England outside the universities: policy funding and management' and a letter to DES dated 9 December 1981 entitled 'Management of local authority higher education in England'
CDP	'Views on the structure and governance of higher education'
IMS	Letter dated 30 June 1982
CLEA	Response to the consultative document: *Higher Education in England Outside the Universities*

Open
University

'Response to the Report of the Select Committee on *The Funding and Organisation of Courses in Higher Education*'

Department
of Industry

Paper by the Department for the Leverhulme Programme

As part of the discussion the SRHE Leverhulme seminar on structure and governance received statements from Christopher Price, MP, as Chairman of the Select Committee and from Phillip Whitehead, MP, Labour shadow minister for higher education on the Labour Party working party on higher and further education.